Expertise...
Know-How...
Skills

On your Side

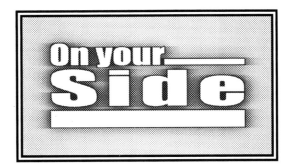

Lotus Notes 6 User

ISBN: 2-7460-2068-8
Original edition: ISBN: 2-7460-1811-X

Editions ENI

BP 32125
44021 NANTES Cedex 1

Tél : 02.51.80.15.15
Fax : 02.51.80.15.16

e-mail: editions@ediENI.com
http://www.editions-eni.com

Author: Béatrice DABURON
English edition by Adrienne TOMMY
On Your Side collection directed by Corinne HERVO

Foreword

This book is for anyone who uses the Lotus Notes 6 messaging and groupware program. The Notes client used for the research of this title was connected to a Lotus Domino 6 server.

This book is designed so you can look up the task you want to perform and find a clear description of how to go about it.

The screens illustrating the pages clarify the explanations by showing the dialog box corresponding to a particular command or by giving a precise example.

This book is made up of 11 parts:

Foreword

Document text .... p. 203 to 218

Create impressive documents, by entering and editing text, then selecting and formatting it. Set up your printouts by creating headers and adjusting margins.

Other document contents .... p. 219 to 236

Use advanced document features such as permanent pen, tables, hotspots and links.

Replication .... p. 237 to 254

Learn how to set up and use replication to create and share several copies of a file. This chapter describes full and partial replicas, how to manage the replicator and schedule or turn off replication.

Security .... p. 255 to 277

Protect your work, by setting up security precautions for your user ID and password, controlling who accesses your files and encrypting documents or databases with secret keys.

In the **appendix** you will find a list of useful Notes 6 shortcut keys.

The final pages of the book contain an **index** of the topics covered, where you can look up the information you need.

Typographic conventions

To help you find the information you require quickly and easily, the following conventions have been adopted.

These typefaces are used for:

bold indicates the option to take in a menu or dialog box.

italic is used for notes and comments.

Ctrl represents a key from the keyboard. When two keys appear side by side, they should be pressed simultaneously.

Foreword

The following symbols indicate:

- an action to carry out (activating an option, clicking with the mouse...).

 a general comment on the command in question.

 a useful tip.

 a technique which involves the mouse.

 a keyboard technique.

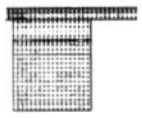 a technique which uses options from the menus.

Foreword

Table of contents

Lotus Notes

Table of contents

Database management

Views

Mail database

Table of contents

Other databases

Table of contents

Documents

Document text

Table of contents

Lotus Notes

part one

What is Lotus Notes 6?

The Lotus Notes environment can be a great help for effective teamwork, as it enables you to share and distribute information easily between team members or within a company.

Lotus Notes is a multi-faceted product:

- It contains e-mail and discussion tools.
- It can be used to share files and data, such as procedures, catalogues, reports, etc.
- It has remote working features.
- It provides optimized networking.
- It gives access to the Internet.

How Lotus Notes works

Lotus Notes keeps information in **databases**. Each database contains a specific type of information. This type is determined by the person who creates the database. The information "type" refers to its format, such as text files, forms and so on.

Starting Lotus Notes

This book has been produced using a Windows XP environment. If you are using an earlier version of Windows, you may find that some of your application features may appear differently to those shown in our illustrations, but they should function in an identical way.

- From the Windows taskbar, click the **start** button (or **Start** for versions of Windows earlier than XP).
- Point to the **All Programs** option (or **Programs** for versions of Windows earlier than XP) then to the **Lotus Applications** option.
- Click the **Lotus Notes** option.

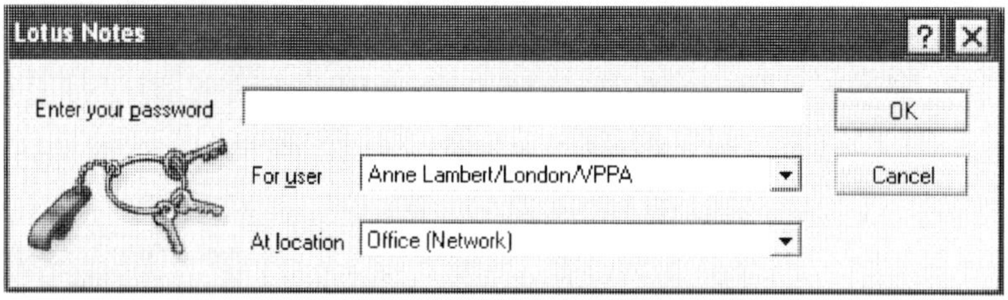

Your network manager would have created a user ID for you, to enable you to log on to Notes. This identification file, which has a .ID file extension, stores all the items Notes requires to identify you, such as your user name, your password and so on.

- **Enter your password**, using the text box of the same name, taking care to use the correct upper and lower case characters.

  The letter x appears instead of the characters you type in, so that your password cannot be seen on screen.

- Open the **For user** list and select your Notes user name. If your name does not appear in the list, choose the **Other** option then use the **Choose User ID to Switch to** dialog box to find your ID file.
- Open the **At location** list and choose the location from which you wish to log in to Notes.

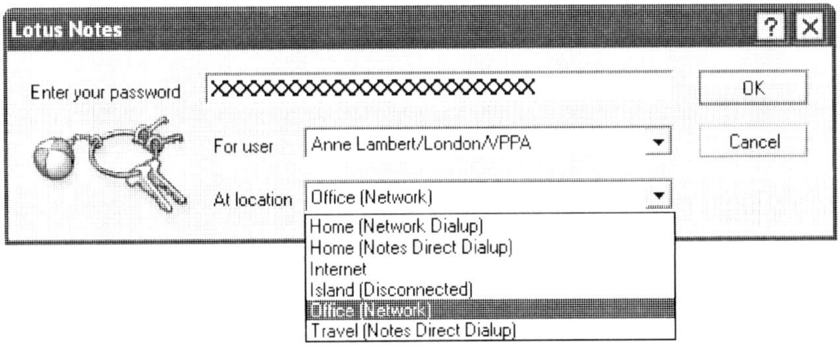

The number of options and their names may have been customized by your network manager. Depending on the chosen site, the active connection method can differ (by modem, network card, or even no connection).

- Click **OK** to open the Notes application.
- If the chosen site needs to be accessed by modem, fill in the **Time and Phone Information** dialog box if necessary then click **OK**.

  *The first time you start Notes 6, the Lotus window contains a **Welcome** page, from which you can create a new Welcome page, look at the new features of Notes 6 or start working using the default values.*

- Make your choice by clicking the number or symbol for the required option:

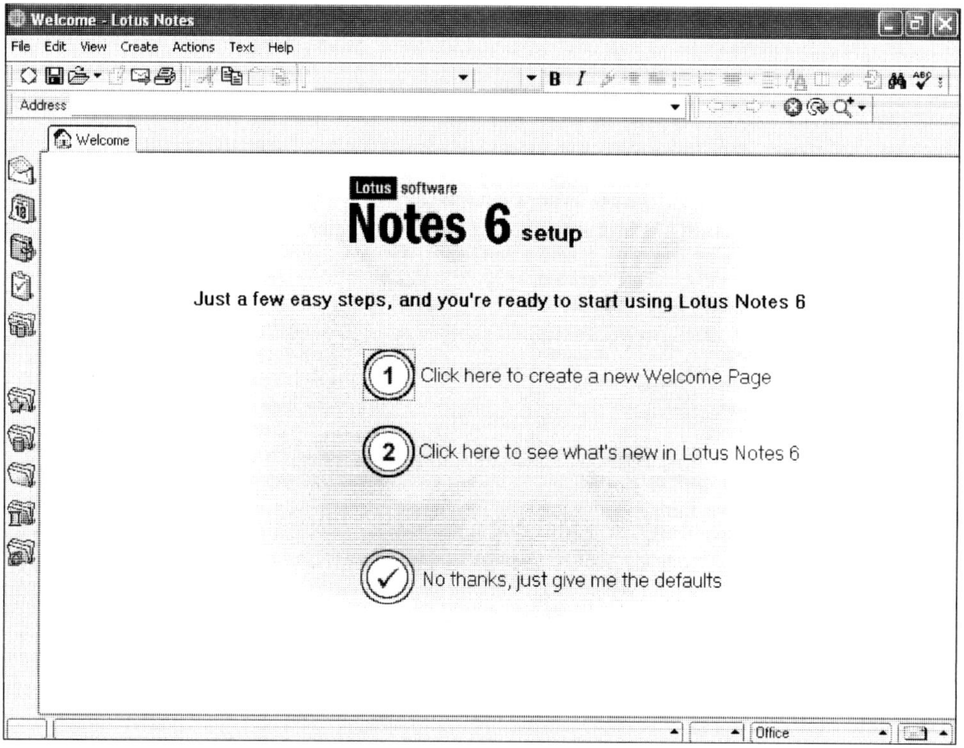

How to create a custom Welcome page is discussed later in this book; for now we will use the default values offered.

- To use the default values, click the **No thanks, just give me the defaults** option.

The default Welcome page appears and you can use it to make a search or to access your mailbox, calendar, personal address book, list of tasks to do or journal.

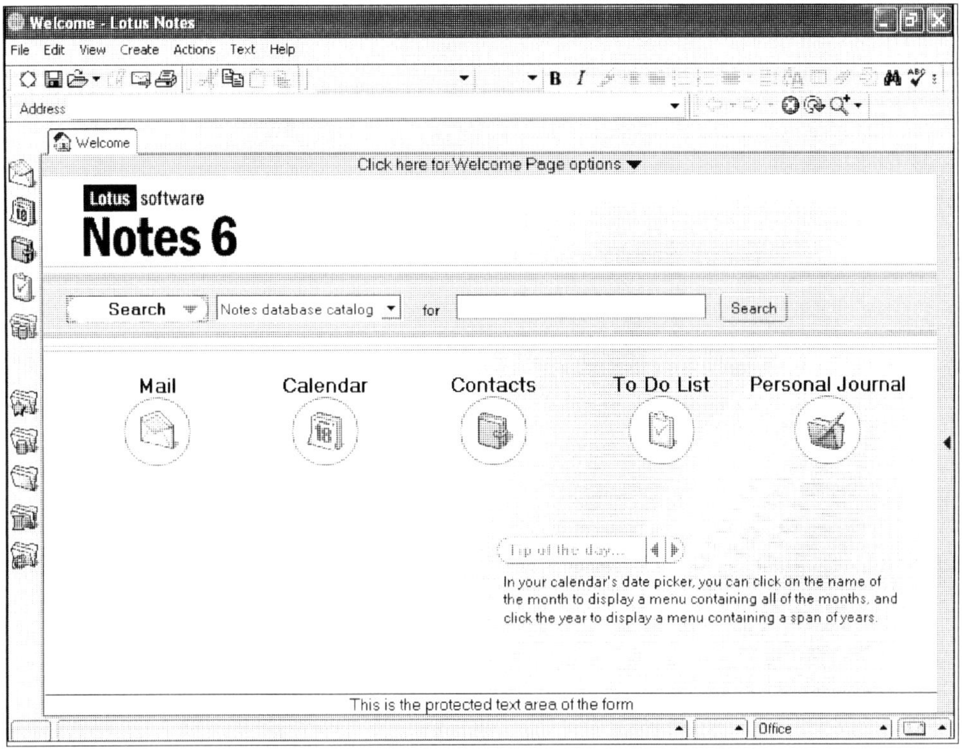

As you can customize this welcome page, do not be surprised if the one that appears in your application is not exactly the same as the one presented here. Your Lotus administrator may have already modified it.

Description of the workscreen

The Lotus Notes 6 window contains the following items:

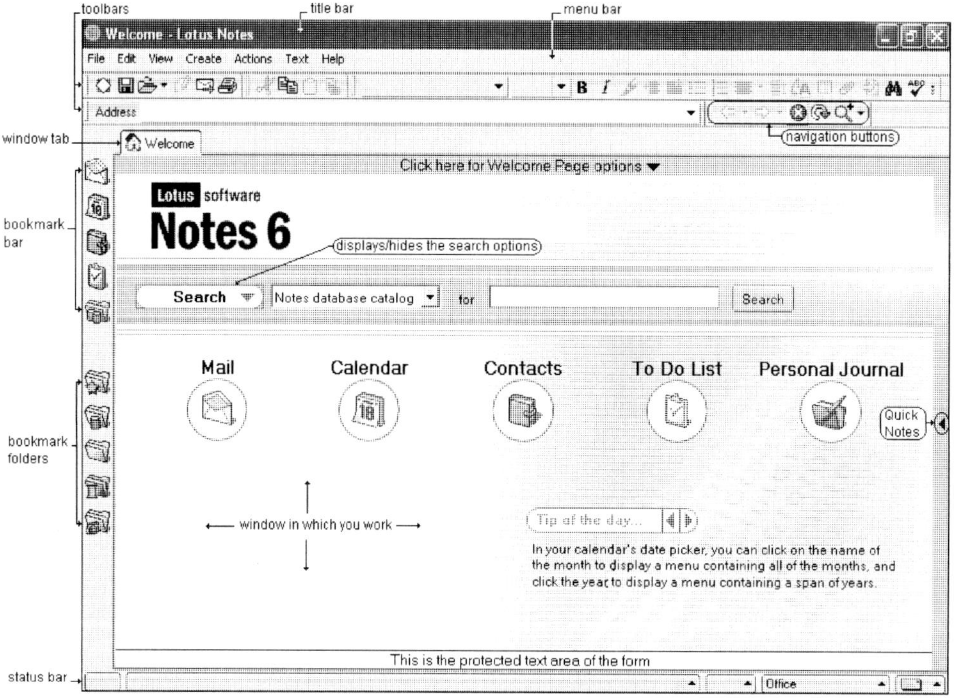

- The Notes application window has a **title bar**, which contains the name of the active page followed by the application name. This bar also contains three buttons that you can use to resize the window (to minimize the window, to restore it or to return to full screen size) and to close the application.
- The **menu bar** offers five menus permanently (**File**, **Edit**, **View**, **Create** and **Actions**) and other menus that appear or change according to a currently selected item, such as the **Help** menu, **Text**, **Table**, **Attachment**, **Picture** and so on.
- The **toolbars** appear on two lines. By default, the **Universal**, **Editing** and **Text Properties** bars sit on the first line and the **Address** and **Navigation** bars are on the second line. A move handle can be seen at the start of each bar . Other bars may appear, depending on the preferences you have set (cf. Shortcuts - Toolbars).

- The **navigation buttons** (**Go Back**, **Go Forward**, **Stop**, **Refresh**, **Search**) are used to move between database pages or web pages.
- Each time you open your mail, a database or a document, a **window tab** appears on the workscreen. To pass from one window to another, click the corresponding tab.
- The **bookmarks** give you rapid access to Notes or Internet items. By default, five bookmarks are placed on the bookmark bar on the left of the screen. If you point to a bookmark, its name appears in a screen tip.
- The **bookmark folders** (of which there are five by default) contain all the bookmarks, and also appear on the left of the screen. If you point to a bookmark folder, its name appears in a screen tip.
- The contents of the **status bar** vary according to the task at hand. Here is an example of what it can display:

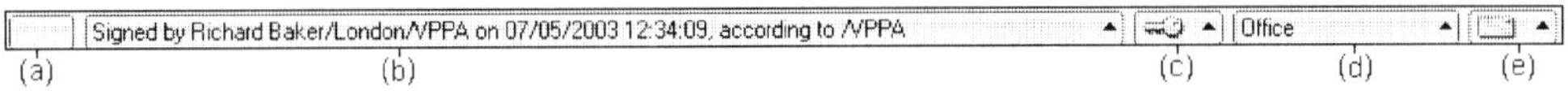

(a) Whether or not a network connection is currently being made. If this is the case, a lightning bolt icon appears.

(b) A list of the last messages in the session.

(c) Your access level for the active database.

(d) The name of the current location: use this zone to switch to another location.

(e) A menu of common tasks, in which you can choose to create a memo or read new mail etc.

- By default, Notes displays the Welcome page as the default view when you open the application.

Modifying the status bar preferences

- **File**
  Preferences
  Status Bar Preferences

  *You can also right-click the status bar and choose the **Status Bar Preferences** option.*

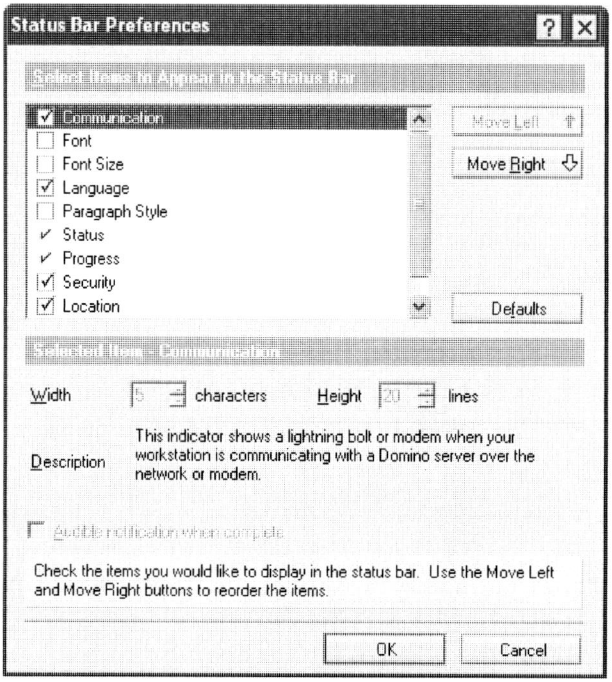

Items set to appear in the status bar are ticked in the ***Select Items to Appear in the Status Bar*** *list.*

- To choose an item to display on the status bar, tick the check box next to its name.

You can see that a ***Description*** *of the selected item (****Communication*** *in this example) appears in the lower half of the dialog box.*

- If necessary, set the **Width** and/or the **Height** of the status bar button for the selected item, using a number of **characters/lines.**

If you tick the ***Progress*** *check box, you can go on to activate the* ***Audible notification when complete*** *option if you want to hear a beep when a task (for example, a replication) is finished.*

- To reorganise the list of items shown on the status bar, click the item you want to move then use the **Move Left** and **Move Right** buttons.

The item that appears at the top of the list will be seen on the far left of the status bar.

- If you no longer want an item to appear on the status bar, deactivate the corresponding check box.
- Click **OK** to confirm your changes.

The **Defaults** button on the **Status Bar Preferences** dialog box resets the original status bar settings and undoes any changes you have made to the preferences.

Getting. help on Notes

Notes help comes in two forms: online help and locally available help. Local help can be obtained in two ways, as context help or as a complete list of the application help texts.

Consulting context help

Context help is specific to the task you are currently performing.

- To see context help, which directly relates to the work you are carrying out, press the F1 key on your keyboard. You can also use the **Context Help** command in the **Help** menu or click the question mark icon ? located in the top right corner of dialog boxes or property info boxes.

  The context help immediately appears in a separate window.

- To close the help window once you are done, click the button on the far right of its title bar.

Consulting the complete application help locally

- Click **Help** on the menu bar then choose the **Help Topics** option.

  The ***Lotus Notes and Domino Help...*** *window opens. The buttons on the window offer various methods for using the help:* ***Contents***, ***Index***, ***Search*** *or* ***Tips***.

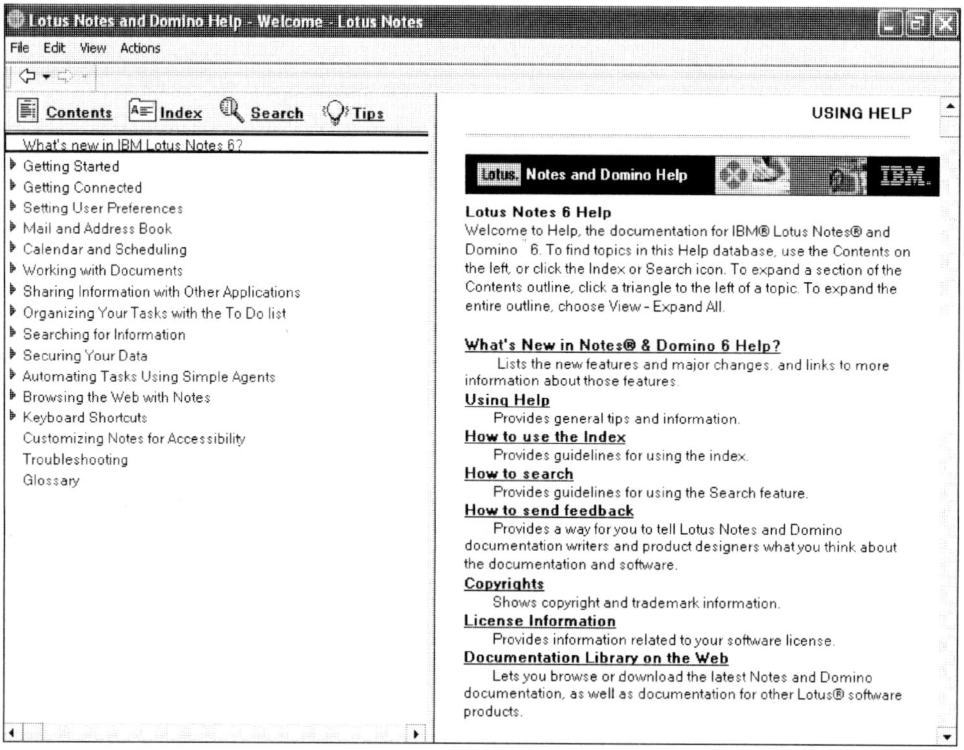

- Choose your method by clicking the corresponding button:

Contents This lists a hierarchy of help topics in the left pane of the window.

Index This gives you an index of keywords which you can explore. Each keyword is listed in alphabetical order and has a right-facing arrow before it. Click a keyword to see the attached topics. Some have secondary keywords attached, which you can continue to click to see one or more associated topics.

Search This is a search feature that will look for topics based on one or more words. Enter your word in the text box then click the **Search** button to see any corresponding help topics.

- To see a full help text, click the arrow on an index entry then click the topic that interests you.

The help text appears in the right hand pane of the window.

- You can click the navigation buttons under the menu bar to move from the active help page to the next or previous one.
- Once you have looked at a help text, you may like to print it by taking the **File** menu's **Print Topic** option or Ctrl **P**. If you do, adjust the options in the **Print View** dialog box, if necessary then click **OK** to start printing.
- Close the help window by clicking the button on its title bar.

If no help is available locally, Notes opens the help located on your mail server. When you consult this help (as topics or context help), make sure that the search bar contains a green dot followed by the word **Indexed**. If this is not so, ask your network administrator to generate a text search index in the help.

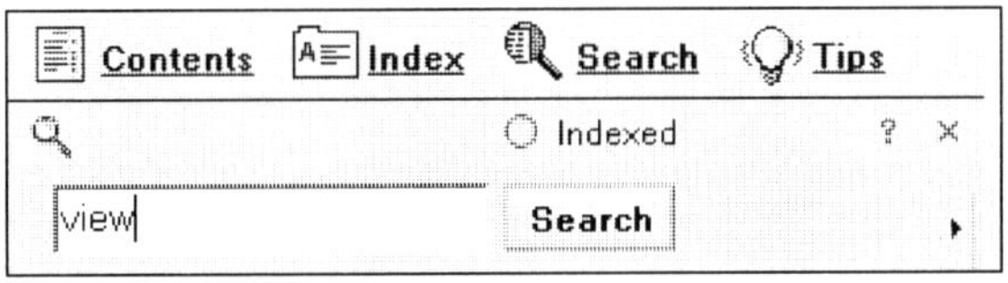

Looking for help on the Internet

When the integrated help found locally in your Notes application does not provide the solution you are seeking, you can search one of a number of Lotus Internet sites.

- Make sure your Internet connection is open.
- Open the **Help** menu and point to the **Lotus Internet Resources** option:

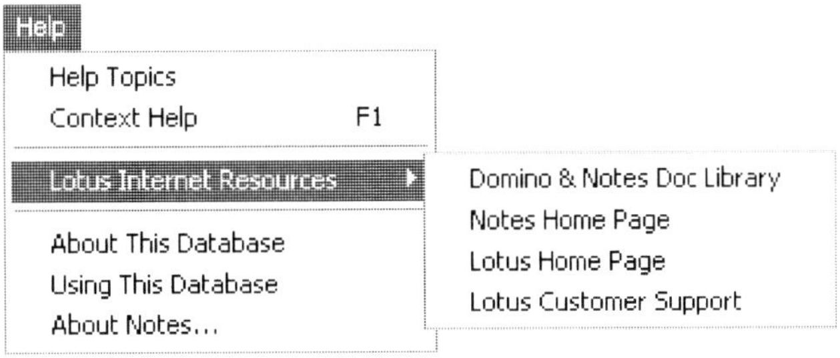

- Choose one of the four options on offer.

The IBM web site opens in the Notes workscreen.

- To look for help based on a keyword, enter the word in the **Search** text box.
- Use these tools on the Navigation bar:

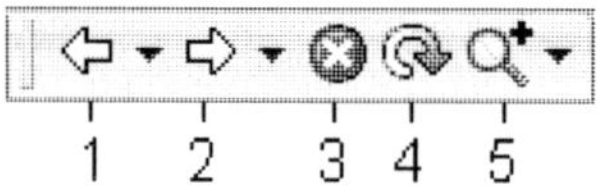

1. to scroll back through the last pages visited.
2. to scroll forward through the list of pages visited.
3. to stop the page downloading.
4. to refresh the current page.
5. to start a new search.

- To close the web help page, click the cross on the tab of the page in question or use the **File - Close** command.

You can also display a web page by entering the complete site address in the **Address** box and confirming with the Enter key.

Leaving Notes

File
Exit Notes

Click ☒ on the Notes window

Alt F4

Opening an existing Welcome page

*As explained in the introduction, Lotus Notes 6 opens on a **Welcome** page, whose layout is initially predefined by Notes. You can customise this page or create a new one.*

- To activate the Welcome page, click the window tab: Welcome.
- If the Welcome page tab cannot be seen, you can open the **Favorite Bookmarks** folder by clicking its icon, then choose **Welcome.**

By default, the Welcome page predefined by Notes appears.

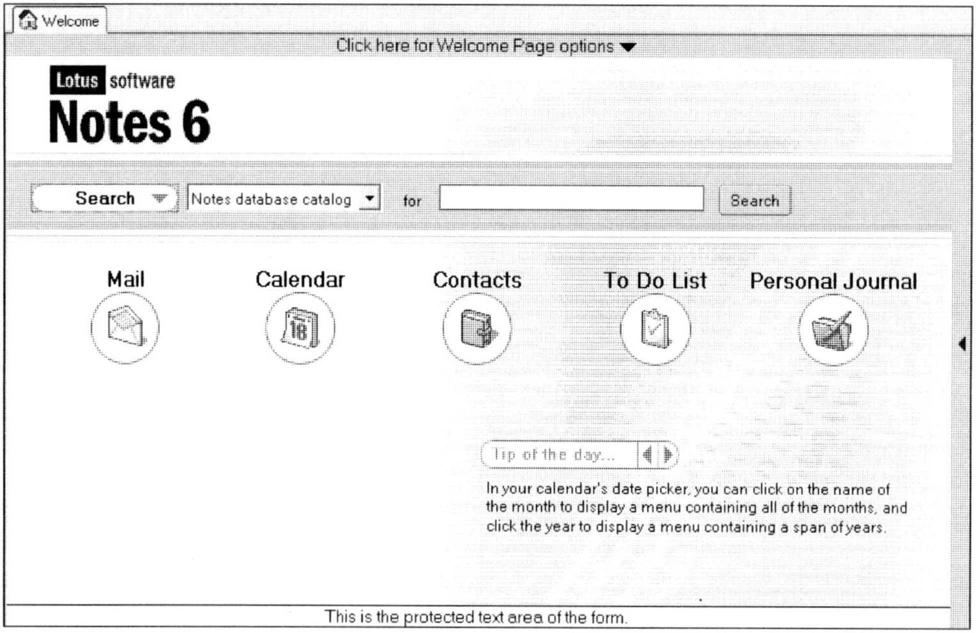

Various buttons and options are there for you to access the search feature, your mailbox or calendar or contacts or even a useful tip, updated regularly.

*You may also notice a blue arrow at the extreme right of the screen. This reduces the central part of the page and expands the **Quick Notes** section. To return to the original layout, click the blue arrow again.*

- To see the previous or following tip of the day, use one of the arrows in the **Tip of the day** frame.

- To change the Welcome page or edit its presentation, click the **Click here for Welcome Page options** link at the top of the page.

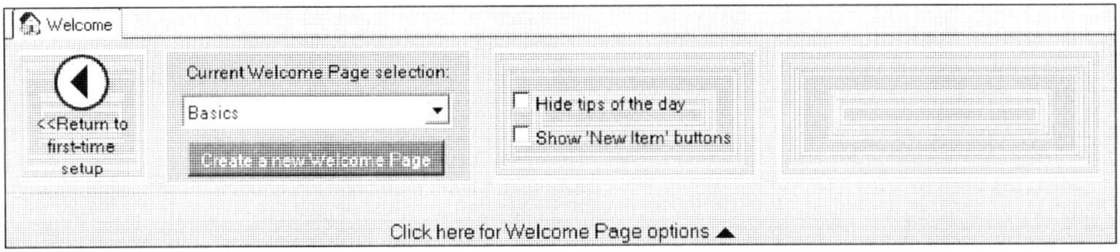

*The **Return to first-time setup** option displays the very first setup screen that appeared when you started Notes for the first time (cf. Lotus Notes overview - Starting Lotus Notes).*

- If you no longer want to see the tip of the day on the Welcome page, tick the **Hide tips of the day** check box.
- To activate a different Welcome page, open the **Current Welcome Page selection** drop-down list and click the required page.

*The Welcome page that Notes offers by default is called **Basics**.*

- To hide the page options, click the **Click here for Welcome Page options** link.

When you open Notes, it displays the last Welcome page that was active during your previous work session.

Creating a new Welcome page

Before you learn how to create a new Notes Welcome page, you may need to know that there are two possible types of page:

- a page made up of several frames. Frames are resizable rectangular areas in which you can include database views, action buttons, preview panes, file system folders, web pages or a control panel from which you can directly access Notes or Web links.

- a single-frame page. This is also called a personal page, and it takes a less structured form. You can include pictures, rich (formatted) text, Java applets or integrated elements such as a date selector.

- If you are in the Welcome page, click the **Click here for Welcome Page options** link then click the **Create a new Welcome Page** button.

- If you are in the first-time Notes setup screen (cf. Lotus Notes overview - Starting Lotus Notes), click on **Click here to create a new Welcome Page.**

  A wizard opens to help you create a Notes Welcome page:

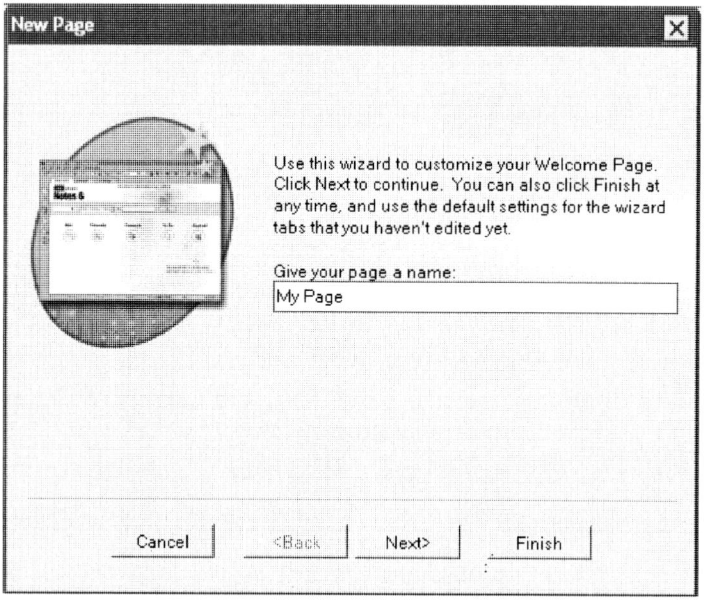

- Enter a name for the new page in the **Give your page a name** box then click the **Next** button.

The second step of the wizard asks you to choose a page type:

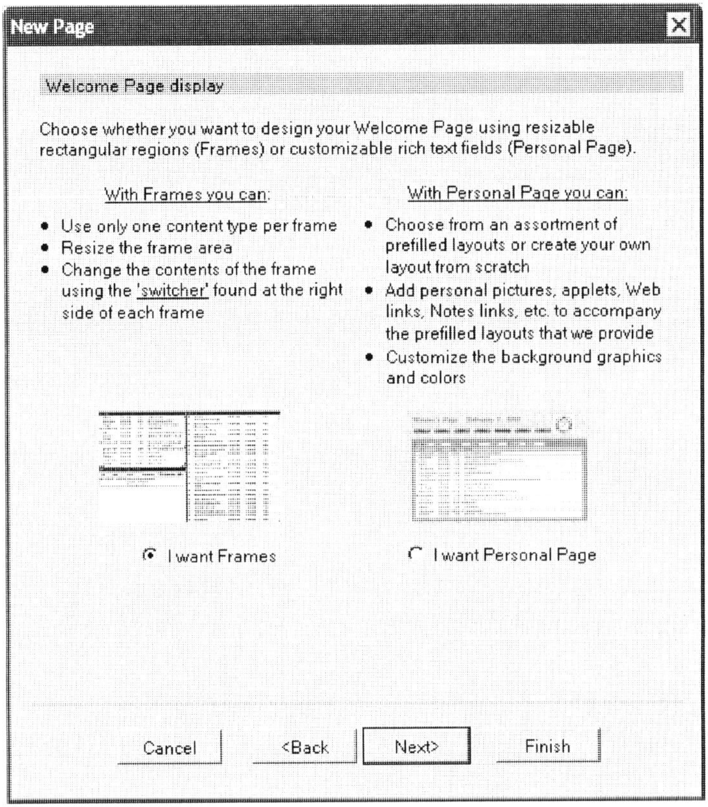

- Activate **I want Frames** for a page with frames or **I want Personal Page** for a page without frames, then click **Next**.

*The **Back** button can be used to go back to previous steps in the wizard if you want to check or edit your settings.*

*The **Finish** button confirms the changes you have made in the current and previous steps: if you click it before the end, the wizard will apply the default settings to any steps that you have not yet reached.*

The steps differ depending on the type of page you have chosen.

A personal page

*If you activated the **I want Personal Page** option in the **New Page** dialog box, this screen will appear:*

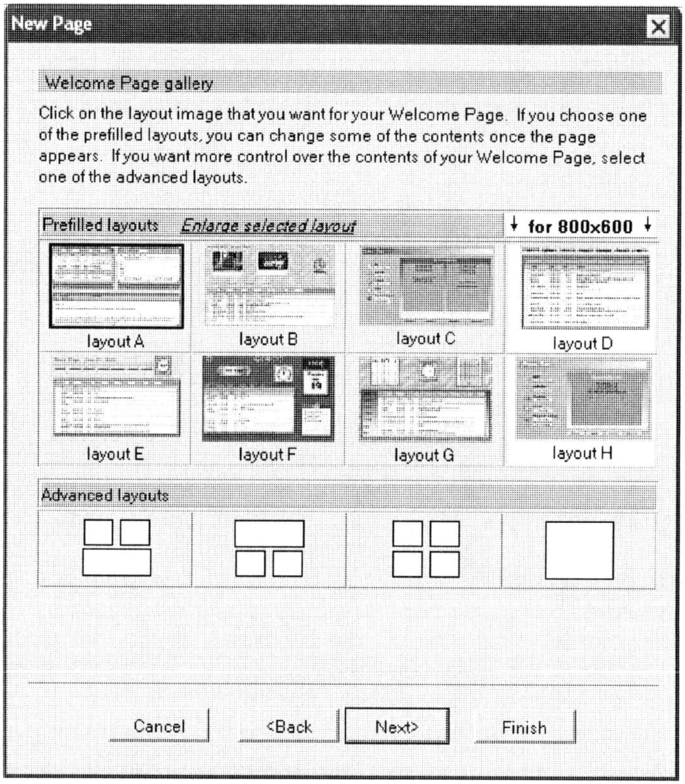

- Click one of the presentations on offer: these are divided into **Prefilled layouts** with specific content and **Advanced layouts.**

  *The **Enlarge selected layout** link (only for prefilled layouts) lets you have a closer look at the chosen presentation and view its contents.*

- Click the **Next** button.

- If you chose an advanced layout, choose a graphic background, if required, by clicking the required option; otherwise tick the **I do not want to use a graphic background** option and click **Next.**

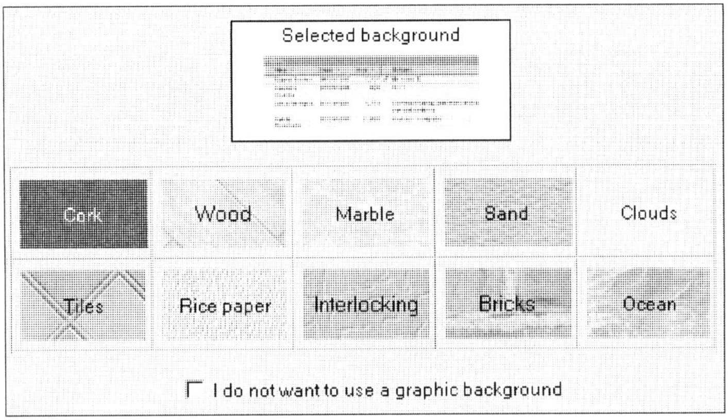

Notes tells you when you have reached the end of the page creation process:

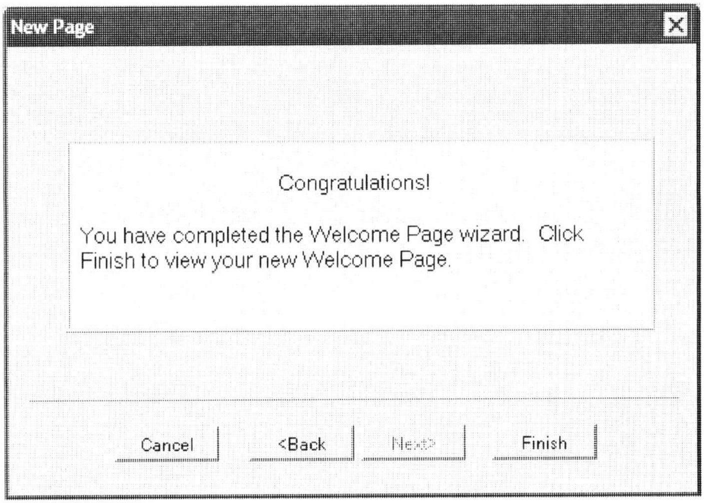

- Click the **Finish** button.

The new Welcome page instantly appears:

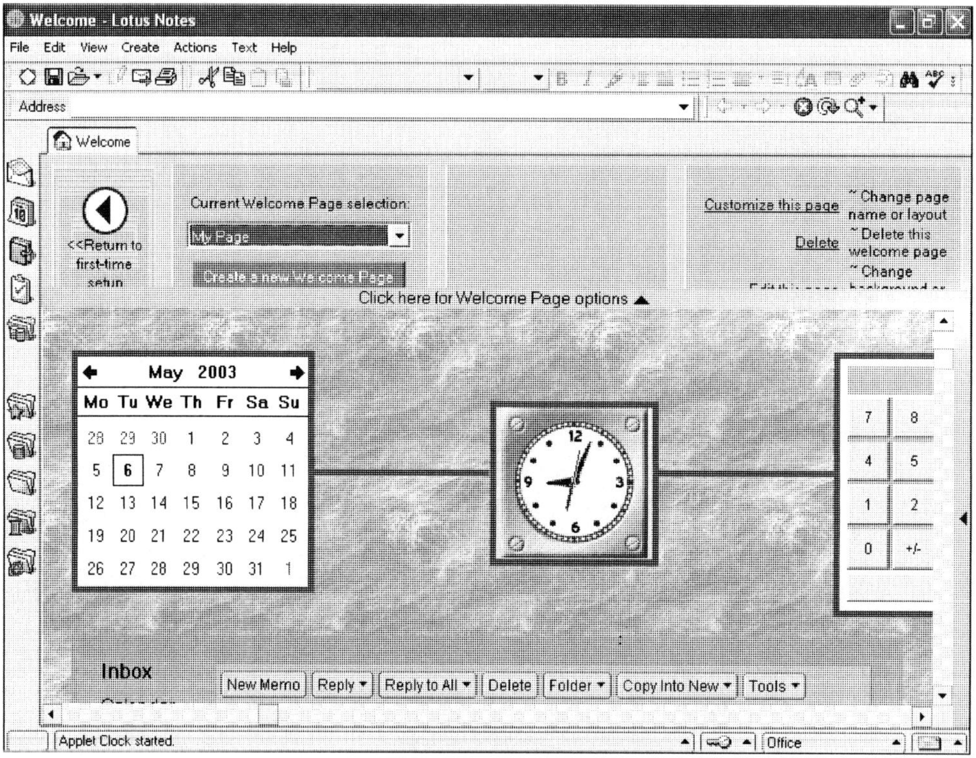

*In this example, a **Prefilled layout G** has been chosen.*

A framed page

*If you activated the **I want Frames** choice in the **New Page** dialog box, this screen will appear:*

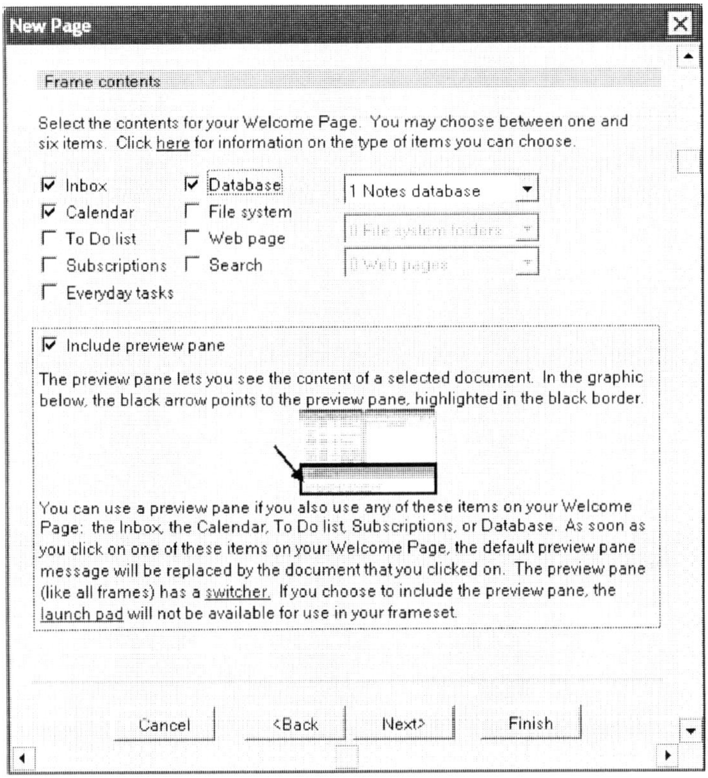

- Define the **Frame contents** with the corresponding options (a maximum of six). To get more details about the options on offer, click the **here** link and then the name of the option concerned.

  *If you choose to display your **File system** in your new Welcome page, you must set Microsoft Internet Explorer as your default browser to display the information correctly.*

- To insert a preview pane in the Welcome page so you can see the contents of a selected document, tick the **Include preview pane** option.
- Click the **Next** button.

- In the following steps, use the various options to set up the **Frame layout**, **Content placement**, **Launch Pad** and **Action bar buttons.** Use **Next** to go from one step to another.
- When you have set all the options, click **Finish**.

Deleting a Welcome page

- Open the Welcome page that you want to delete (cf. Welcome page - Opening an existing welcome page).
- If necessary, show the Welcome page options by clicking the **Click here for Welcome Page options** link at the top of the workscreen.
- Click the **Delete** link.

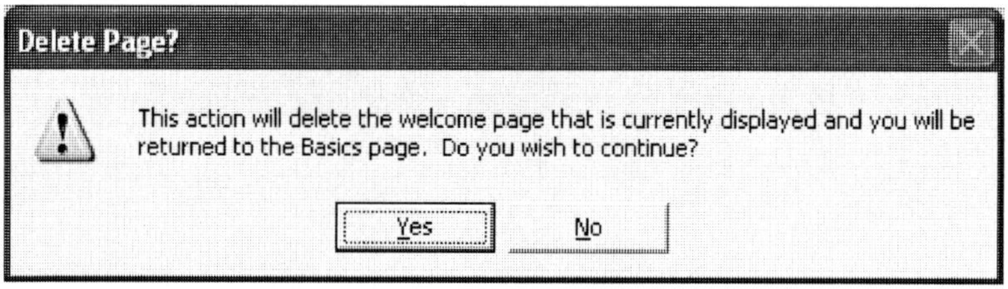

- Click the **Yes** button to confirm the deletion.

  *The page disappears and is replaced by the **Basics** Welcome page.*

Only the Welcome pages you have created yourself can be deleted.

The name of a deleted Welcome page does not disappear from the **Current Welcome Page selection** list in the Welcome page options until you restart Notes.

Editing a Welcome page

This feature offers so many variations that only the basics can be described here.

- Open the Welcome page that you want to modify.
- If necessary, click the **Click here for Welcome Page options** link.
- To change the Welcome page's name and/or presentation, click the **Customize this page** link then make the changes in the same way as for creating a new page.
- To change the contents and/or background of the Welcome page, click the **Edit this page** link.

*A new actions bar with **Save and Cancel** buttons appears: right-angled brackets show where the frames will be.*

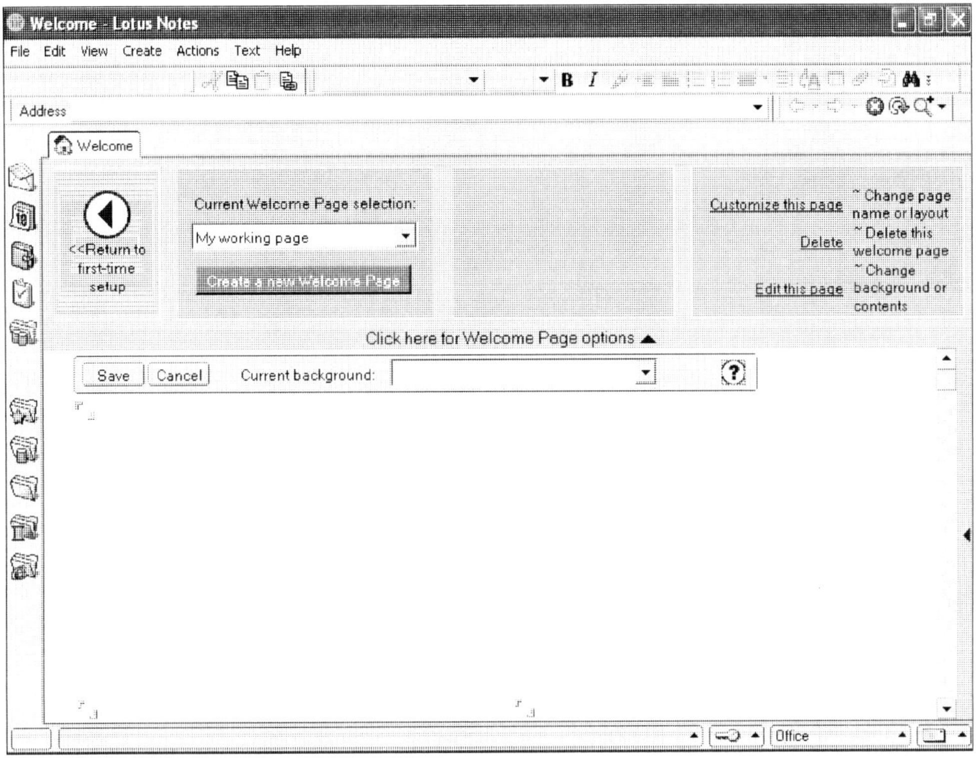

To see the editing options more clearly, this example shows a personal Welcome page with three (empty) frames and no background.

- To change the **Current background**, open the list of the same name and make your choice.
- To change the contents of a frame, click between the right-angles that symbolize the frame and use the menu options to insert an image (**Create - Picture**), format text (**Text** menu) or carry out other actions.
- Click the **Save** button to finish editing the page and save your changes.

Using a bookmark as the home page

Notes can use an existing bookmark (cf. Lotus Notes - Shortcuts - Bookmarks) as a "home page" (the first page you see). When you open Notes, it will go directly to the database, document or web page concerned.

Setting a bookmark to be the home page

- Right-click the bookmark concerned to see its shortcut menu.
- Click the **Set Bookmark as Home Page** option.

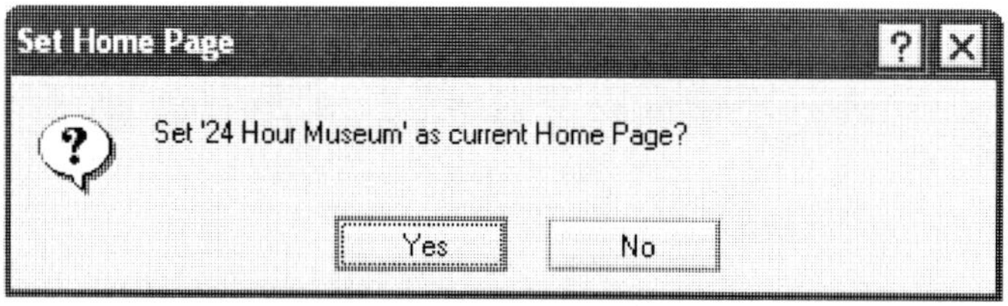

- Click **Yes** to confirm using this bookmark as the home page.

Restoring the Welcome page as the home page

- Click the **Favorite Bookmarks** icon to see the corresponding list.
- Right-click the **Welcome** bookmark and choose the **Set Bookmark as Home Page** option.

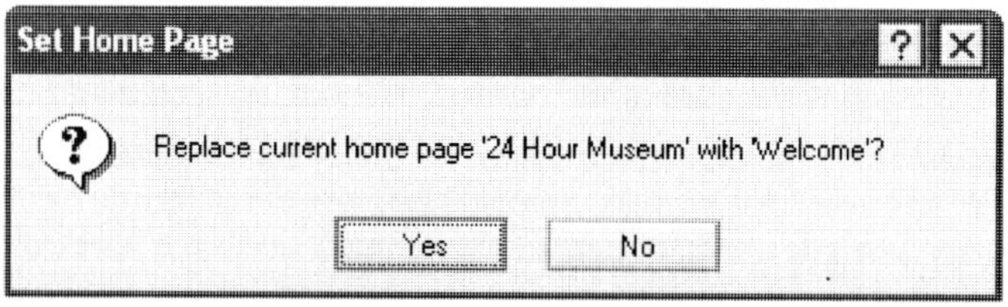

- Confirm changing the home page by clicking **Yes.**

Opening/closing the workspace

The workspace is the user interface traditionally used with older versions of Notes. It contains database icons. This interface is accessible from a bookmark bar folder.

- Click the **Databases** bookmark folder ( ) then click **Workspace**.

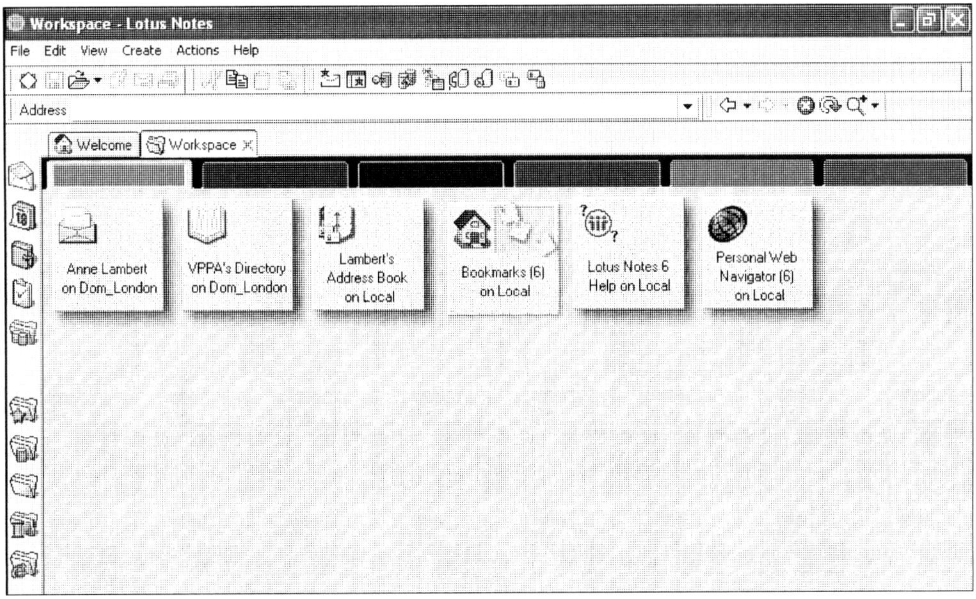

The workspace consists of 6 pages on which you can group related databases. These pages are represented by different coloured tabs.

By default, your screen configuration permitting, the workspace has a three-dimensional appearance.

- To close the workspace, click the cross ☒ at the right of the **Workspace** window tab.
- To move through the workspace pages, click the page tab in the workspace or press Ctrl → or Ctrl ←.

Changing the appearance of the workspace

- **File**
  Preferences
  User Preferences
- If necessary, activate the **Basics** page.

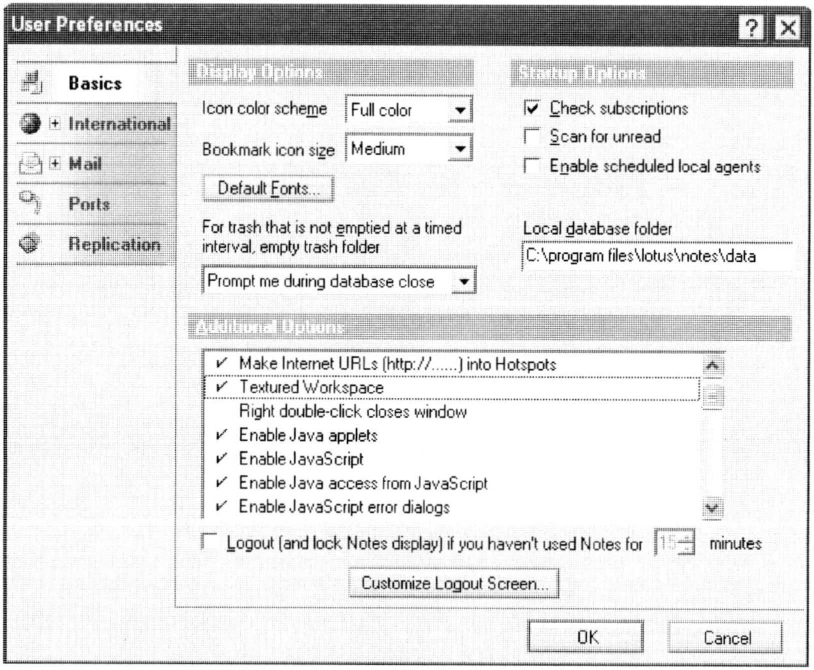

- To activate/deactivate the workspace's relief appearance, use the vertical scroll bars to scroll through the **Additional Options** list and tick the **Textured Workspace** option to show the workspace in relief or deactivate this option to use a flat workspace.

  *Initially, and if your screen configuration supports it, the **Textured Workspace** is active by default.*

- Click **OK** to confirm.

- Click **OK** if the following message appears:

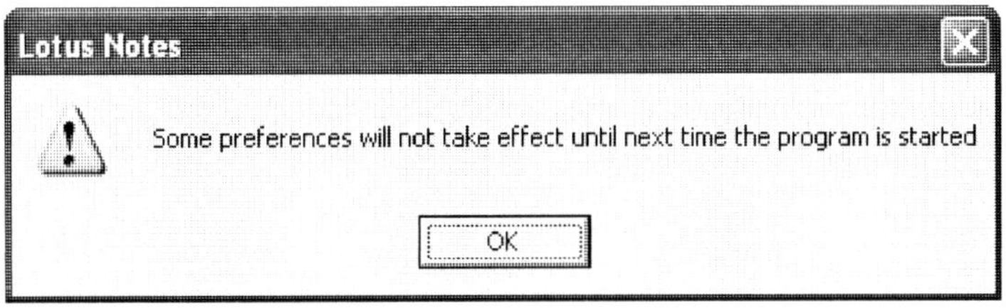

Changing the colour of workspace page tabs

- Double-click the tab concerned.
- Check that the **Workspace** properties box opens and that its i tab is active.
- Choose the required **Tab color** from the list.
- Click the cross on the properties box title bar to close it and confirm your changes.

Deleting a workspace page

- Right-click the tab of the workspace page you wish to delete.
- Choose the **Remove Workspace Page** option.
- Confirm the deletion by clicking **Yes.**

  The database icons on the deleted page are removed from the workspace when you delete the page.

Adding a workspace page

- Right-click the tab of the workspace page before which you are inserting the new one.
- Click the **Create Workspace Page** option.

  If this is the first time you have added a workspace page, Notes asks you if you want to update your desktop file.

- If necessary, click **Yes** to confirm.

You can use up to 32 workspace pages.

Naming a workspace page

- Double-click the tab of the workspace page you wish to name.
- Check that the **Workspace** properties box opens and that its [i] tab is active.
- In the **Page name** field, enter the text that should appear on the tab:

- Confirm the title by clicking [X].

The tab's size adjusts to the length of the text you enter. A title can contain up to 32 characters.

What are shortcuts?

- Shortcuts are techniques for obtaining faster access to your frequently-used commands, bases, documents, web pages and so on.
- These include:
  - shortcut menus,
  - keyboard shortcuts (or shortcut keys),
  - bookmarks,
  - window tabs,
  - toolbars.

Shortcut menus

- Right-click with the mouse (providing the right button is your secondary mouse button; if you are left-handed, you may have switched the buttons. If so, click the designated secondary button).

  The contents of a shortcut menu are specific to the active item.
- Each option in a shortcut menu has an equivalent in a traditional menu. For example, the **Open Database** option in the workspace shortcut menu has the same effect as the **File - Database - Open** command.

Shortcut keys

- Shortcut keys are combinations of keys on your keyboard that you press to perform an action or command: this can be quicker than using the menus.
- For example, by pressing the Ctrl and **O** key, you start the procedure to open a database. This corresponds to the **File - Database - Open** command.

Toolbars

Moving a toolbar

- Point to the bar's move handle (the vertical line at the start of the bar).

  The mouse pointer will take the shape of a four-headed arrow.
- Drag the handle to the place where you want the toolbar to be.

If you move a toolbar into the central window, the bar becomes an independent window that you can move and/or resize. This is a "floating" toolbar.

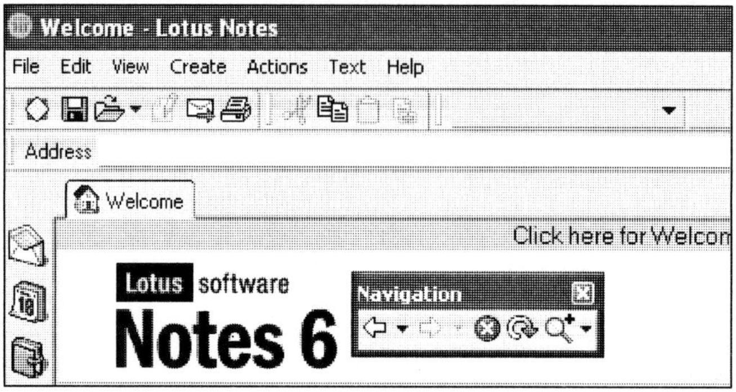

*In this example, the **Navigation** toolbar is floating.*

- To dock (or anchor) a floating toolbar, drag its window to an edge of the workscreen.

  The window changes shape and becomes a horizontal/vertical toolbar again.

Hiding/showing a toolbar

- **File**
  Preferences
  Toolbar Preferences
- Activate the **Toolbars** page.

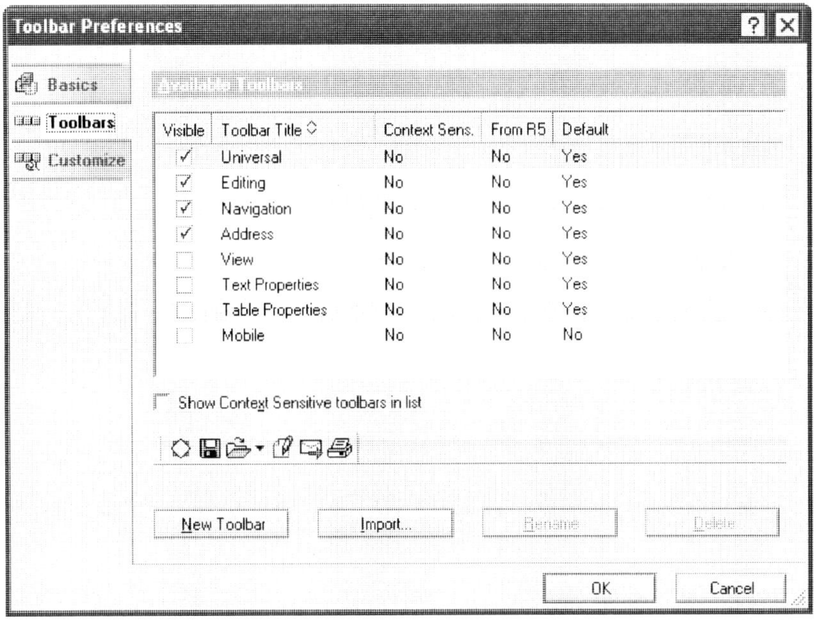

Notes offers 8 predefined, non-contextual toolbars; four of these are visible by default (these are ticked in the ***Visible*** *column).*

- To see what tools a bar contains, click the bar's name. A preview appears below the list.
- To display a bar in the Notes window, tick the check box next to its name; click to remove the tick if you want to hide a visible toolbar.
- To **Show Context Sensitive toolbars in list**, tick the option of the same name.

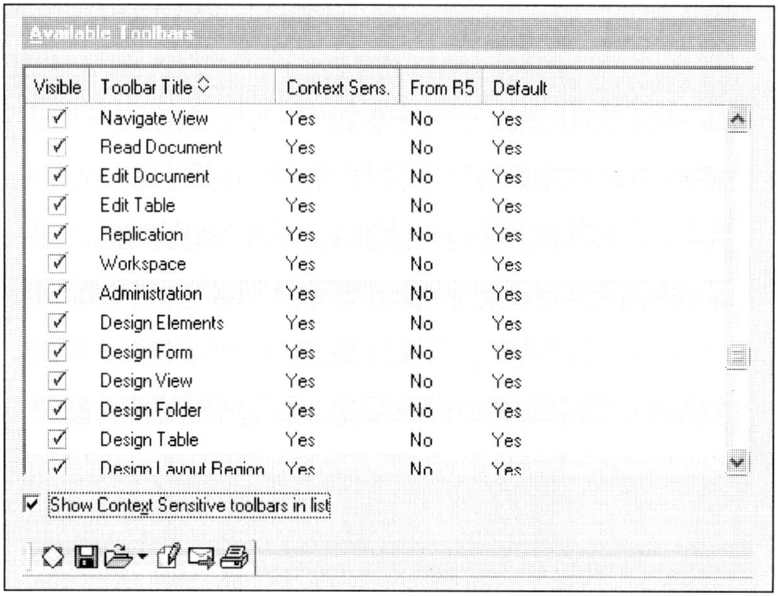
Available Toolbars
Visible
Toolbar Title
Context Sens.
From R5
Default
Navigate View Yes No Yes
Read Document Yes No Yes
Edit Document Yes No Yes
Edit Table Yes No Yes
Replication Yes No Yes
Workspace Yes No Yes
Administration Yes No Yes
Design Elements Yes No Yes
Design Form Yes No Yes
Design View Yes No Yes
Design Folder Yes No Yes
Design Table Yes No Yes
Show Context Sensitive toolbars in list

Fifteen new contextual toolbars appear in the list; these are ticked by default. These toolbars are integrated into the Notes workscreen according to the task currently at hand.

- Click **OK** to confirm your changes.

You can also hide or show toolbars by right-clicking a currently-displayed toolbar and activating/deactivating the name of the toolbar concerned. The **Toolbar Preferences** option in this shortcut menu displays the dialog box of the same name.

Creating a new toolbar

You can create a new toolbar and add tools to it that are relevant to what you are working on. You create a toolbar in two stages: you give a name for the bar then you customize the bar by adding tools.

- **File**
  Preferences
  Toolbar Preferences
- Activate the **Toolbars** page.
- Click the **New Toolbar** button.

- There is an empty field in the **Toolbar Title** column; enter your toolbar's name here. Next, click outside the field to confirm the name.
- Activate the **Customize** page.

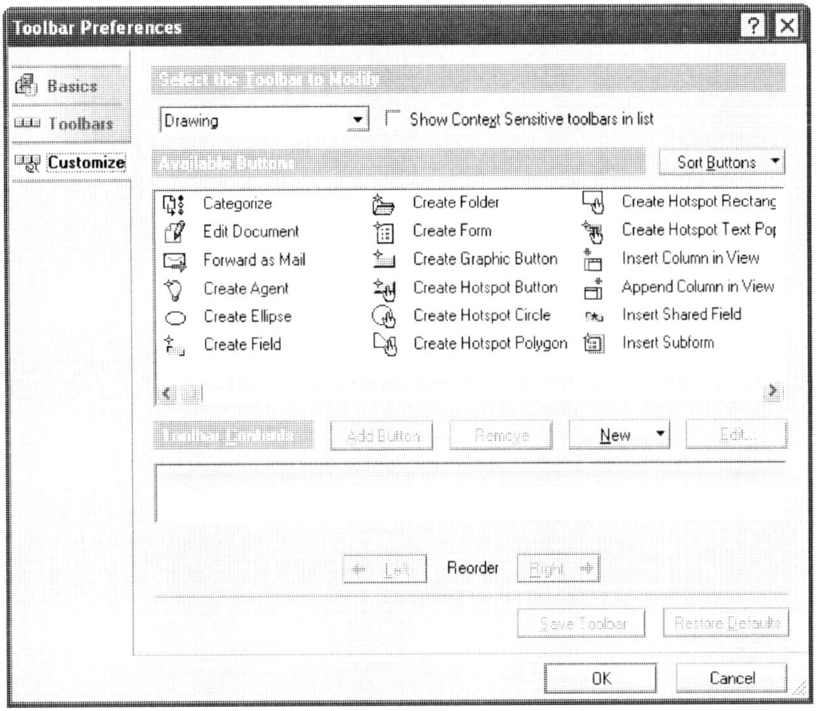

- Open the **Select the Toolbar to Modify** list and click the name of the new bar.
- In the **Available Buttons** list, click the tool that you want to insert into the new toolbar then click the **Add Button** button.
- Repeat this procedure for each new tool that you want to add.
- Click the **Save Toolbar** button then **OK** to confirm.

Modifying a toolbar

- **File**
  Preferences
  Toolbar Preferences
- Activate the **Customize** page.

- Open the **Select the Toolbar to Modify** list and click the name of the bar in question.
- To work on one of the tools on the bar, click that tool in the **Toolbar Contents** list then click a button:

Remove	to delete the tool from the bar,
Edit	to rename the tool or change its icon,
Left	to move the tool to the left on the bar,
Right	to move the tool to the right on the bar.

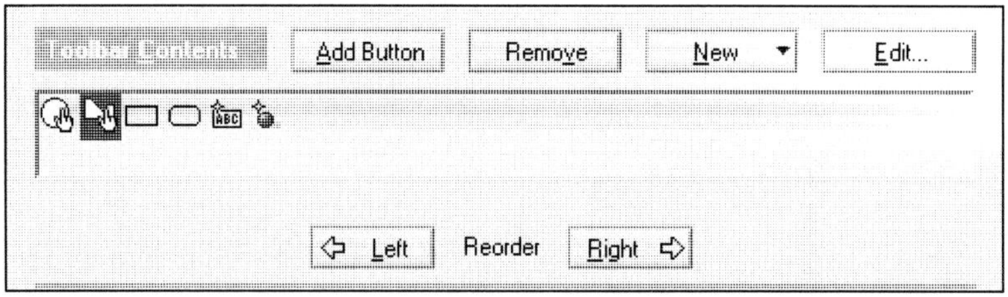

- To add a tool, click the tool in the **Available Buttons** list then click **Add Button.**
- Click the **Save Toolbar** button then **OK** to confirm.

To rename a toolbar, open the **Toolbar Preferences** dialog box, activate the **Customize** page, select the name of the toolbar concerned and click the **Edit** button. Make the required changes and click **OK.**

Importing SmartIcons from Notes version 5

In Notes 5, SmartIcons were used as shortcuts for commands and common tasks. In version 6, toolbars have replaced these.
Notes 6 allows you to import the SmartIcons that may have created in version 5 of Notes, so you can use them as toolbars.

- **File**
  Preferences
  Toolbar Preferences
- Activate the **Toolbars** page.
- Click the **Import** button.

*The **Choose SmartIcons Set** dialog box opens:*

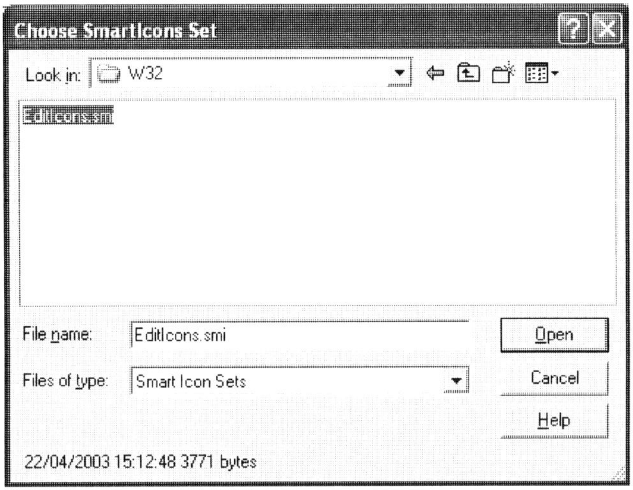

- Using the **Look in** list, look for the folder in which the SmartIcons palette file is stored.
- Select the name of the file you want to import.

  SmartIcons palette files have a .smi file extension.
- Click the **Open** button.

  *The SmartIcons palette is added to the **Available toolbars** list and you can then use it as any other toolbar.*

Window tabs

Each open element has a window, topped with a window tab.

- To activate a certain task, click the corresponding window tab.

- To close that window, click the [X] on the right of its tab.

The [F11] key closes the current task and the [Ctrl][⇄] keys go from one task to the next.

Bookmarks

Bookmarks create links to Notes or Internet elements such as databases, views, documents, web pages and discussion forums. The Bookmark bar on the left of the Notes workscreen (cf. Lotus Notes overview - Description of the workscreen) is by default made up of bookmarks that give access to the ***Mail****,* ***Calendar****,* ***Address Book****,* ***To Do*** *and* ***Replication*** *pages. The bar also contains bookmark folders, such as the* ***Favorite Bookmarks*** *folder in which you can keep your most-used bookmarks.*

- When you point to a bookmark or a bookmark folder, its name appears in a screen tip.
- To activate a bookmark, click the bookmark on the bar to open the application or corresponding page or click the bookmark folder to display its contents.
- To create a bookmark on the Bookmark bar, drag the item's window tab towards the Bookmark bar. Release the mouse button when the black horizontal line, or insertion point, is in the correct position.
- To insert a bookmark into an existing bookmark folder, drag the window tab towards the folder but only release the mouse button once the folder's contents are displayed.
- To manage a bookmark, right-click the bookmark to see its shortcut menu and choose to **Remove Bookmark**, **Rename Bookmark** or **Change Bookmark Icon**.
- To use a bookmark as your home page, right-click the required bookmark and click the **Set Bookmark as Home Page** option.

The corresponding database, document or page will open automatically when you start Notes.

What are properties boxes?

- You can open an item's specific properties in a small dialog box (or properties box) which contains a series of tabs, dividing the properties thematically.
- This remains open on the screen until you close it.
- The changes you make in properties boxes take effect immediately, there is no **OK** button to confirm your work.

Displaying a properties box

- Select the element whose properties you wish to see or edit.
- Press [Alt][Enter] or [Ctrl] Y or right-click the item concerned and choose the **Document Properties** option.

  *The **Document** properties box opens immediately:*

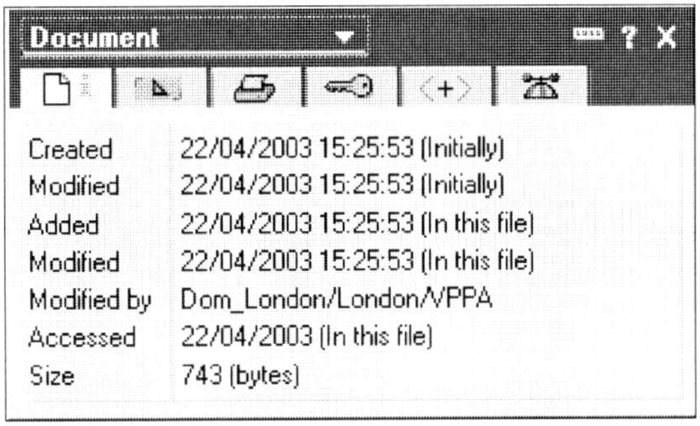

The contents differ according to the item selected.

Minimizing/maximizing a properties box

If you want to keep properties boxes on the screen, they will take up less space if you minimize them.

- Minimize the box by double-clicking its title bar or clicking .

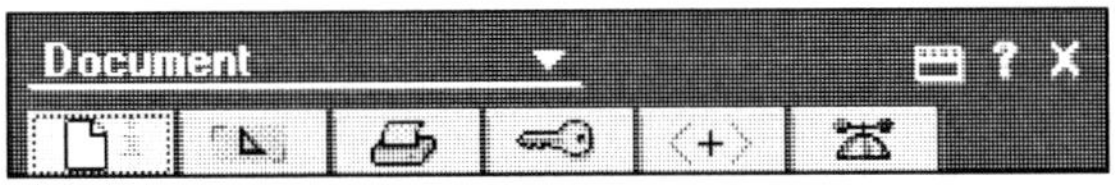

- Maximize the box by double-clicking the title bar again or by clicking .

Moving/closing a properties box

- To move a properties box, drag it by its title bar.
- To close a properties box, click its close button.

Selecting another properties box

Sometimes you may have a box relating to one item on the screen, but want to see the properties for a different item. You do not need to close the first box to open another.

- Click the arrow on the title bar to see the list of options.

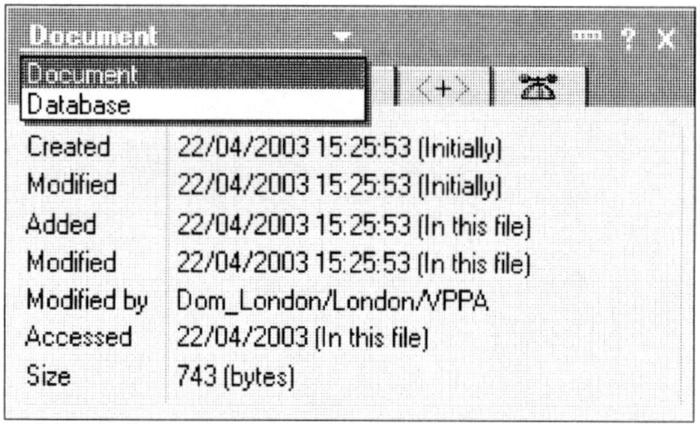

- Select the item whose properties you wish to see.

You also use the ↓ and ↑ keys to activate the next or previous properties box.

Database management

part two

What is a database?

- A **Notes database** usually contains documents concerning a particular subject, such as articles for a journal, after-sales service procedures etc. You could think of databases as filing cabinets in which you can store your papers.
- Databases can be private (stored locally) or public (on the server).
- A Notes database is a unique file made up of one or more documents relating to the chosen subject. These documents can be text, images, objects or other sources of information.
- When you create a database, a new bookmark is added to the **Databases** bookmark folder. You can access a database by clicking this bookmark or you can add an icon to the workspace. In any case, to open a database you must have the appropriate permissions.

Opening a database

Using the File menu

- **File**
  Database
  Open — Ctrl **O**
- To give the name of the **Server** on which the database is stored, enter the name directly or open the drop-down list on the field and click the name of the required server. If the database is on your hard disk, choose the **Local** option.

  By default, the drop-down list only shows the servers that you have accessed previously. If the required server name does not appear in the list, use the ***Other*** *option to display further names.*

The databases on the selected server are represented by a symbol and database folders by a symbol.

- In the **Database** list, double-click to open the folder in which the required database is stored (if necessary) then select the database concerned.

  *The **Browse** button can help you to find the database's file path and name.*

- Click the **Open** button.

Using a bookmark

- Select a bookmark folder in the Bookmark bar on the left of the Notes window.

A list of corresponding bookmarks appears:

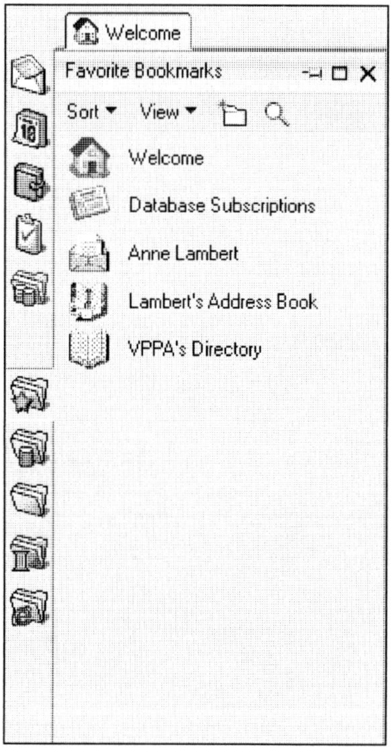

In this example, the ***Favorite Bookmarks***  *folder has been opened.*

- If necessary, select the folder in which the required database's bookmark is stored.
- Click the bookmark for the required base.

From the workspace

- Display the workspace (cf. Workspace - Opening/closing the workspace).
- Activate the tab of the workspace page on which the database icon is located.

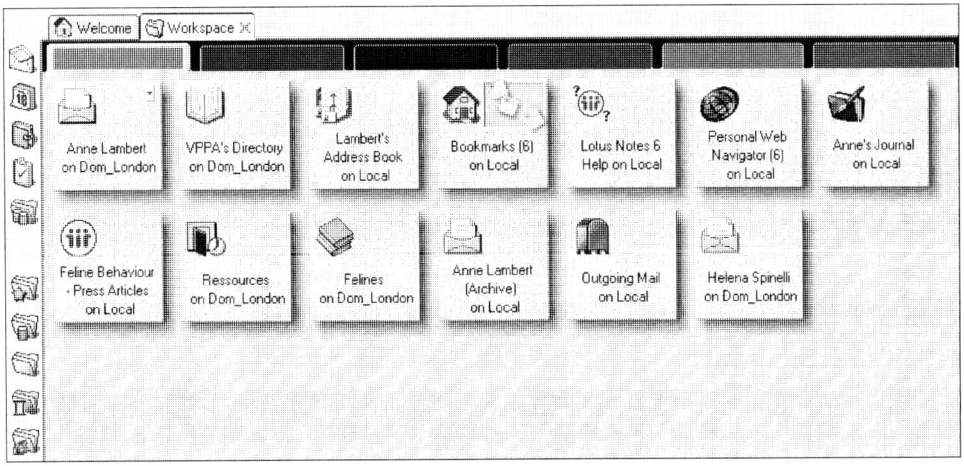

- Double-click the name of the database you wish to open.

Closing a database

When you have finished working on an open database, you can close it.

- **File** Ctrl **W**
  Close
  or
  Click the [X] button on the open database's window tab.

Getting information about the database

Seeing a brief presentation of the database

- Select the database icon on the workspace.
- Open the **Help** menu and click the **About This Database** option.

  The "About..." document opens on the screen. This contains mainly information about the object and the base's contents.
- Read and/or print (**File - Print**) the displayed text.
- Close the document by clicking the [X] button on its window tab.

Seeing more detailed information

- Select the database icon on the workspace.
- Open the **Help** menu and click the **Using This Database** option.

  The "Using..." document contains more detailed information. It gives instructions on how to use forms, views and other aspects of the selected base.
- Read and/or print (**File - Print**) the displayed text.
- Close the document by clicking the [X] button on its window tab.

Seeing information about the database file

- Right-click the database icon, point to the **Database** option then click **Properties.**

  *You can also select the database icon and use **File - Database - Properties**.*
- Activate the **Database Basics** tab to see the general characteristics of the database (name, server, general settings etc.).
- Activate the **Info** tab to see details of the file's size and the date and time it was created and last modified.

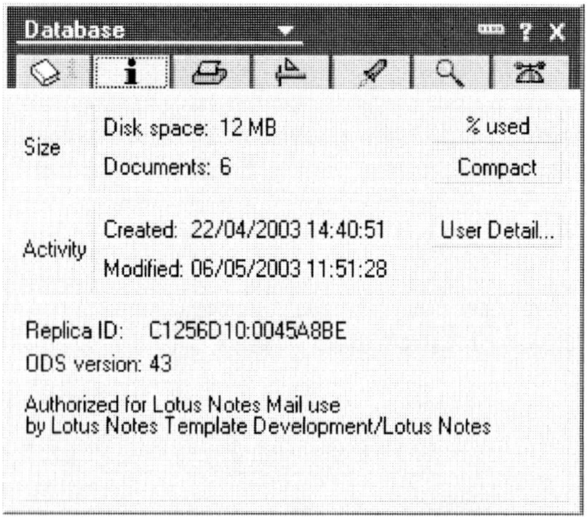

Creating a database from a template

*A **template** could be described as a database "skeleton", containing a basic structure but no actual data. When you use a template to create a database, the original template is unaffected and you can use it as many times as you wish.*

- **File** Ctrl N
  Database
  New
- Open the **Server** drop-down list and choose the **Local** option if you want to create a database on your hard disk; otherwise, choose the name of the server (on which you must have database creation permissions).
- Give a **Title** to your new database. This must not exceed 96 characters and will appear in the bookmarks.

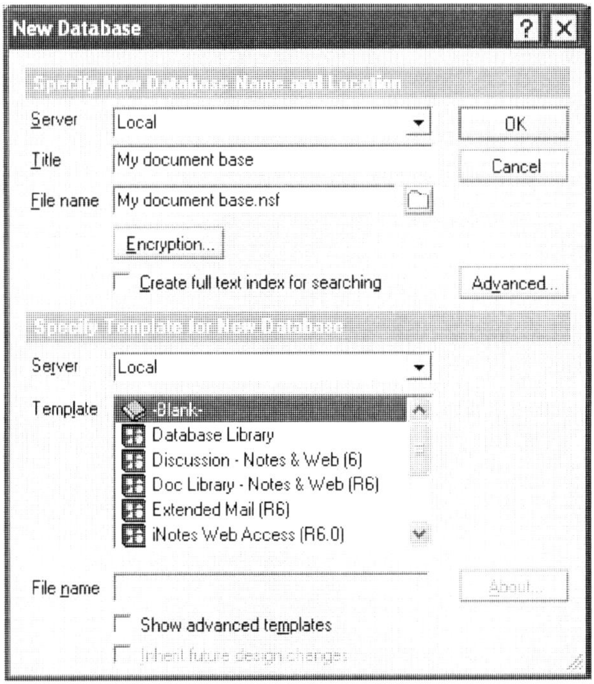

*By default, Notes will use the title as the **File name**.*

- To change the suggested **File name**, select the contents of the field and enter the name of your choice. This must not exceed 32 characters and be followed by a .nsf extension (e.g. my new base.nsf).

  Proceed according to where the new base is to be stocked:

  – on your hard disk: precede the file name by the name of the drive then the folder in which it will be stored (e.g. C:/My Documents/my new base.nsf). Otherwise the new base will be automatically placed in the working folder (data).

  – on a server: specify the server or folder concerned by the new base.

  *The **Encryption** button can be used to encrypt the new base (cf. Security - Encrypting local databases).*

- It is a good idea to tick the **Create full text index for searching** option which will speed up searches on the new base.

  *Depending on the selected **Server**, the list of available Notes templates will vary.*

- If necessary, choose another **Server** to see the list of templates it offers in the **Template** frame.
- To see a complete list of the templates available on the selected server, tick the **Show advanced templates** option.
- To use a particular **Template**, click its name. If you do not wish to use a template, choose the **Blank** option. However if you do, you will have to create all the forms and views in the new base "manually".

  *The **About** button gives you a general description of the database created with the **Template** selected in the list.*

Notes templates have a .ntf file extension.

Creating a new database by copying an existing one

- Select the icon of the database you want to copy.
- **File**
  Database
  New Copy
- In the **Server** list, choose where you want to create the new base.
- Give a **Title** for the new base.

- If required, enter a new **File name** and use the 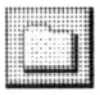 button to choose where to store the file.
- It is a good idea to tick the **Create full text index for searching** option which will speed up searches on the new base.
- **Specify What to Copy** in the corresponding frame.

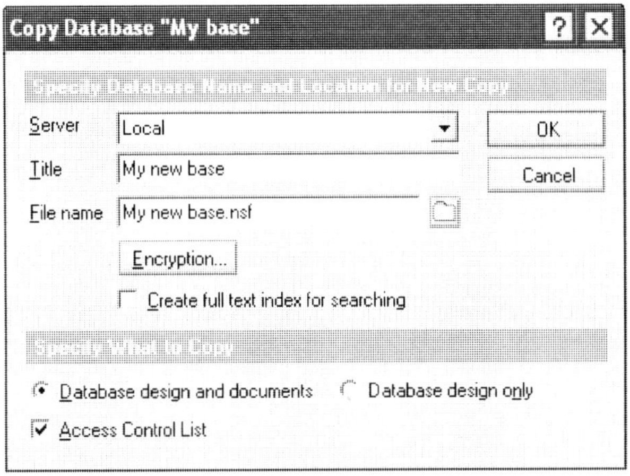

- Click **OK** to confirm.

Notes shows the copy's progress on the status bar:

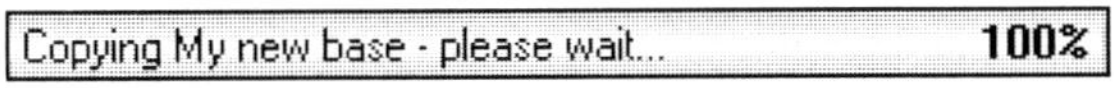

When the copy is finished, the database icon is inserted on the workspace.

- If necessary, move the icon onto the required workspace page.

Moving an icon on the workspace

You can move workspace icons within a page or onto another workspace page.

- Select the icon you want to move.
- To move an icon on its workspace page, drag the icon to the required place.
- To move it onto another workspace page, drag it onto the tab of the required page.

You can use **View - Arrange Icons** to let Notes lay out the icons as it sees fit.

Choosing which information is displayed with icons

- Right-click the workspace to see its shortcut menu.
- To show/hide the database's location on the icon (on local or a server), activate/deactivate the **Show Server Names** option.

  A tick indicates the option is active.
- To display the name of the database file, hold down the Shift key and click the **Show Server Names** option.
- To show the number of unread documents, activate the **Show Unread** option.

If you display the number of unread documents, you can update the number by right-clicking the workspace and choosing **Refresh Unread Count.**

Changing the title of a database

You can change the titles of local databases, or of those for which you have at least ***Designer*** *rights. Do not confuse the title with the file name.*

- Right-click the database icon concerned, point to the **Database** option and then click **Properties.**
- If necessary, activate the **Database Basics** tab.
- Enter the database's **Title** in the corresponding text box.

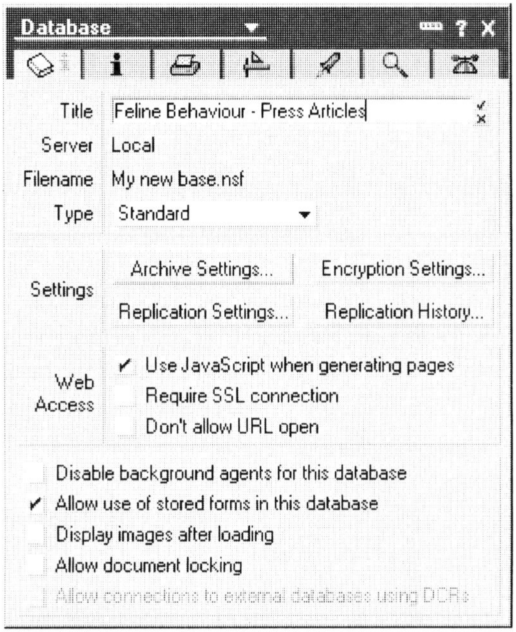

- Press Enter to confirm.
- Close the properties box by clicking its X button.

Selecting database icons

A single icon

- On the workspace, click the icon you want to select or type the initial letter of its title.

When several bases start with the same letter, move from one to the other by typing the initial several times.

Several icons

- On the workspace, click the first icon to select it.
- Select the next icons by holding down the Shift key and clicking the other icons.

You can only select several icons within the same workspace page.

Opening a database automatically on startup

You can set Notes to display a database when it first starts, instead of the Welcome page. To do this, you must first create a bookmark for the database in one of the bookmark folders (cf. Shortcuts - Bookmarks)

- Activate the **Databases** bookmark folders.
- Right-click the bookmark for the database that you want to open on startup.
- Click the **Set Bookmark as Home Page** option.
- Click the **Yes** button to confirm your choice.
- To restore the default Welcome page, follow the instructions in the section Welcome page - Using a bookmark as the home page.

Removing a workspace icon

You can at any time remove one or more workspace icons, without destroying the corresponding databases.

- Select the icon(s) you want to delete.
- **Edit** Del
  Delete
- Confirm with the **Yes** button.

If you delete the icon of an open database, this will only take effect once you close the base.

Deleting a database permanently

You can delete any database that is stored locally; if it is on a server, you must have Manager access.

- If the database is open, close it.
- Select the icon of the database you want to delete.
- **File**
  Database
  Delete
- Click **Yes** to confirm.

If you delete a database which is the only document in the folder containing it, the folder will also be destroyed.

Any bookmarks for deleted databases remain in the bookmark folders and have to be deleted manually.

What is a database library?

- A database **library** is a base containing lists of other databases.
- It only lists data-bases which have been published in it.
- Libraries make it easier to find databases, even when the bases have been moved, as libraries search, not with the file path, but with a unique replication ID.

Creating a library

You can create a database library on a server so other users can access it and add bases if you wish. You can also create a library on your local disk for your personal use.

- **File** Ctrl **N**
  Database
  New
- Use the **Server** list to specify the library file's destination. The **Local** option saves the database library file on your hard disk.

  If you want to create a library on a server, you must have appropriate permissions.
- Give a **Title** and if necessary a **File name.** This must not exceed 32 characters and be followed by a .nsf file extension.
- If you wish, use the button to show where the file should be stored.
- If necessary, tick the **Show advanced templates** option to see a complete templates list.
- Select **Database Library** (dblib4.ntf) as the **Template.**

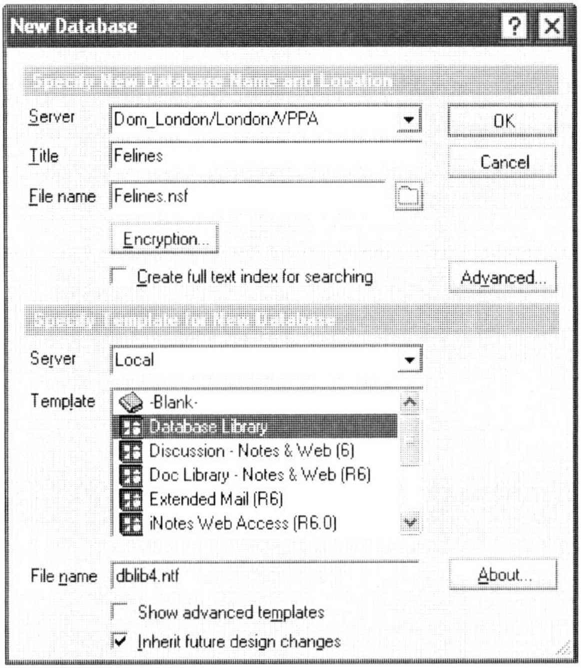

- Click **OK** to confirm.

  The "About..." document presentation appears on the screen.
- Read the presentation document and/or print it with **File - Print - OK.**
- Close the document by clicking ☒ on the corresponding window tab.

  The library view appears on the screen.
- Close the view.

On the workspace, library icons have a symbol.

If you are the creator of a library database, you automatically become its librarian and a **Manager** type access will be assigned to you in the access control list.

By default, users have **Author** access to a library created on a server and **Reader** access if the library is created locally.

If you do not want users to be able to publish directly into a library located on a server, give a **Reader** default access in the access control list. If you do this, when a user tries to publish a base to the library, Notes will create a publication request in an e-mail automatically, which the user can then send to the librarian.

To change a library's access control list, proceed as for an ordinary database (cf. Protection - Defining who is allowed to access a database).

Assigning librarians

Librarians can publish databases into a library and delegate other librarians. You are the default librarian for libraries that you create and you can create as many librarians as needed.

- Open the library to which you want to assign librarians; double-click its icon on the workspace or with **File - Database - Open**.
- Activate the **Librarians** view.
- Click Edit Librarians.
- In the **Librarian List**, give the full names of the persons you want to list, separating names with a semi-colon.

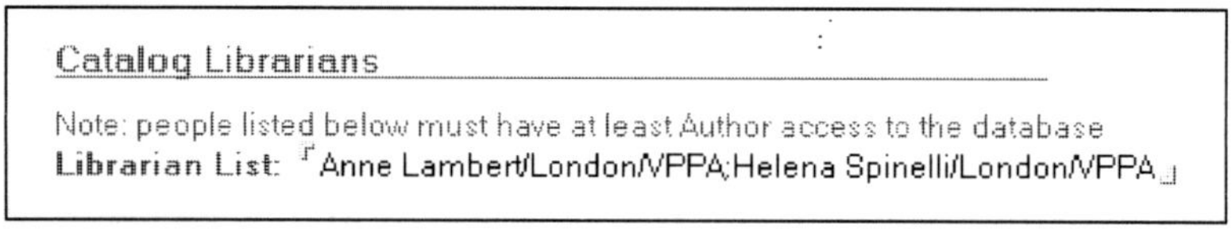

- Click the Save Document button.
- Click the Close button.

Publishing a database in a library

When you publish a database into a library, you ensure that the base reference appears in the library. You can do this if you have at least ***Author*** *access.*

- In the workspace, select the icon of the database you wish to publish.
- **File**
  Database
  Publish
- In the **Available libraries** list, choose the destination library.

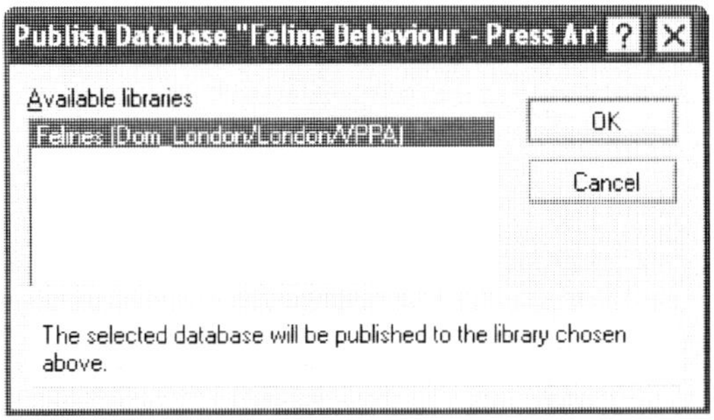

The name of the database being published appears on the title bar.

- Click **OK** to confirm.

With Author access or higher

When you publish the database, a form appears in which you can give identifying information about the base, such as an abstract.

- Fill in the database information form by clicking between the right-angled brackets on the **Abstract** and **Long Description** fields and entering your text.

*The information entered in the **Abstract** field will be reproduced in the library view:*

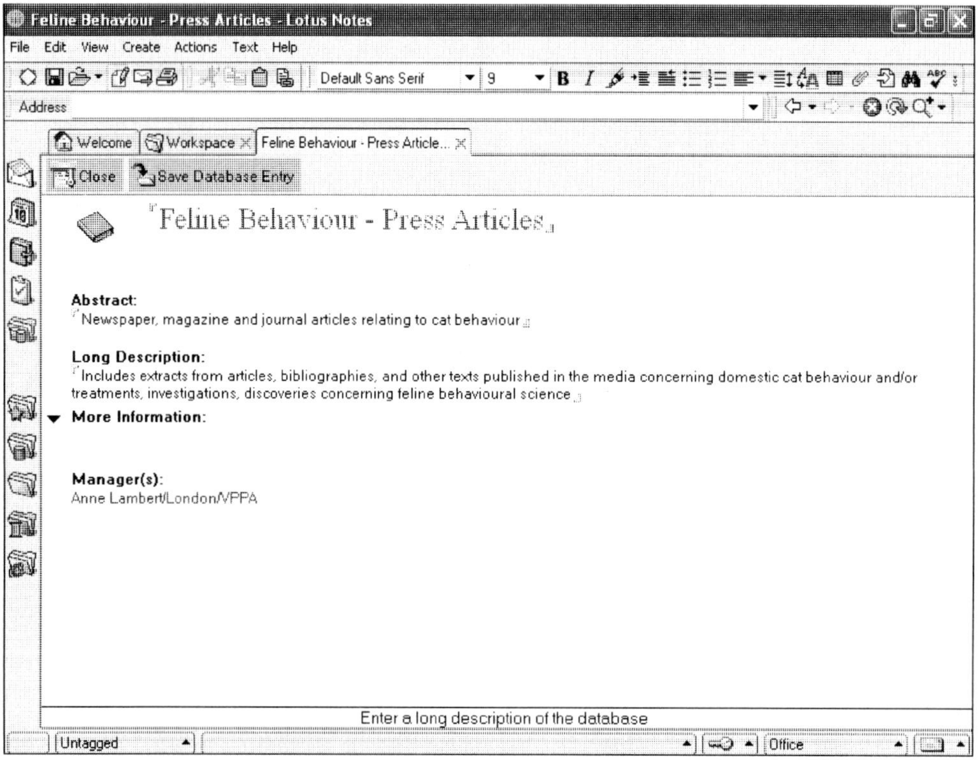

- Click the  button.
- Click the  button.

With lower access levels

If you do not have Author access or higher, the following message appears:

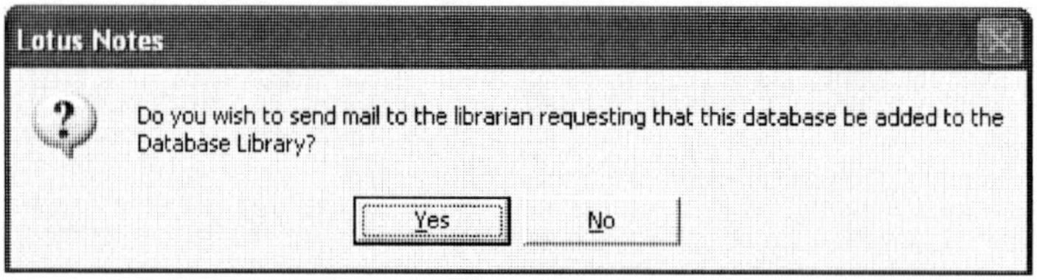

- Click **Yes** to accept creating a publication request.

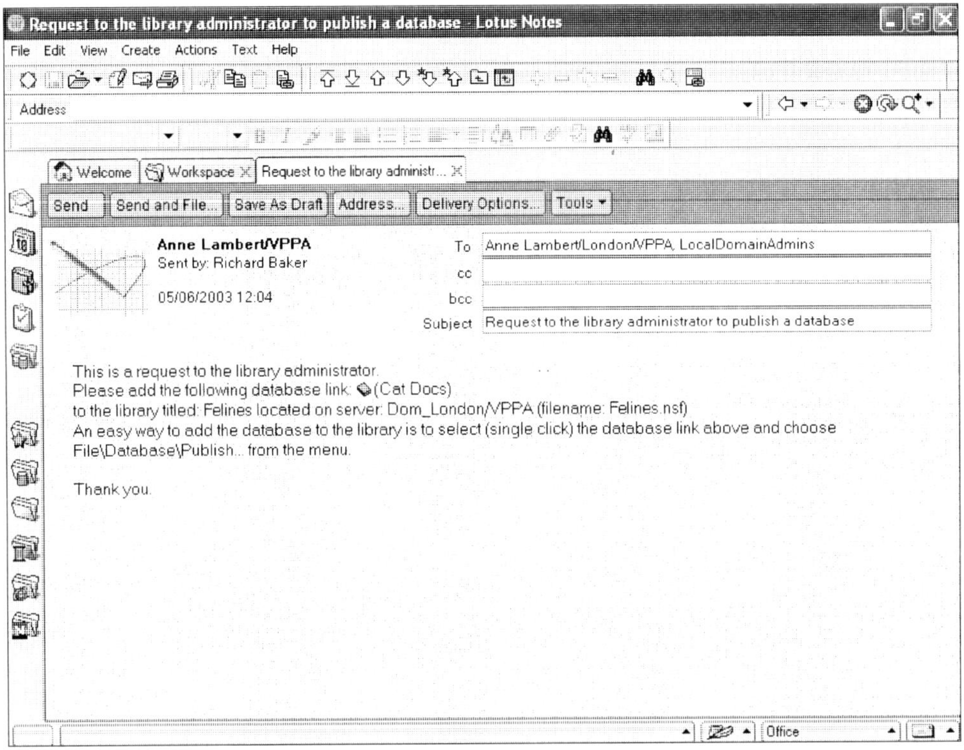

A standard notification message opens.

- If you wish, edit the proposed message and send it with **Send** or **Send and File**.

Using database libraries

Libraries help you to locate databases. You can use any library as long as you have at least Reader access.

Listing the databases in the library

- Open the library from the workspace by double-clicking its icon; otherwise use **File - Database - Open**.
- If necessary, activate the **Databases by Title** view.

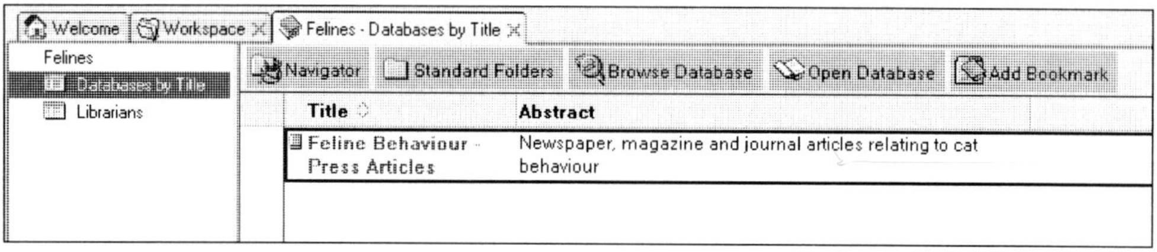

*Notes mentions the **Title** of each database published and a summary of its identification form (in fact, the contents of the **Abstract** field).*

Viewing the information sheet of a published base

- Display the library view.
- Double-click the **Title** of the database concerned.

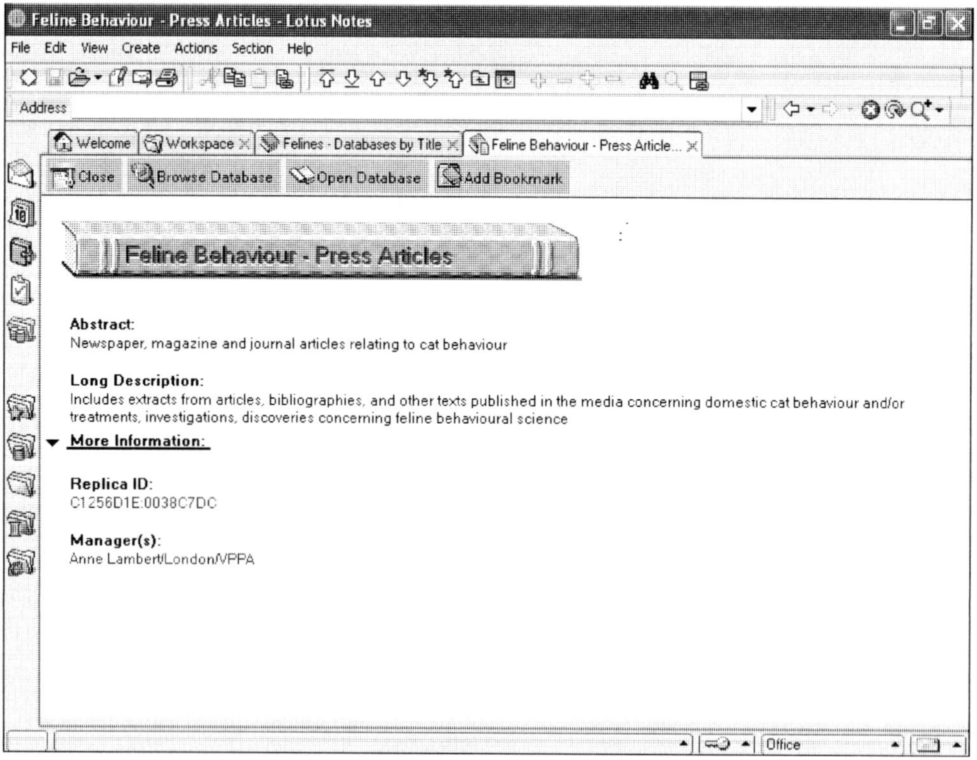

The database's information sheet appears.

- If you want to change details on this sheet, double-click the text you want to modify, to display the field brackets then make your required changes.
- Save your changes with the Save Database Entry button then click Close.

Listing the contents of a published database

- Display the library view and selected the required database.
- Click the Browse Database button.
- Close the view by clicking the ☒ button on the corresponding window tab.

You can also access this button from the database's information sheet.

Removing databases from a library

Whether or not you can remove a database from a library depends on your access permissions. With Author access you can remove a database that you have published, but you will need Editor permissions to remove bases that other users have posted.

Library entries are only shortcuts to the real database; if you remove a database from the library, you do not delete the actual database.

- Open the library concerned.
- Select the database(s) you want to remove.
- Press the Del key or use **Edit - Delete**.
- Close the library by clicking ☒ on its window tab.
- Click **Yes** to confirm removing the entry from the library.

Remember that this procedure removes the database entry but does not actually delete any database files!

Views

part three

What is a view?

- When you open a database, Notes displays it in a **view**.
- The view shows the different elements in the database and gives you information about the documents it contains, such as the author's name, its creation date and so on.
- In a view, you can select, sort or class documents.
- A view can show all the documents or merely a selection.
- Each type of database has its own view.
- A view can be made up of three elements:
  - the **navigation pane**, in which you can select a view or folder.
  - the **view pane**, in which you can select or open documents within the active view/folder.
  - the **preview pane**, in which you can preview the contents of a selected document without having to open it. This pane only appears when you ask for it specifically.

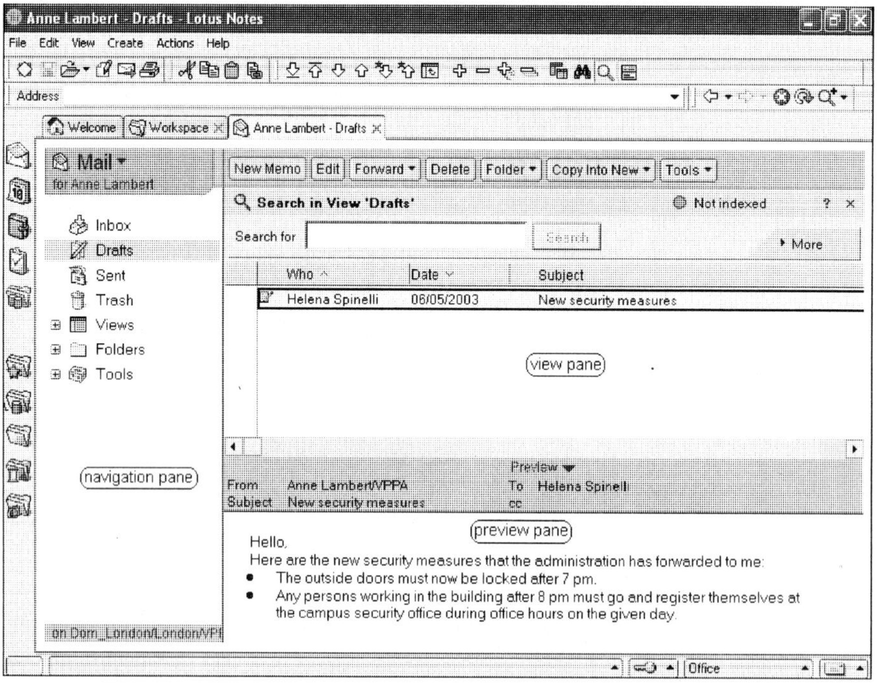

- Most views have action bars, such as the one below:

You can use these actions to carry out specific tasks on selected documents without opening them.

Looking at the navigation pane

- The navigation pane shows a list of the views and folders where documents are stored.
- To go to a specific view or folder, click its icon or its name in the navigation pane, or,

  Use the **View - Go To** command, select the name of the view or folder that you want to go to and confirm with **OK**.
- Certain databases can display the contents of the navigation pane in Navigator view. To do this, click the 

 button.

  The appearance of the Navigator varies from one base to the next:

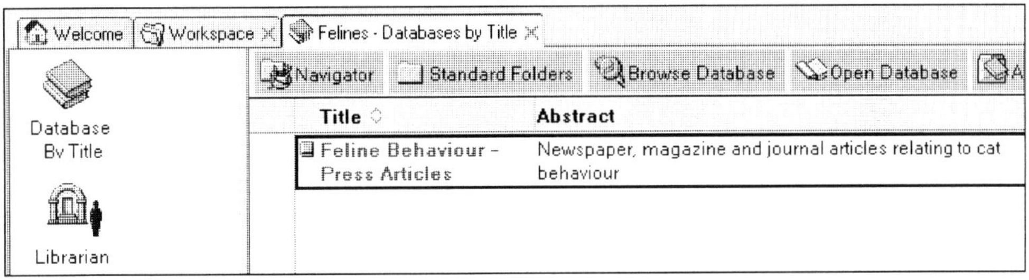

- To return the navigation pane to its standard appearance, click the 

 button.

Looking at the view pane

- The view pane contains the list of documents from the view or folder selected in the navigation pane.
- Its first column, which has no header, is called the **selection margin**. It shows icons that help you identify the type of document and its status.

Customising a view's appearance

- Activate the view concerned.
- **View**
  Customize This View

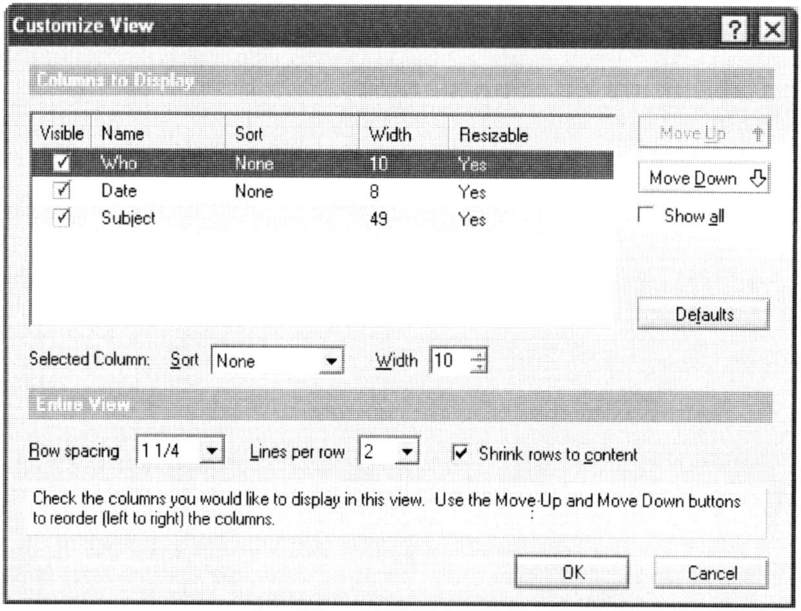

- To hide a column, remove the tick from the **Visible** column next to its **Name.**
- To move a column, select its **Name** then use the **Move Up** button to move it to the left or **Move Down** to move it to the right.
- If you wish, you can change the column's **Width** (under **Selected Column**). The **Sort** option offers a selection of sort orders.
- Click **OK** to confirm.

You can also modify a column's width by pointing to the vertical line to the right of the column header and dragging right or left to widen or narrow it.
Another way of sorting a column's contents is to click the column header, providing this has an arrow on it. Click once to sort in ascending order. To return to the original order, click the header once more.

Refreshing a view

Refreshing a view updates its contents to show the documents added or deleted since the view was opened. If you see a message telling you that you have mail, refresh the view if you want to read it.

- **View** F9
  Refresh

Printing a list of documents

- Select the folder or view you want to print.
- If necessary, select the documents that you want to print in a list.

  If you do not select any specific document, Notes prints the list of all the documents in the view or folder.

- **File** Ctrl P
  Print
- Activate the **Printer** tab if necessary.
- In the **What to Print** frame, choose to print the **Selected view** or just the **Selected documents**.

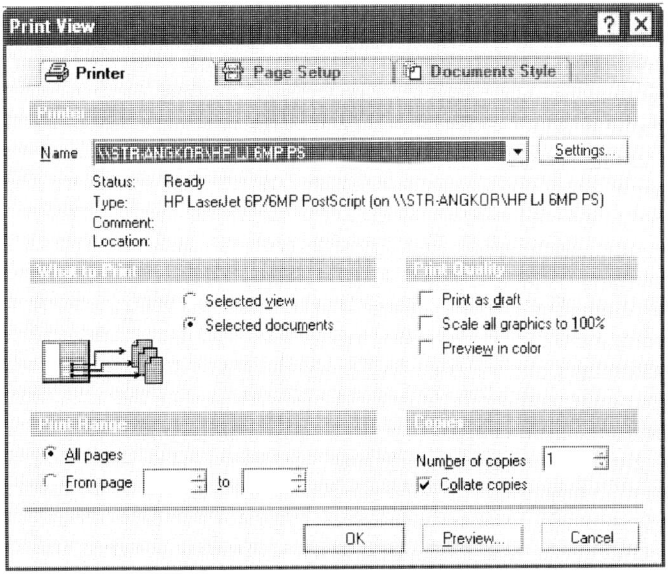

- Click **OK** to confirm.

Managing categories

A view can contain a large number of documents; to make organising and finding them easier, Notes can compile them into categories. Categories can then be sorted in alphabetical or numerical order or by date.

Creating a category

- Select the document(s) you want to categorize.
- **Actions**
  Categorize
- Click the **Add category** field and give the name of the new category.

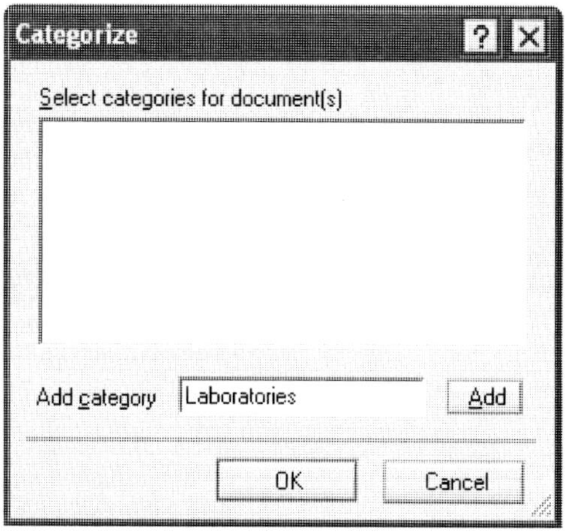

- Click the **Add** button to confirm the entry.
- Add all the necessary categories in the same way.
- When you have added all the categories, click **OK** to close the dialog box.

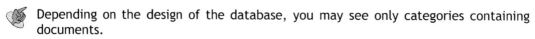

Depending on the design of the database, you may see only categories containing documents.

Creating a subcategory

- Select the document you want to categorize.
- **Actions**
  Categorize
- Click the **Add category** field and enter the name of the category, then a backslash (\) then the name of the new subcategory.

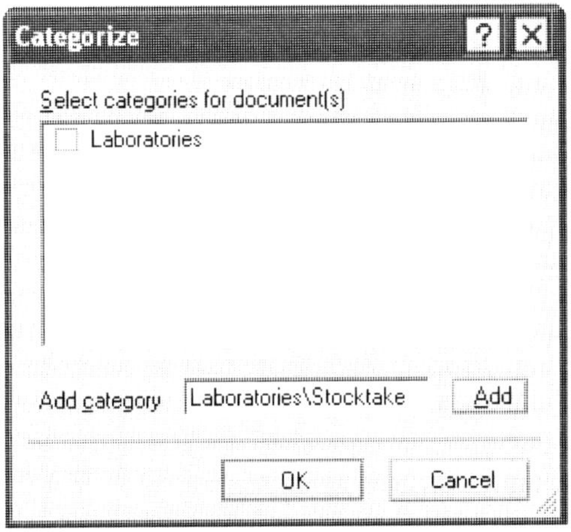

You can enter several levels of subcategory, separating each one with a backslash, for example Laboratories\Stocktake\April.

The subcategory is indented below the category name:

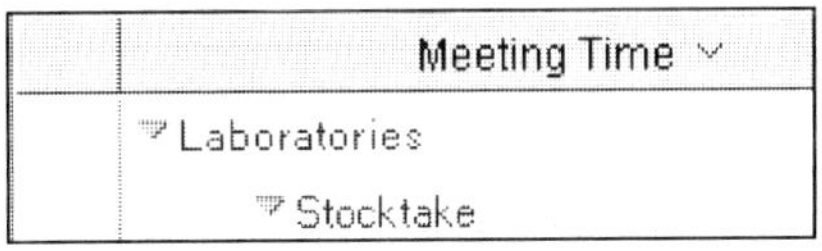

Showing only categories

- **View**
  Show
  Categories Only

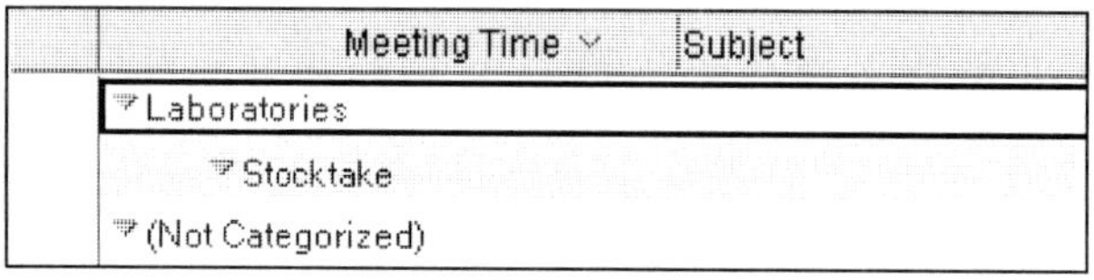

To see the name of the documents again, use **View - Show** again and deactivate the **Categories Only** option.

Deleting a category

The database's manager has to give you permission to remove the name of the category from your list of categories.

- Select all the documents in the category you want to delete.
- **Actions**
  Categorize
- In the **Select categories for document(s)** frame, deactivate the name of the category you want to remove.
- Click **OK** to confirm.

*The documents now appear under the **Not Categorized** header.*

Mail database

part four

What is the Mail database?

*The **Mail** database is mainly used for sending and receiving electronic mail via Notes.*

- The **Mail** base can create several different types of message, including:

Memo	to create a standard message.
Reply	to reply to a selected message.
Reply With History	to reply to a message and keep a copy of the original.
To Do	to note things you need to do or to ask a favour of someone else.
Calendar Entry	to note appointments, meetings, reminders, events, anniversaries etc.
Phone Message	to take a message for another user.
Link Message	to send a reference to a document.
Send Memo to Database Manager	to contact the database's manager.

- To access the Mail database from the workspace, double-click this icon:

- To access the Mail database from the Welcome page, click this icon:

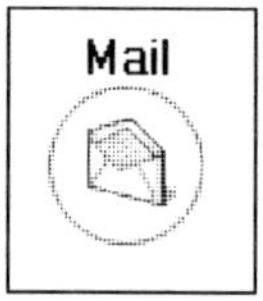

Once you have opened the base, use the views and folders in the navigation pane.

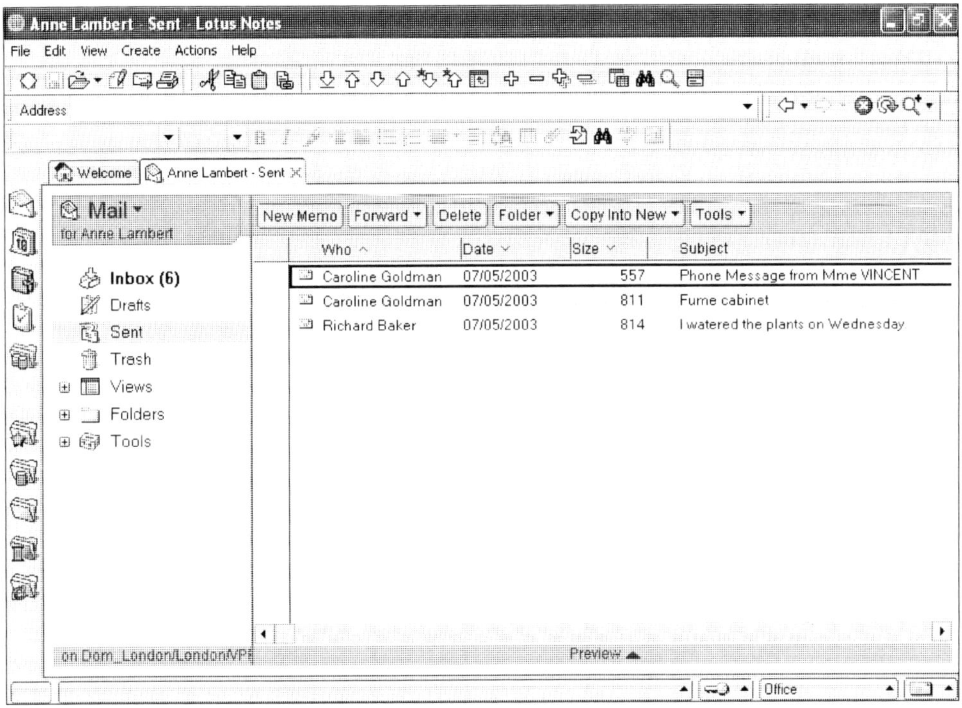

Most of the points covered in this chapter deal with all types of mail, except for To Dos which work in a slightly different manner.

Creating a memo

*A **memo** is the most common type of message.*

There are several different ways in which you can create a memo, such as:

– opening the Mail database and clicking the **New Memo** button.

– clicking the button on the status bar and choosing **Create Memo**.

– using the **Create - Memo** menu option or Ctrl **M**, if you are in the Mail database; otherwise use **Create - Mail - Memo**.

A blank memo opens on the screen, reminding you of the author's name (you!) and the day's date.

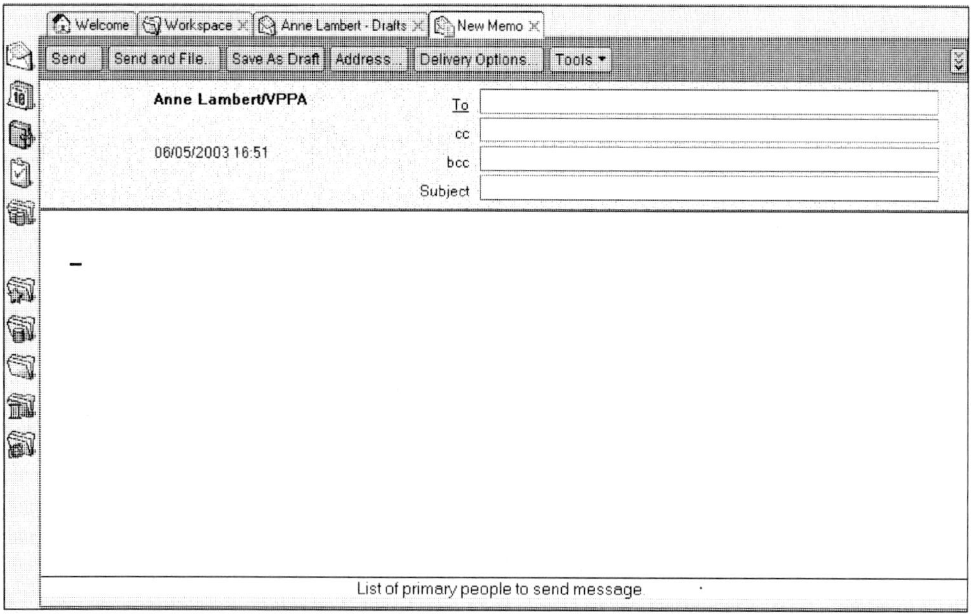

You need to give the name(s) of the recipient(s) in the following fields:

To	This recipient receives the original message; you must enter at least one name in this field.
cc	For "carbon copy"; this recipient receives a copy of the message, meaning you do not really expect a reply. The persons in the **To** and **cc** fields see all the recipients to whom the message has been sent. This field is optional.

bcc For "blind carbon copy"; this recipient receives a copy but this remains a secret. Other recipients cannot see the names in the **bcc** field. This field is optional.

You can fill in these fields by typing in the addressees' names or by selecting them in your address book.

Entering mail recipient names

- Click the field you want to fill in (**To**, **cc** or **bcc**).
- Use the key to go from one field to another or click in the field of your choice.
- If the name of your contact already exists in your address book, enter the first letters of his/her name.

Once you type in the first few letters, Notes searches your address book and suggests a name automatically. If more than one name could correspond, Notes will show a list and you can choose the correct name.

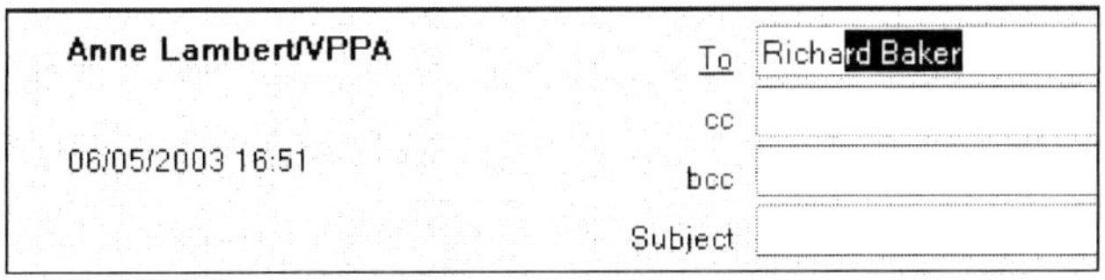

In this example, only one Richard is in the address book, so Notes offers the contact's complete name.

- If your contact's name does not exist in your address book, continue entering the name, giving the full e-mail address, for example paul.smith@mycompany.com.
- To enter several names, separate each one with a semi-colon (;).

If Notes finds your contact's surname, but the person has a different user name, Notes will display the full user name once you leave the field.

Choosing recipients in an address book

- Click the field you want to fill in (**To**, **cc** or **bcc**).
- Click the **Address** button.

*The **Select Addresses** dialog box opens:*

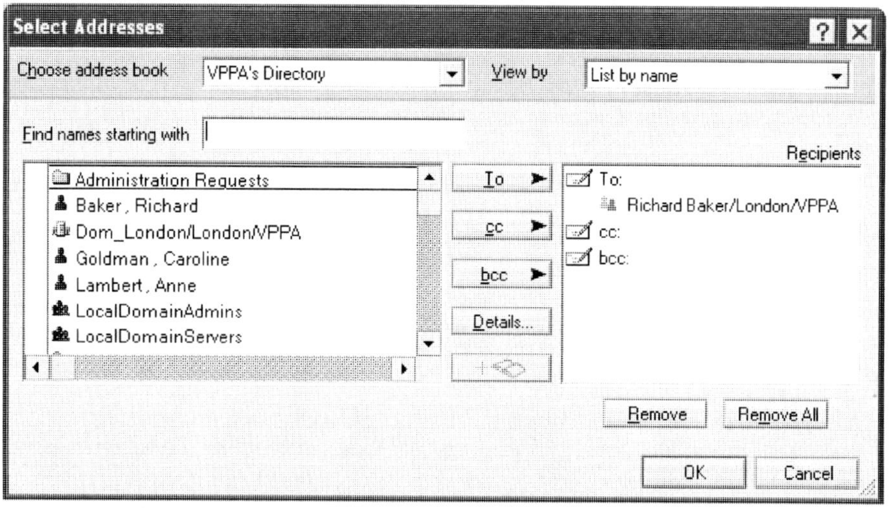

- Choose an address book from the corresponding list.
- In the list on the left, click the name of the message recipient.
- Click the **To**, **cc** and **bcc** button according to how you want to send the message (original, copy, or blind copy).

  *The selected name appears in the **Recipients** box.*
- To remove a recipient from the selection, click his/her name in the **Recipients** list then click the **Remove** button.
- Click **OK** to confirm and close the **Select Addresses** dialog box.

Entering the body of the message

- Click the **Subject** box and enter a brief description of the memo's purpose.

  *The information entered in the **To** and **Subject** fields will appear in the preview pane.*
- Click the next field (the large blank text box) and enter the message text.

  This is a rich text type field.
- If necessary, format the message text.

You can create and send a memo quickly without having to open your Mail base: click the Quick Notes **Memo** button (to see the Quick Notes pane, click the diamond at the extreme right of the Welcome page).

Creating a memo from the personal address book

- Click the bookmark to open your personal **Address Book**.
- Select the addressees for your message.
- Click the **Write Memo** button.
- Finish creating the memo following the usual procedure (see above for details).

Leaving a telephone message

You can inform another user that he/she has received a call or a message during his/her absence.

- If your mail base is open, use **Create - Special - Phone Message**, or use **Create - Mail - Special - Phone Message** if your mail is closed.
- Fill in the relevant fields (**To**, **cc**, **bcc**) to say for whom the message is.
- In the **Contact** box, give the name of the person who called. The **of** field is used to specify that person's company, office etc.
- Use the **Phone** and **Fax** fields to note the corresponding numbers.
- Tick the options to describe how the message should be treated.
- If required, enter a **Message** below the form, in the field brackets.

Types of message

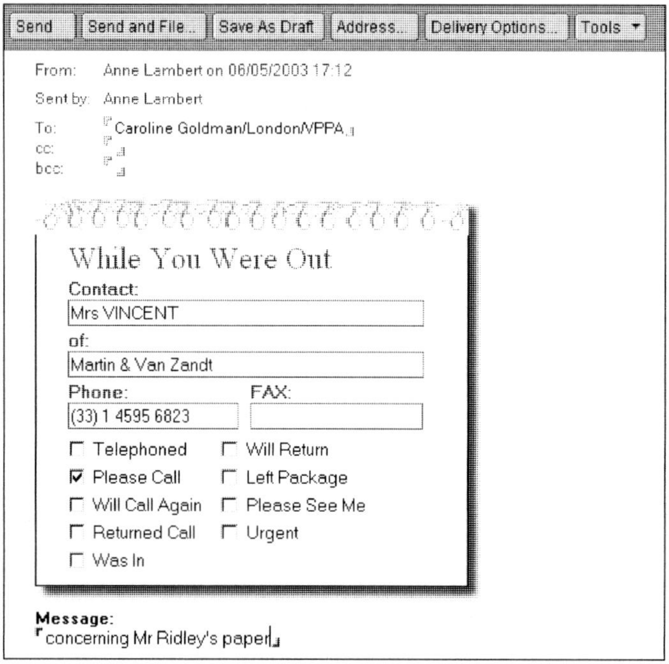

In the recipient's preview pane, the text **Phone Message from** and the correspondent's name will appear in the **Subject** field.

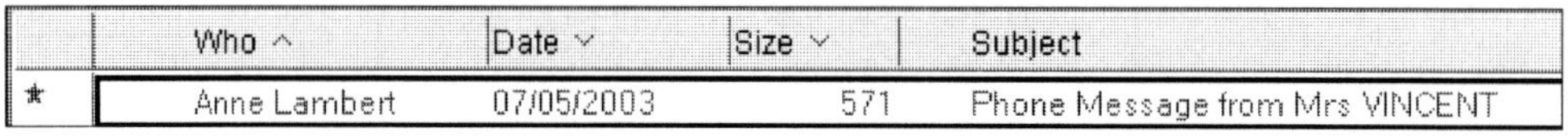
Who
Date
Size
Subject
Anne Lambert
07/05/2003
571
Phone Message from Mrs VINCENT

Creating a memo from a calendar entry

- Select the calendar entry concerned.
- **Actions**
  Copy Into New
  New Memo
- Give the required new information.
- Save the memo as a draft or send it.

Sending a memo

Once you have entered the body of a memo, there are two ways in which you can send it before you close it.

- To send the memo, click the **Send** button.
- To send it then save it in a folder, click the **Send and File** button.

*The **Folders** window opens.*

- Select the folder in which you want to save the memo,
  or
  click the **Create New Folder** button to create one. If you do this, enter the **Folder name** and confirm with **OK**.

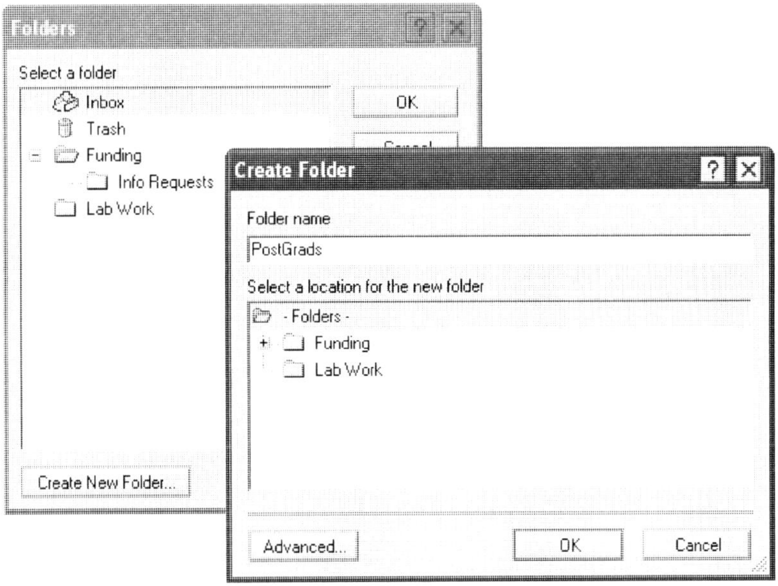

- Click the **OK** button to close the **Folders** window.

Notes sends the message to the addressee's mailbox and displays it in the sender's **All Documents** and **Sent** views.

If you saved the memo in a folder, it can also be seen in that folder.

Sent messages are preceded by a *icon.*

- If you want to postpone sending a memo, click the **Save As Draft** button (cf. below).

Saving an unfinished memo

- To save a memo that you have not yet finished or to send it later, click the **Save As Draft** button.

  *This closes the memo and saves it in the **Drafts** view, accompanied by a*  *icon.*

- To send a memo that is in the **Drafts** view, open this view and double-click the memo in question. Click the **Send** or **Send and File** button as required.

Setting memo delivery options

- Start creating the new message.
- Click the **Delivery Options** button.

  *This opens the **Delivery Options** dialog box.*

- If necessary, activate the **Basic** tab.
- To add a "mood" icon (also known as smileys or emoticons) to your memo, open the **Mood Stamp** list and choose the symbol of your choice.

  Here is a description of the various "moods" available:

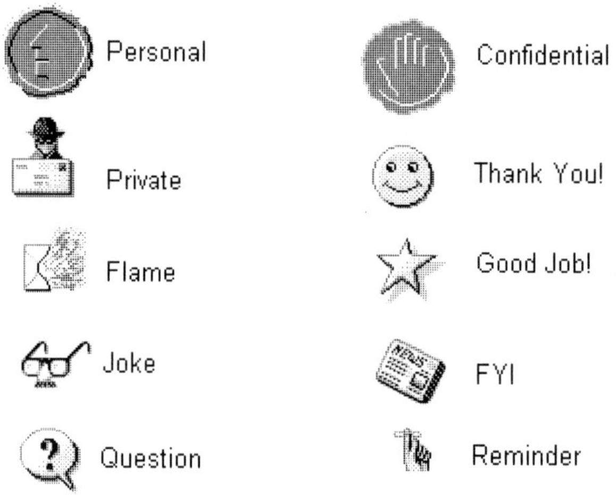

- Give the memo's **Importance** level: **Normal**, **High** or **Low**.

- Using the **Delivery report** list, choose whether you want to receive an information report in your mailbox to describe how successful your mail delivery was.
  You can choose to receive a report **Only on failure**, to **Confirm delivery** or to **Trace entire path** or **None** if you do not require confirmation.
- To specify how quickly your mail needs to be distributed on the network, choose one of the **Delivery priority** options (**Normal**, **High** or **Low**).
- Activate or deactivate the following check boxes:

Return receipt	To see the date and time the message was received by the recipient.
Prevent copying	This protects the message from being copied by the recipient.
Auto spellcheck	To check the message's contents for spelling errors, before sending.
Sign	This adds a unique code, identifying you as the message sender.
Encrypt	To encode the message so that only the addressee can read it (for further details, see the Protection chapter in the Security section).
Save these security options as the default	to save this message's security settings and apply them to all future messages.

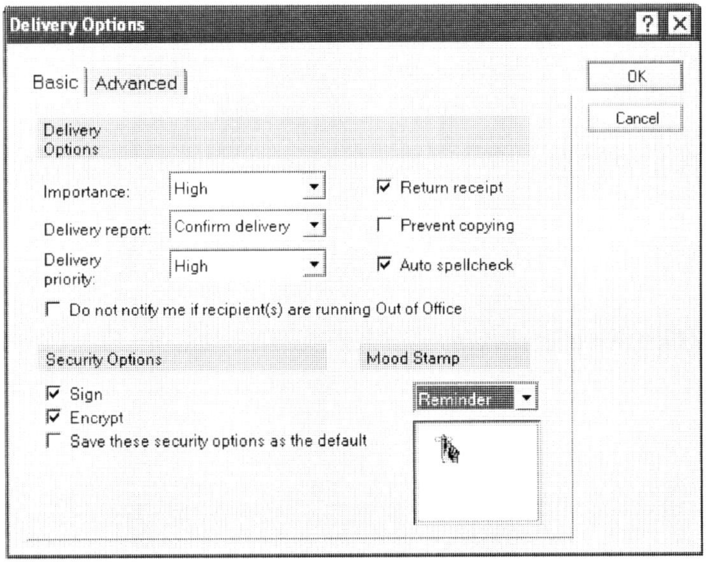

- Click **OK** to confirm.

A **High Importance** message is presented as follows:
-  (in red) for the sender,
- preceded by an exclamation point for the recipient.

Changing the presentation of the author's name

- Open your Mail base but do not create a new document.
- **Actions**
  Tools
  Preferences
- If necessary, click the **Mail** tab and the **Letterhead** tab within the dialog box.
- Choose the required **Letterhead** in the drop-down list.

  *Notes shows you a **Preview** of the selected letterhead:*

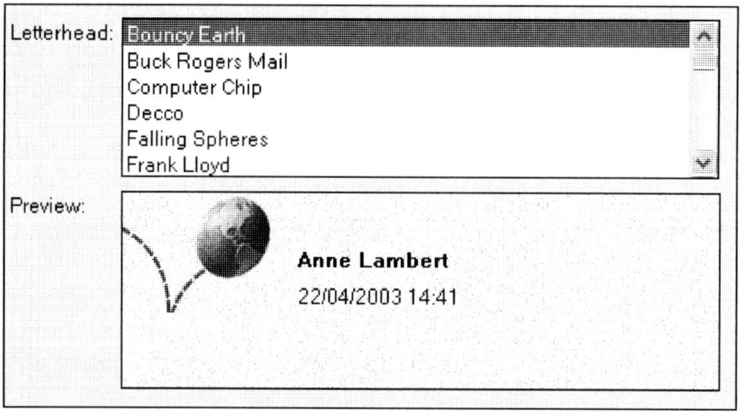

- Once you have made your choice, click **OK.**
- Create a new memo to check the result.

Reading received mail

- In your Mail base, select the **Inbox** folder.

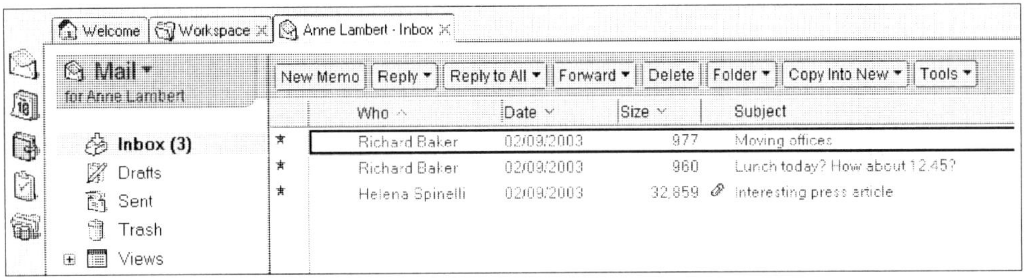

- If necessary, update the view with **View - Refresh** or with the F9 key.

  *Notes lists the mail received, the **Who** column gives the name of the sender and the **Date** column shows the date on which the mail was sent.*
  Unread messages are shown in red and are preceded by a star; high priority messages display an exclamation mark.

- Double-click the red text to open the corresponding message (but do not click the star icon).

Once you have opened a message, Lotus Notes considers it as read.

Configuring how new mail is announced

- **File**
  Preferences
  User Preferences
- Activate the **Mail - General** page.
- To choose how often Notes will check for the arrival of new messages, tick the **Check for new mail every** option then if required, give the interval in minutes in the associated field.
- To choose how you are notified of new mail, activate or deactivate the **Play a sound** and/or **Show a popup** options as required.
- Click **OK** to confirm.

Replying to a message

- Make sure that the message to which you want to reply is either open or selected in the navigation pane.
- To reply to the message's sender and all the other visible recipients, click the **Reply to All** button.

  To reply only to the message sender, click the **Reply** button.
- Choose one of these options:

Reply	to send a reply that contains no part of the original message.
Reply with History	to send a reply that includes the original message plus any previous messages in the same thread.
Reply without Attachment(s)	to send a reply with the message history but not including any attached files.
Reply with Internet-Style History	to send a reply with the message history; the lines of the history elements will be formatted and preceded by a character (usually a > symbol) in the left margin.

*Whatever you choose a **New Memo** view opens.*
*Notes automatically fills in the name of the original sender in the **To** field, and if necessary the names of the other recipients who will receive a copy. The reply will have the same **Subject** as the original message, preceded by the letters **RE:**.*

For replies that include a history, Notes creates a section in the new message that contains a copy of the contents of the original message:

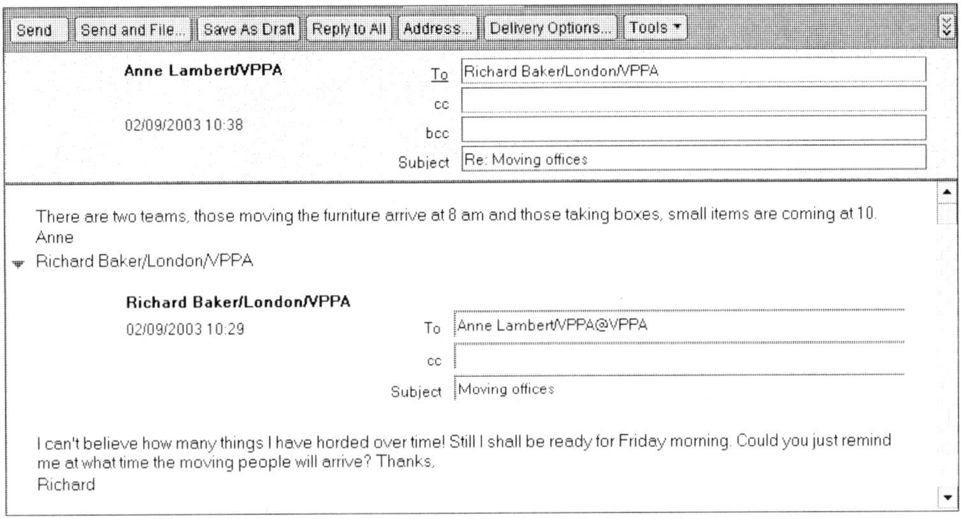

- Enter the reply's text and send the message.

  The reply window closes and the received mail is active once again.

Forwarding a message

You can forward a message to another person, adding new comments if required.

- Make sure that the message you want to forward is either open or selected in the navigation pane.
- To forward several messages together as one single message, select the messages concerned by clicking the selection margin to the left of the title in the view pane.
- Click the **Forward** button and choose the required option:

Forward	to transfer the entire original message.
Forward without Attachment(s)	to send on the original message, but not any attachments it may have had.
Internet-Style Forward	to send on the original message, formatting the line length and marking the left margin with a character (usually the > symbol).

The message appears in the lower part of the screen.

- Enter the necessary forwarding information in the **To, cc** and **bcc** fields and add new comments if you wish.
- Send the new message.

What is the Personal Address Book?

- This database is designed to file information about people, companies, sites or servers with which you regularly communicate.
- Each user has his or her own personal address book.

Opening the Personal Address Book database

- Click the bookmark or double-click the icon for your address book on the workspace:

A user's personal address book is represented by an open diary icon, while the server's address directory has an open book icon.

Creating a contact manually

- Open your address book.
- Click the **New** button then the **Contact** option or use the **Actions - New - Contact** menu command.

The ***New Contact*** *window opens, in which you can see a frame with fields and four tabbed pages.*

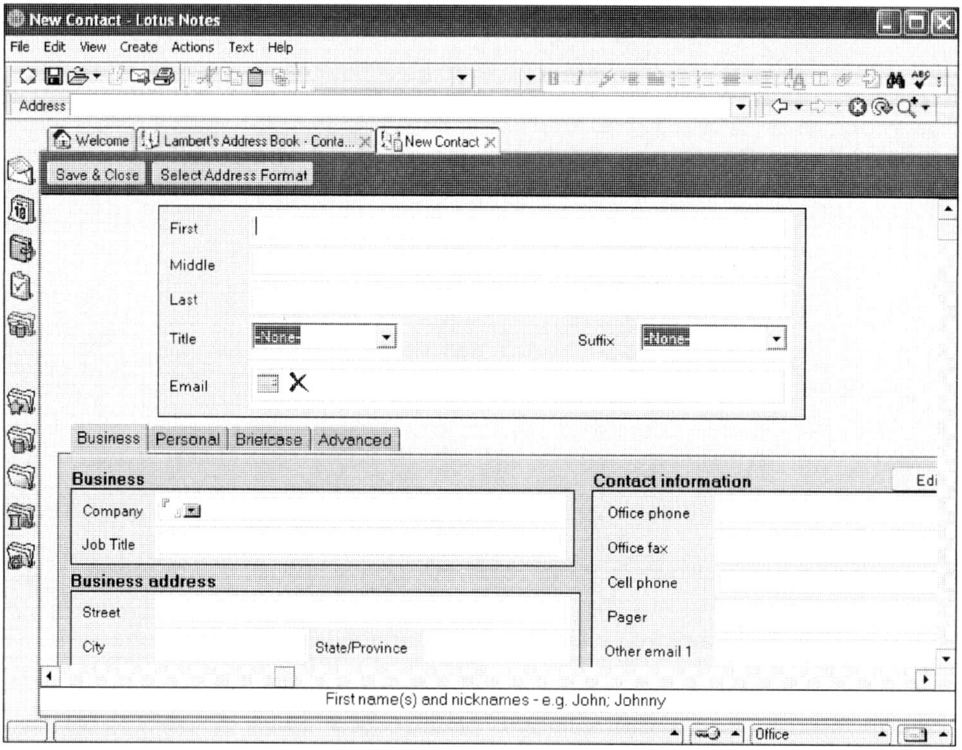

- Fill in the **First** and **Last** names of the new contact.
- If required, also give the **Middle** name, a **Title** and/or a **Suffix**.
- Enter the person's **Email** address.

You can use the  *button on the* ***Email*** *field to choose the type of messaging system used by the contact. This can help Notes to send mail to that person but this is not a compulsory detail.*

The  *button on the* ***Email*** *field deletes any information you have entered there.*

- If necessary use the **Business** and **Personal** pages to give extra information about the contact, such as his/her company's name and address, telephone numbers and even his/her birthday. If you supply this, the contact's name appears automatically in the address book's **Birthdays & Anniversaries** view.
- If required, use the **Briefcase** page to insert any files, pictures or texts associated with the contact entry. This can useful for items such as a map of the person's company or a CV and so on.
- If required, use the **Advanced** page to give more complex information about the contact, such as his/her **Certified public key** or to customise how the contact's information is displayed (in the **Organize** frame).
- Click the **Save & Close** button to confirm the entry.

You can create a new contact quickly without opening the address book base, by using the **Contacts** button in Quick Notes (from the Welcome page).

Creating a contact from an open message

- Open your Mail database then the message from which you want to create a new contact.
- **Actions**
  Tools
  Add Sender to Address Book

  *The **Add Sender to Address Book** dialog box opens and automatically copies the details of the messages sender.*
- If necessary, fill in the **Basics** and **Advanced** pages.

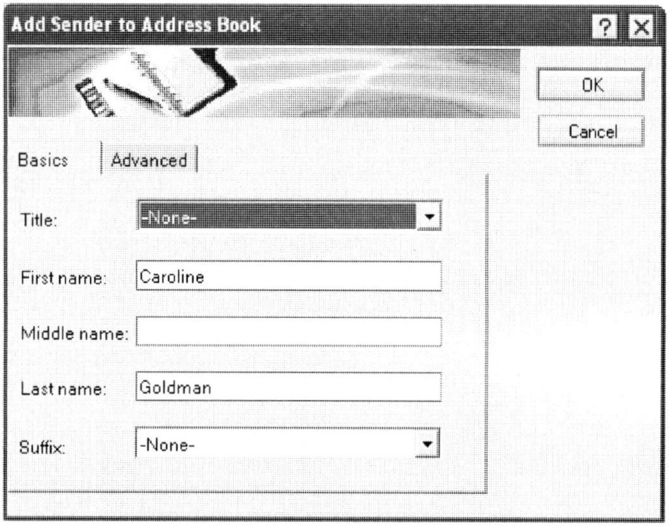

- If the contact is already in your address book, choose one of the available options to **Skip** adding the contact or to **Update** the existing information:

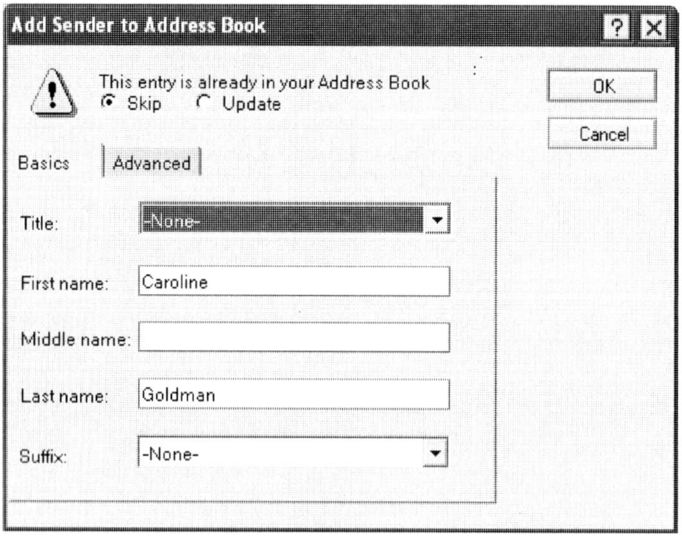

- If necessary, fill in the **Basics** and **Advanced** pages.
- Click **OK** to confirm.

Copying users from a public address book into a personal address book

As you create a message

- While the message is still being composed, click the **Address** button.
- In the **Choose address book** list, select the address book containing the required contact.
- Click the name of the contact you wish to add to your address book.
- Click the button.

A message tells when the copy has been completed:

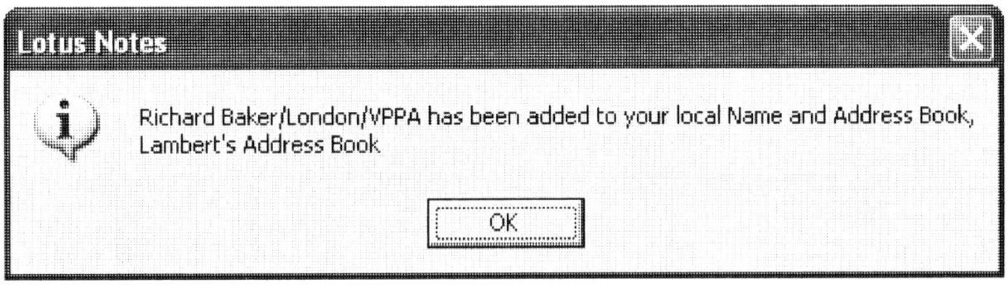
Lotus Notes
Richard Baker/London/VPPA has been added to your local Name and Address Book, Lambert's Address Book
OK

- Click **OK.**

Directly from the public directory

- Open the public directory from the workspace (icon) or use the **File - Database - Open** menu command.
- Activate the **People** view.
- Select the names you want to copy into your personal address book.
- Click the **Copy to Personal Address Book** button.

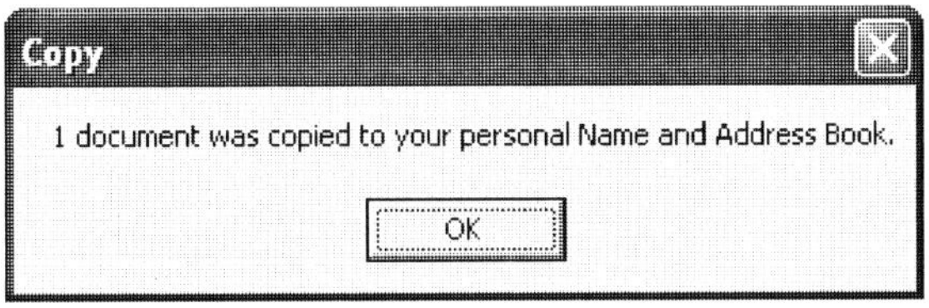
Copy
1 document was copied to your personal Name and Address Book.
OK

A message confirms the action.

- Click **OK.**

Creating a mailing list from a personal address book

This is an interesting technique if you often send messages to a certain group of users.

- Open your personal address book.
- To create a mailing list directly from contacts already in your address book, select them then click the **Tools** button and choose the **Copy Into New Group** option.
- To create a mailing list using new contacts, use the **Actions - New - Group** menu command.

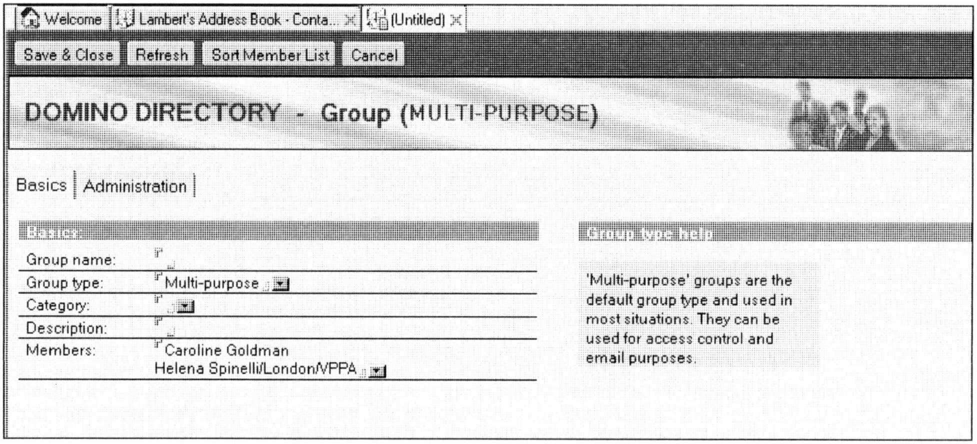

- Enter the **Group name.**
- Click the arrow next to **Group type** and choose the **Mail only** option.
- If you want to organise your groups, select or create a **Category**.
- If you wish, enter a **Description** of the new group.
- Check or enter the names of the **Members** of this group. If you type the names in, press the [Enter] key after each name. To select names from an address book, use the drop-down arrow on the **Members** field.
- Click the **Save & Close** button.

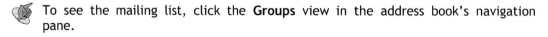

To see the mailing list, click the **Groups** view in the address book's navigation pane.

Creating a mailing list from the Mail database

You can create a mailing list made up of message senders and recipients, meeting invitations and tasks.

- Open your Mail database.
- Select the document containing the names of the users that you want to save in a new mailing list.
- **Actions**
  Add Recipients to new Group in Address Book
- Enter the **Group name** and, if you wish, a **Description.**
- Check the **Members** list for the new group. If you do not want to include one of the members in this group, deactivate the check box next to the name.

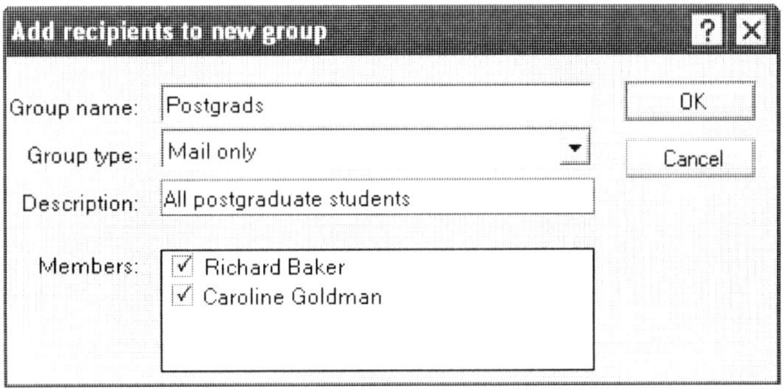

- Click **OK** to confirm.

What is a To Do?

- Creating To Dos (tasks that have to be done) helps you organise your time more efficiently and allows you to delegate work to other users.
- Notes manages two types of To Do: one that you assign yourself, which is a **personal To Do**, and those that you assign to one or more people, along with an assignment notice, which are known as **group To Dos**.

Creating a personal To Do

A personal To Do is one that you assign only to yourself.

- Open the list of current To Dos, by clicking the 

icon on the Welcome page or by clicking the 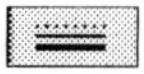 bookmark.
- **Actions**
  New To Do Item
  or
  click the arrow on the  tool button and choose the **New To Do** option
  or
  click the **New To Do Item** button.

*The **To Do Item** form opens:*

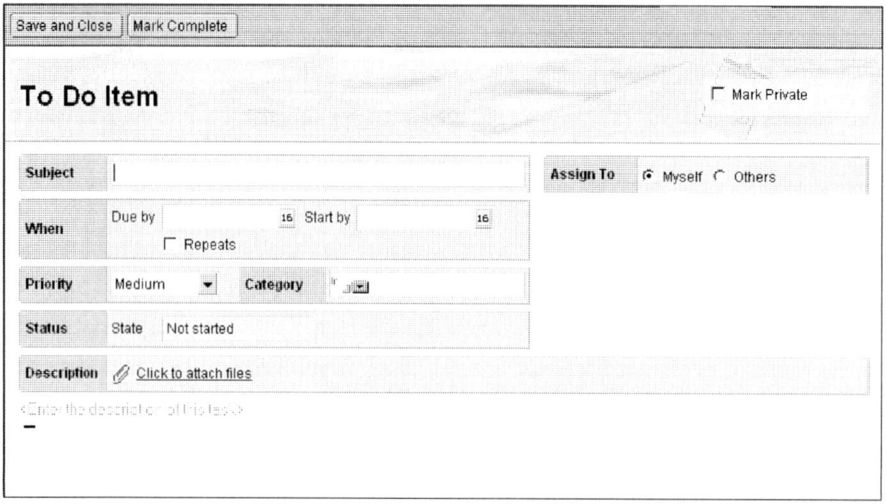

- In the **Subject** field, enter a brief description.
- Make sure that the **Myself** option is active in the **Assign To** frame.
- If necessary, enter or select a **Due by** and/or **Start by** date.
- If the entry should recur, tick the **Repeats** option and set the recurrence options in the corresponding dialog box.

  *Take note that a repeating entry cannot be turned into a non-repeating task once you have saved it, and vice versa. You must simply create a new entry. You can do this by copying the original entry (**Actions - Copy Into New - New To Do**) then change the settings on the new entry before saving it.*

- If you wish, open the **Priority** list and choose to set a **High, Medium** or **Low** importance, or **None** at all.

  *Depending on the priority ranking you choose, the current To Do appears in the list of To Dos, accompanied by a value of **1** for High, **2** for Medium, **3** for Low or no value for None.*

- If required, assign a **Category** to the entry.
- If necessary, add text, links, file attachments, objects and/or images using the **Click to attach files** link.
- If you wish, click **Enter the description of this task** and give a precise description of the item.
- Tick the **Mark Private** option at the top right of the form if you want to prevent displaying the To Do to those users who may have access to your calendar. They will only see the To Do's date and time.
- Click the **Save and Close** button.

  *A personal To Do appears in the **Personal** folder in the **To Do** view.*

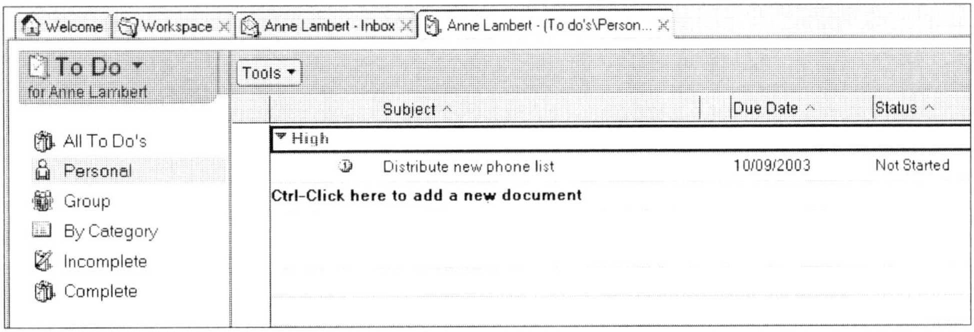

Creating a group To Do

A group To Do is one that you can assign to one or more other users.

- Open the list of current To Dos, using a technique such as clicking the icon on the Welcome page.
- **Actions**
  New To Do Item
  or
  click the arrow on the tool button and choose the **New To Do** option
  or
  click the **New To Do Item** button.

  *The **To Do Item** form opens.*
- In the **Subject** field, enter a brief description.
- Activate the **Others** option in the **Assign To** frame.
- Fill in the **Participants** frame:

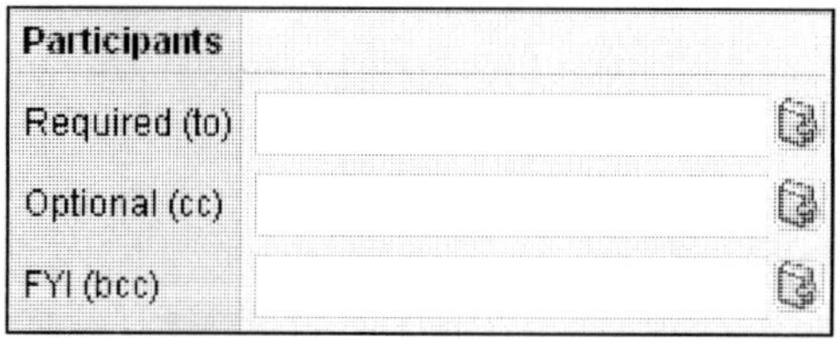

  – You must fill in the **Required (to)** field with the names of the people who should receive an assignment notice, which will give the reply options: **Accept**, **Decline**, **Delegate**, **Propose new date** and **Completed.**

  – In the **Optional (cc)** field, give the names of the people who are invited to participate but who do not have to. They will also receive an assignment notice, with reply options: **Accept**, **Decline**, **Delegate**, **Propose new date** and **Comple-ted.**

  – If necessary, fill in the **FYI (bcc)** field with the names of people who should simply be informed of the item. They will receive a message that will not contain the reply options mentioned previously, but they will be able to add the item to their list of To Dos, if they wish. The names of these people will not be seen by the other message recipients.

- If necessary, enter or select a **Due by** and/or **Start by** date.

- If the entry should recur, tick the **Repeats** option and set the recurrence options in the corresponding dialog box.

  *Take note that a repeating entry cannot be turned into a non-repeating task once you have saved it, and vice versa. You must simply create a new entry. You can do this by copying the original entry (**Actions - Copy Into New - New To Do**) then change the settings on the new entry before saving it.*

- If you wish, open the **Priority** list and choose to set a **High**, **Medium** or **Low** importance, or **None** at all.

  *Depending on the priority ranking you choose, the current To Do appears in the list of To Dos, accompanied by a value of **1** for High, **2** for Medium, **3** for Low or no value for None.*

- If required, assign a **Category** to the entry.
- If necessary, add text, links, file attachments, objects and/or images using the **Click to attach files** link.
- If you wish, click **Enter the description of this task** and give a precise description of the item.
- Tick the **Mark Private** option at the top right of the form if you want to prevent displaying the To Do to those users who may have access to your calendar. In this case, they will only see the date and time.
- If you want to receive a text or sound alarm before the item's deadline, tick the **Notify Me** option and set the alarm options in the **Alarm Notification Options** dialog box.

This option appears only if you have set a ***Due by*** *date:*

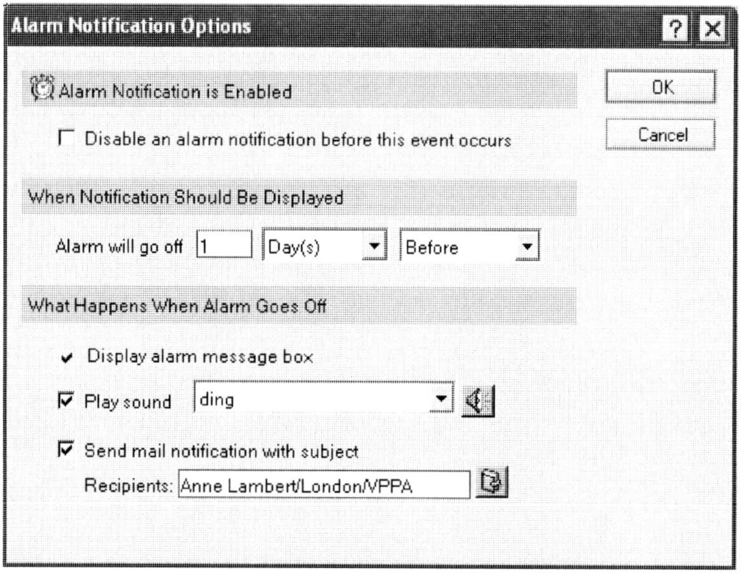

- Click **OK** to confirm the alarm options.
- Click the **Save and Send Assignments** button.

Managing To Dos

- Open the To Do database by clicking the  button on the Welcome page.

- Each To Do has a **Status**:

Overdue a task that has not been stated as finished, even though its due date has passed.

In Progress a task that has no due date or whose start date has passed but not its end date.

Not Started a task whose start date has not yet come around.

Completed a task that has been declared finished by all those concerned with it.

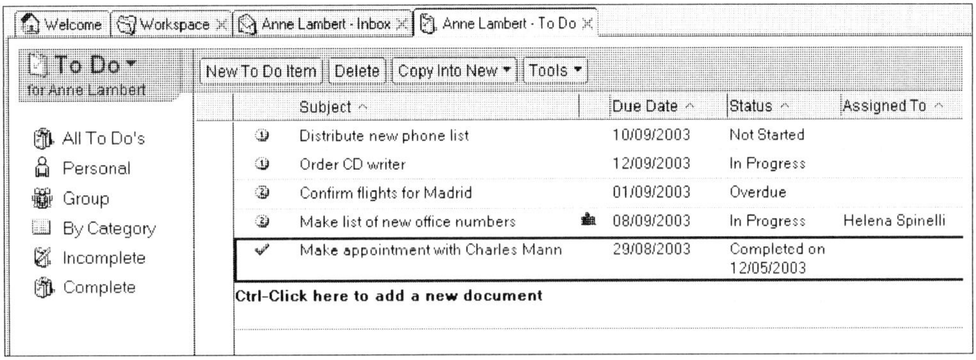

- The priority given to each To Do is represented by a number:

no value	None
1	High
2	Medium
3	Low

Declaring a To Do as completed

- In the **To Do** view, select the finished tasks.
- Click the **Mark Complete** button.

*Each To Do concerned is instantly given a **Completed** status, followed by its actual end date.*

Deleting a To Do

- In the **To Do** view, select the tasks you want to delete.
- Click the **Delete** button or use the **Edit - Delete** command.

Be careful, as deleting To Dos is immediate and cannot be undone.

Replying to a To Do request

- Open the message that has been sent to you to check whether or not a reply is required.

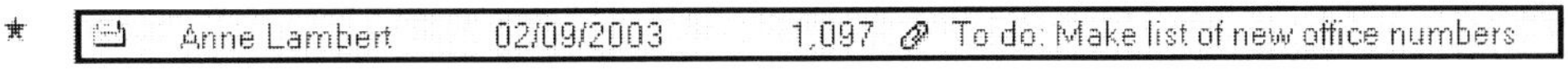

If the buttons shown below are visible, the sender wants you to answer the request:

- Click the **Request Information** button if you want to receive further details about the task at hand.

  Notes opens a blank information request form, so you can send comments to the task's owner. Fill this in and click ***Send*** *to send it. A word of caution: this action cannot be undone. If you change your mind, you cannot close the form, you can only continue sending the message but without any comments.*

- To reply to the sender, click the **Respond** or **Respond with Comments** button then choose one of these options:

Accept	to accept the To Do as it is.
Decline	to refuse the To Do.
Delegate	to send the request to another person whom you will specify.
Propose New Date	to suggest a change in the date.
Completed	to change the request status.

- If you chose to **Respond with Comments**, enter your text then click **Send.**

Converting a calendar entry into a To Do

- Select or open the calendar entry that you want to convert into a To Do.
- **Actions**
  Copy Into New
  New To Do

  The form for creating a new To Do opens.

- Finish creating the new To Do.

Introduction

By archiving your mail, you gain space in the Mail database without losing your information. Increasing the free space can significantly improve the performance of your messaging system.

Depending on the archiving policies set up by your administrator, your mail may be configured to archive automatically. However your administrator can also allow you to set your own private archiving criteria, distinct from those put in place on your company network.

Checking the archive settings

- Open your Mail database.
- **Actions**
  Archive
  Settings
  or
  File
  Database
  Properties - Archive Settings button

  The ***Archive Settings for*** *dialog box appears, containing three pages (****Basics****,* ***Settings*** *and* ***Advanced****).*

  Your access permissions for mail archiving depend of the archiving policy put in place by your network administrator. One of several situations may occur.

  Before presenting a specific example, let's see what situations may occur.

Looking at archiving possibilities

What appears on the page			
Basics	**Settings**	**Advanced**	**What this means**
Options are greyed-out. Message informs you that your administrator does not allow archiving.	Options are greyed-out.	Options are greyed-out.	Any type of private archiving is prohibited.
Options are greyed-out.	Options are greyed-out + padlock icon appears next to the set of criteria in the list.	Scheduling options are available.	You can control the archive schedules defined by your administrator that will occur on your computer.
Options are greyed-out.	Add button is available + padlock icon appears next to the set of criteria in the list.	Options are greyed-out.	An archiving administration policy exists but you can still specify other personal criteria.
Options are available.	Options are available.	Options are available.	You can configure your own mail archiving.

Checking or configuring mail archiving

For this example, imagine that no specific archiving policy is in place and you can configure mail archiving yourself.

- Open the Mail database.
- Open the **Archive Settings** dialog box.
- If necessary, activate the **Basics** tab.

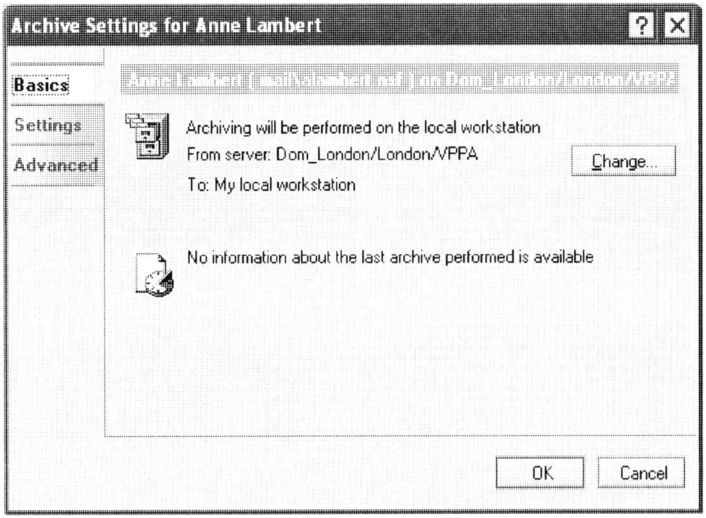

This page tells you where the archive base is located and gives information of the last archive made (if there was one).

- To change the location of the archive base, click the **Change** button.

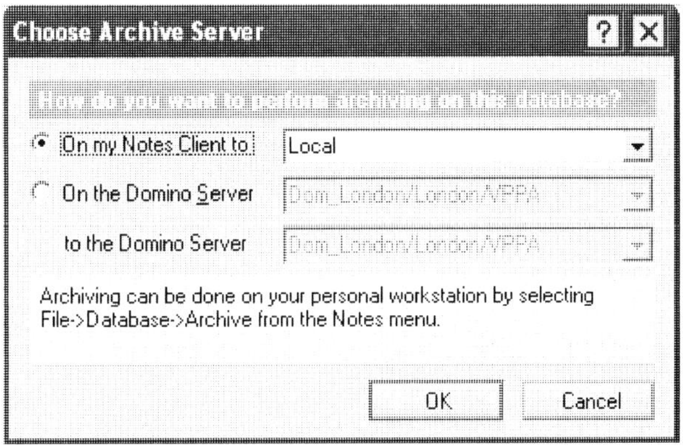

- To archive your mail database onto your computer (client archiving), activate the **On my Notes Client to** option. To archive your mail database onto a Domino server (server archiving), activate the **On the Domino Server** option and give the name of the server (for which you need access permissions).
- Click **OK** to confirm.
- Activate the **Settings** page.

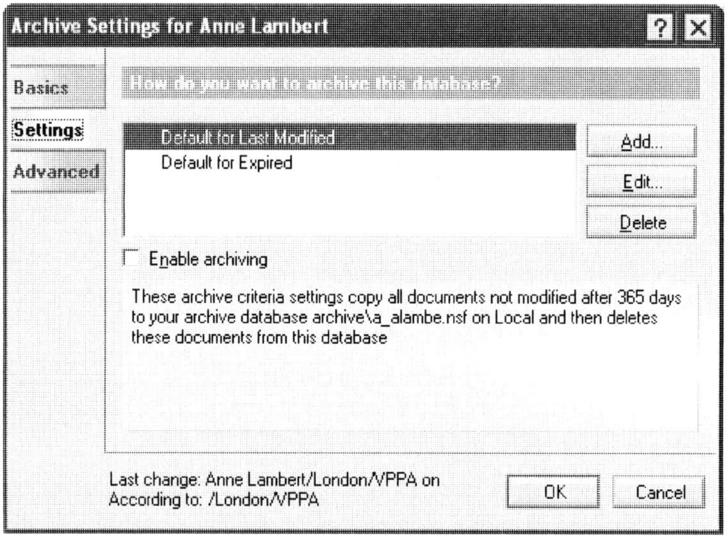

On this page, you can choose one of the archiving criteria sets supplied by your company.

- Click the required criteria set to select it.

  A description of the selected set appears in the yellow frame.

- Use the **Edit** button to work on the settings for the selected criteria set.

  Any criteria set that is preceded by a padlock symbol cannot be modified.

- To create your own set of archiving criteria, click the **Add** button and define your settings as required.
- To **Enable archiving** using the selected criteria set, tick the option of the same name.
- If necessary, activate the **Advanced** page.

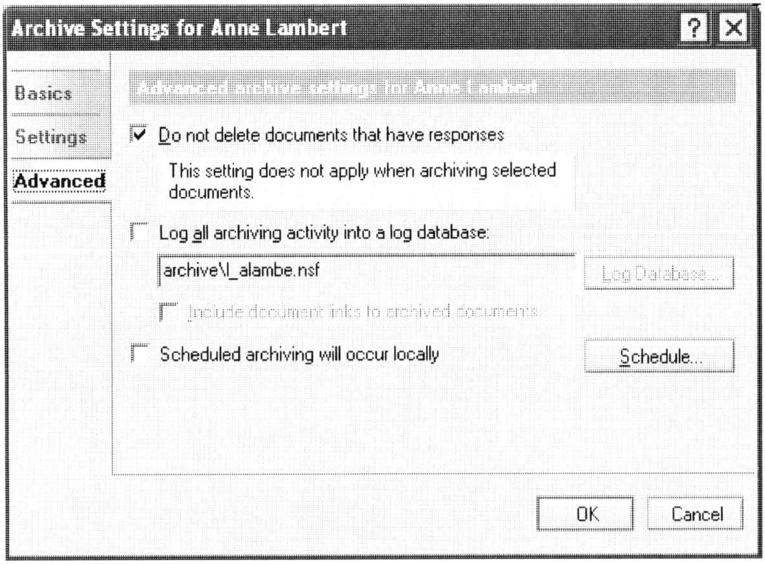

- Set the mail archiving settings and set up an archiving log.

  Be careful, as these advanced settings will apply to all the criteria sets.

- Click **OK** to confirm and close the **Archive Settings for...** dialog box.

Running archiving manually

Even if you have set up an archiving schedule, you can still carry out archiving on your database in Notes whenever you like.

<u>All the documents in the base</u>

- Open the database that you want to archive.
- Make sure that a set of criteria is assigned to it and that the set is active (cf. Checking the archive settings).
- **Actions**
  Archive
  Archive Now
- Click the **Yes** button to start archiving.
- Close the database then open it again.

A selection of documents

- Open the database that you want to archive.
- To archive the documents that are selected in a view or folder, use:

  Actions
  Archive
  Archive Selected Documents

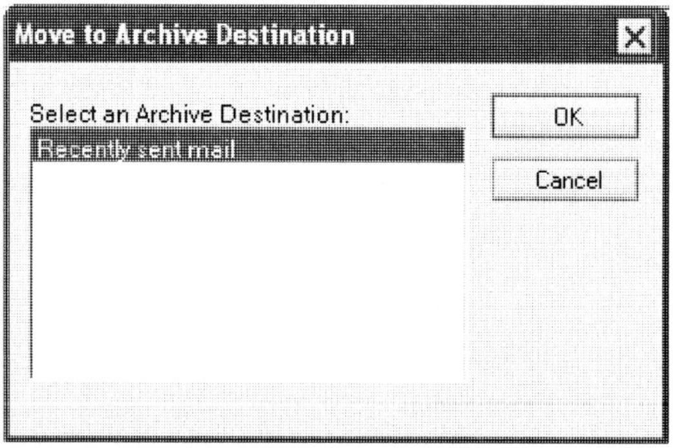

- If necessary, click the criteria set you wish to use for archiving then click **OK**.

  *You can also drag the selection towards any archiving criteria set listed in the **Archive** subfolder (in the **Tools** folder):*

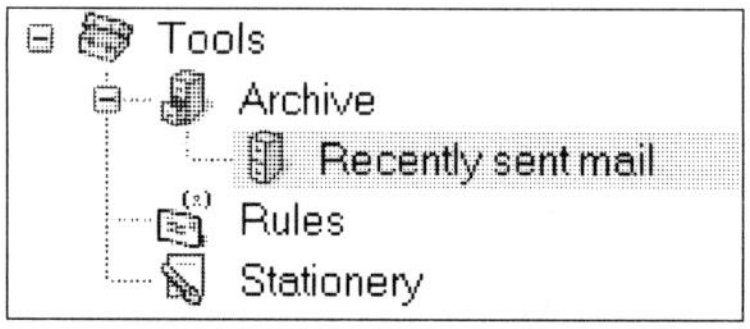

- If you wish to archive documents from several views or folders in the Mail database, you will first need to create a criteria set that selects those views or folders. You can then use the **File - Database - Archive Now** command, using the **Yes** button to confirm archiving.

Managing archived documents

From an archive database, you can permanently delete any documents you like. You can also restore them, to recover them in the base from which they were originally archived.

Recovering an archived document

- Open the Mail database.
- In the navigation pane, open the **Tools** folder then the **Archive** subfolder.
- Click the criteria set that corresponds to the archive base you wish to open.

  This opens the archive base associated with the selected criteria set:

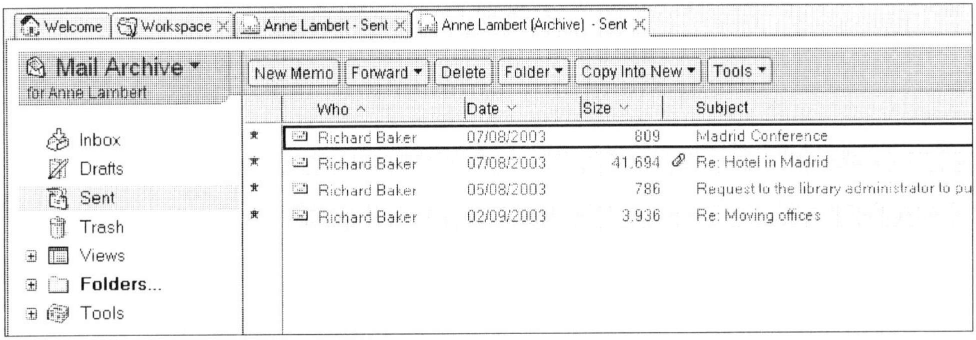

- In the navigation pane of the **Mail Archive** view, open the folder or subfolder containing the documents you wish to retrieve.
- Select the document(s) that you wish to restore.
- **Edit**
  Copy
- Open the database then the view or folder into which you want to recover the selected document(s).
- **Edit**
  Paste

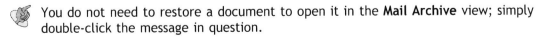

You do not need to restore a document to open it in the **Mail Archive** view; simply double-click the message in question.

Deleting an archived document

- Open the Mail database.
- In the navigation pane, open the **Tools** folder then the **Archive** subfolder.
- Click the criteria set that corresponds to the archive base you wish to open.
- In the navigation pane of the **Mail Archive** view, open the folder or subfolder containing the documents you wish to remove.
- Select the document(s) that you wish to delete.
- Click the **Delete** button.

  *If you selected the **Sent** folder, this message appears:*

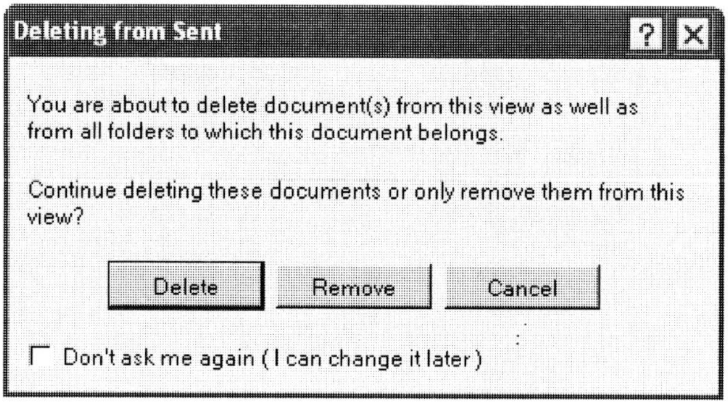

*This window appears only if the **Always Ask** option is active in the **Delete/Remove Preference for Sent View** frame, under **Actions - Tools - Preferences**.*

- If the message appears, click the **Delete** button to send the selected document to the trash. Otherwise, click **Remove** to take it out of the Sent view, but keep it in other views and folders.

Calendar

part five

What is the Calendar?

- The Calendar is a view of the Mail database used for managing your time schedule.
- You can add calendar entries for meetings, appointments, reminders, events and birthdays or anniversaries. You can also display To Dos there.
- You can also use the Calendar to work with the schedules of other users and to plan meetings (sending invitations, checking replies, reserving resources and so on).

Displaying the Calendar

- Click the  bookmark to open the **Calendar** view,
  or
  In the Mail database, click the arrow next to the **Mail** or **To Do** header and choose the **Switch to Calendar** option:

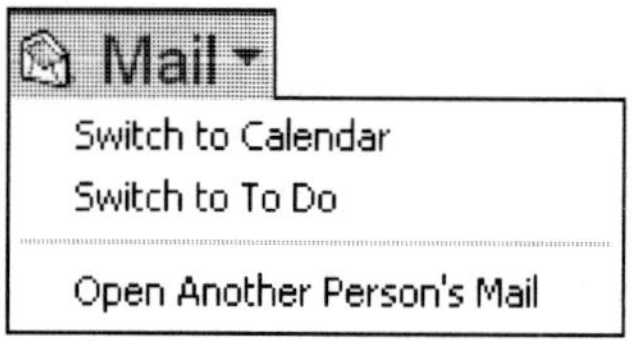

  or
  Click the  button on the Welcome page.

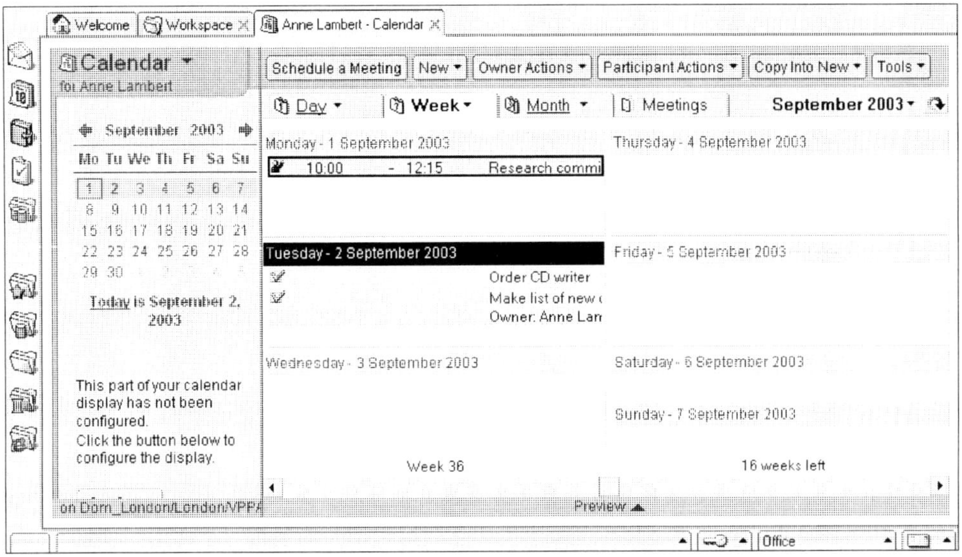

By default, the Calendar displays one week of your schedule. The day's date appears clearly in the navigation pane and at the bottom of the page you can see the week number and the number of weeks remaining in the year.

The Mail pane may be inserted between the Calendar navigation pane and the schedule. If you wish to close this pane, drag its right edge towards the left.

*If the Calendar schedule does not appear, click the **Today** link in the Calendar navigation pane.*

Changing the display format

- Open the Calendar.
- Open the **View** menu, point to the **Change Format** option and click the time period you wish to see:

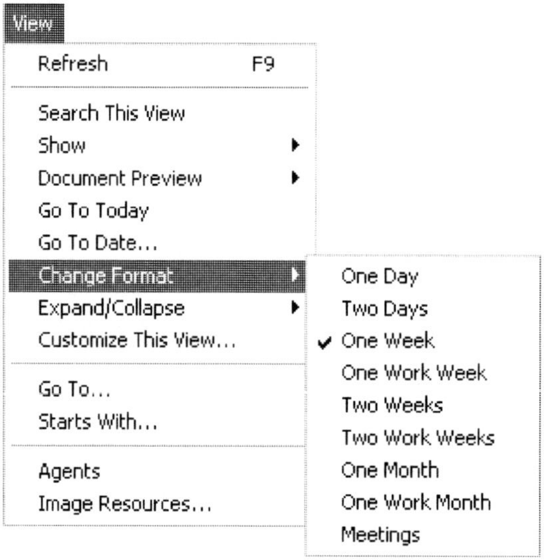

*The **Meetings** option will display only the meetings in your Calendar.*

- You can also choose a display format by using these tabs or lists:

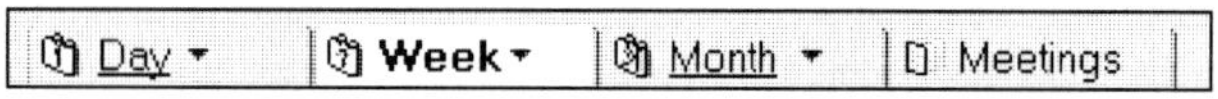

- To go to another day, month or year, click the year or month in the date selector in the left pane of the **Calendar** then select the required item.

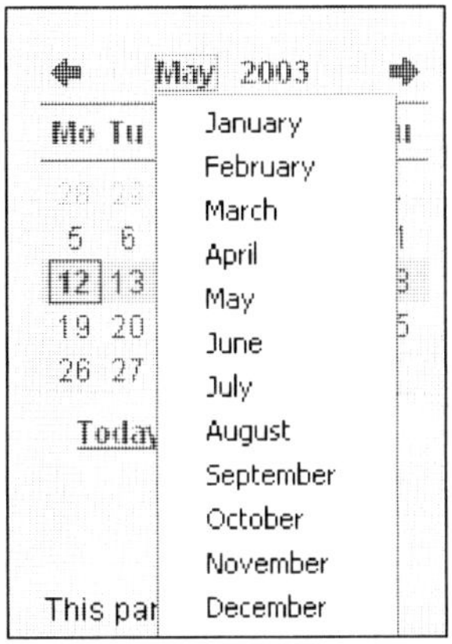

In this example, we want to choose another month than May.

- To go to a specific day, you can also use the **View - Go To Date** command and enter or select the required date.
- To go to today's date, use the **View - Go To Today** command or click the **Today** link in the date selector.

- To activate or deactivate a summary of the entries in the active view, use the **View - Show - Summary** command or click the **Formatting** button (at the right of the Calendar view tabs) and click the **Summarize** option.

Showing or hiding times

- Click the **Formatting** arrow then the **Show Time Slots** option, or use the **View - Show - Time Slots** command.

- Using the  and  buttons, go to the required time slot.

If the times of two appointments overlap, Notes displays a conflict bar at the left of the overlapping entries:

Viewing Calendar entries

- In the **Calendar** view, go to the date you wish to consult.
- If you cannot see the details of the entry immediately, point to the entry's icon so you can see the description in a screen tip.

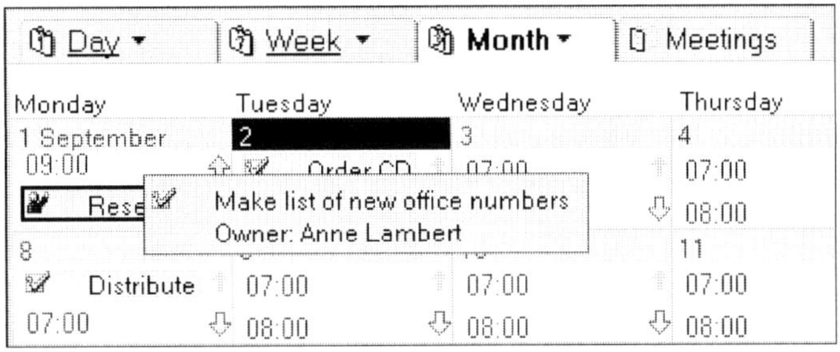

Selecting Calendar entries

- Activate the **Calendar** view.

  By default, the selection bar is inaccessible.

- Shift-click the first entry you want to select.

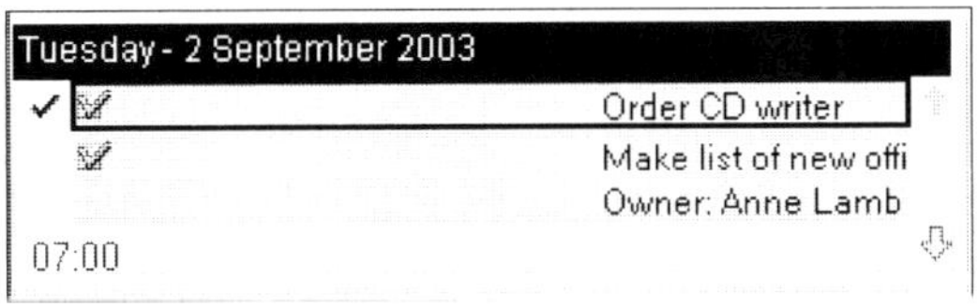

The selection bar appears and the entry appears as ticked.

- Continue selecting as usual.

Printing specific entries

- Activate the **Calendar** view.
- Select the entries you wish to print.
- **File**
  Print — Ctrl **P**
- Activate the **Selected documents** option in the **What to Print** section.

- In the **Print Range** section, activate the **All pages** option to print all the pages, otherwise activate the **From page** option and give the numbers of the pages to print in the adjoining fields.
- If necessary, define the **Print Quality** using the options given.
- If required, give the **Number of copies** that should be printed.

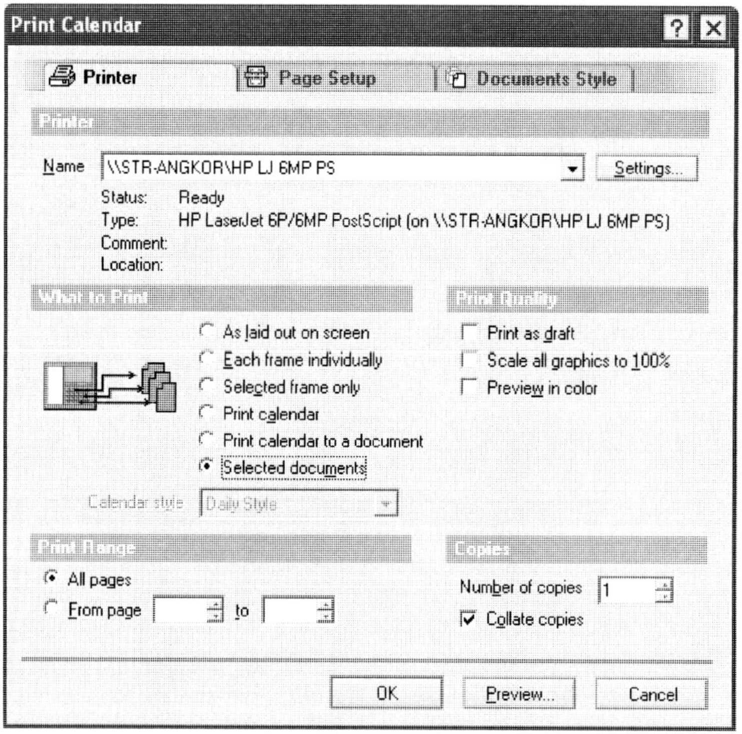

- Click **OK** to start printing.

The **Preview** button in the **Print Calendar** dialog box takes you to a preview of the document before it is printed.

Printing the Calendar

- Activate the **Calendar** view.
- **File** [Ctrl] P
  Print
- In the **What to Print** section, choose the **Print calendar** option.
- In the **Calendar style** drop-down list in the **What to Print** section, choose one of these options:

Daily Style	makes a page break at each new day.
Weekly Style	prints one week per page.
Work Week Style	prints one working week per page (by default Monday to Friday).
Monthly Style	prints one month per page.
Rolling Style	prints the time period indicated in the **Print Range** section, starting with the week containing the day given in the **From** field and ending with the week containing the day given in the **to** field.
Calendar List	prints the calendar entries as a list.
To Do List	prints the list of current To Dos.
Trifold Style	prints the page with three sections, showing the calendar entries for the current day, week and month.

- Click the **Calendar Style** tab and tick the following options as necessary:

Print first line only	this option is inactive by default.
Expand rows, time-slots as needed	increase the height of horizontal timeslots if necessary
Spread week across 3 pages	gives more vertical space to the entries. This option appears only for the **Weekly** and **Work Week** styles.
Use row/column format	to print the calendar as it appears in one-week format. This option appears only for the **Weekly** and **Work Week** styles.
Include weekends	This option appears only for the **Weekly**, **Monthly** and **Trifold** styles.
Print three month banner	prints small calendars of the previous month, the current one and the next month at the top of the page.
Hide private entries	excludes entries marked as private in the calendar from the printout.

- Choose one of the **Page types** to adapt the printed Calendar to fit your day planner.

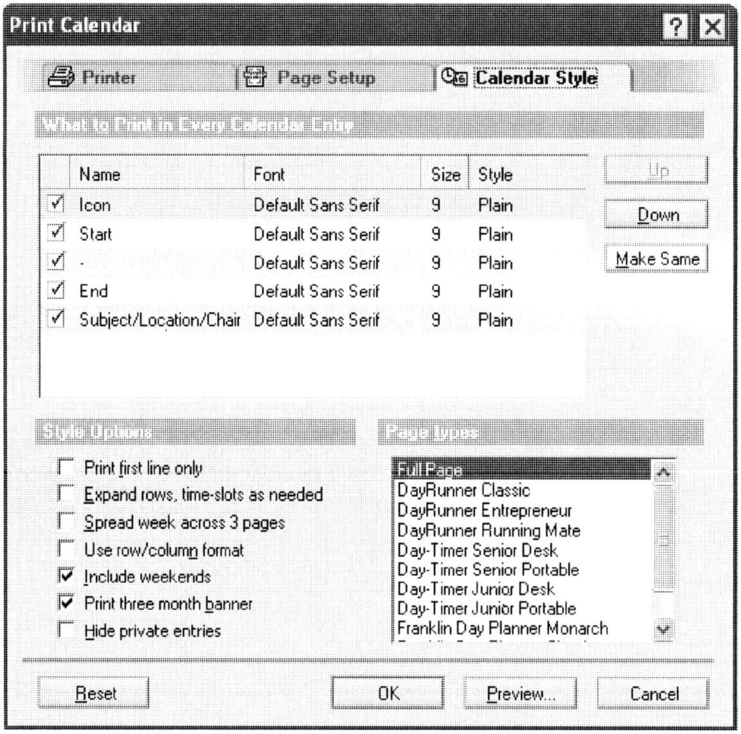

- Click the **Preview** button to see the document before you print.

  *The **Reset** button restores the last settings used to print the current style.*

- Click **OK** to start printing.

Creating a group calendar

- Open your Calendar.
- Click the arrow next to the header:

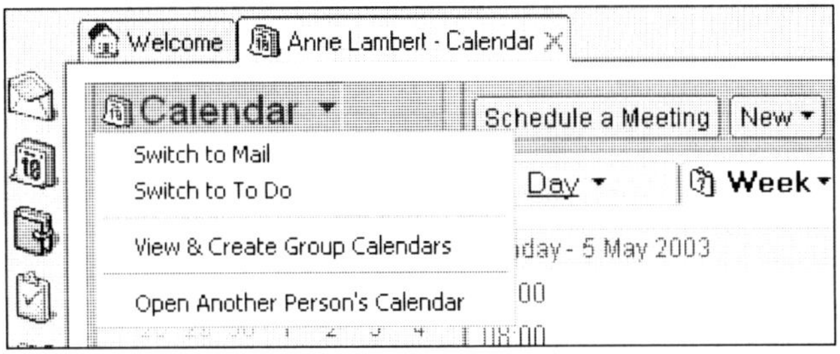

- Click the **View & Create Group Calendars** option.

  *The **Group Calendars** view opens.*
- Click the **New Group Calendar** button.
- Enter the group name in the **Title** field.
- Complete the list of **Members** for this new group by entering their names, or by selecting them in an address book (to do this, click the arrow at the bottom right of the **Members** field).

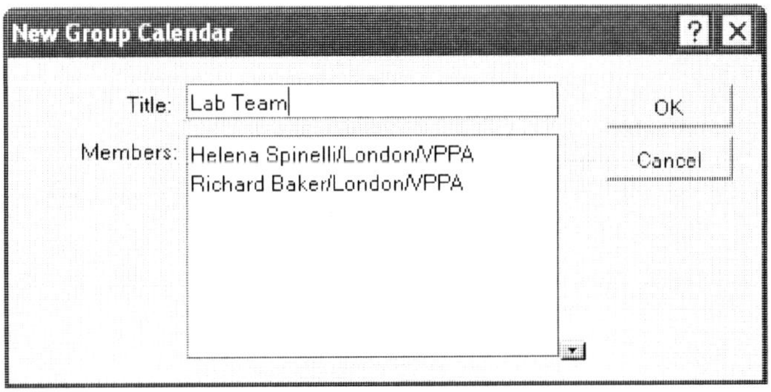

- Click **OK** to confirm.

*The new **Group Calendar** appears in Notes:*

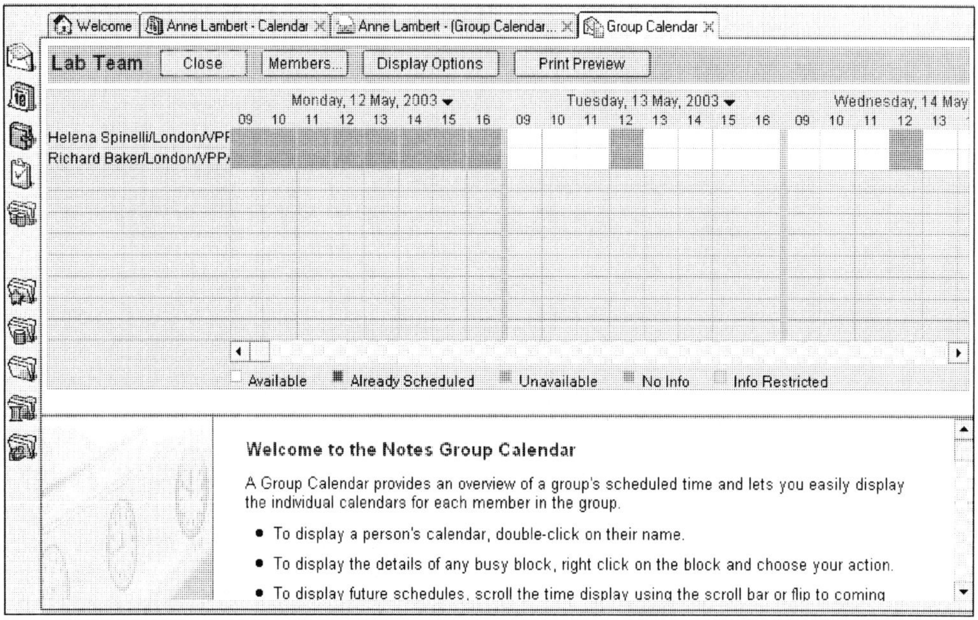

*The new group calendar is also added to the list of group calendars in the **Group Calendars** view:*

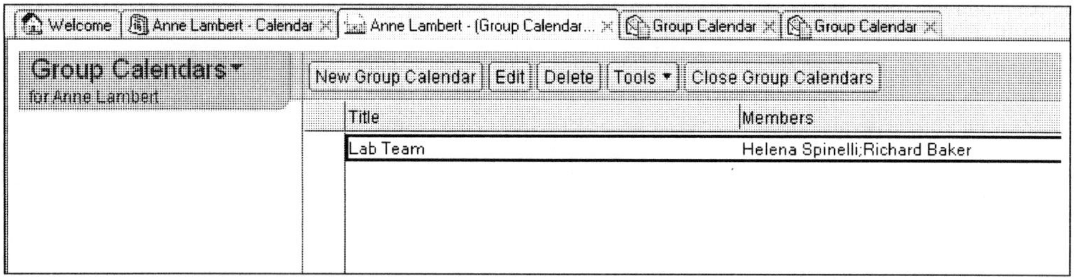

Seeing the calendar of a group member

If you want to see the details of a group member's calendar, you must have the appropriate access permissions.

- Open your Calendar.
- Click the arrow next to the header and click the **View & Create Group Calendars** option.
- Double-click the **Title** of the group calendar to which the required group member belongs.

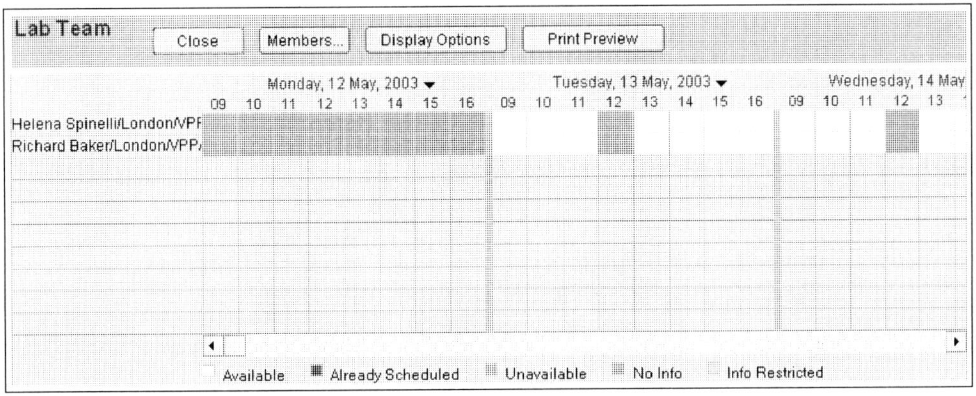

- Double-click the name of a group member to see his/her calendar.

When a group member is shown as busy at a certain time in the group calendar, you can click the busy time slot to see the corresponding calendar entry in Notes, which avoids opening the whole calendar. Of course to do this, you must have the correct permissions.

Creating a Calendar entry other than a meeting

- If you wish, select the date and, if required, the time of the event (appointment, anniversary, reminder, whole-day event).
- Click the **New** button then choose the required type of event:

- Click the **Subject** field then enter the information of your choice.

  The contents of this field are displayed in the Calendar.
- If necessary, change the **Starts** and **Ends** dates of the event.
- If you need to change the times, click the  button on the event's **Starts** or **Ends** fields. Change the time by dragging the small clock icon onto the required time. To see another time range, click the arrowheads.

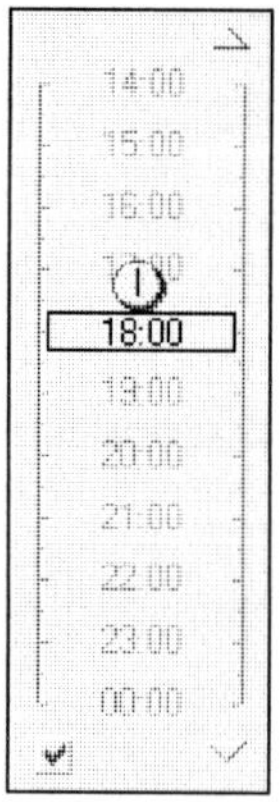

- To confirm your choice, click .

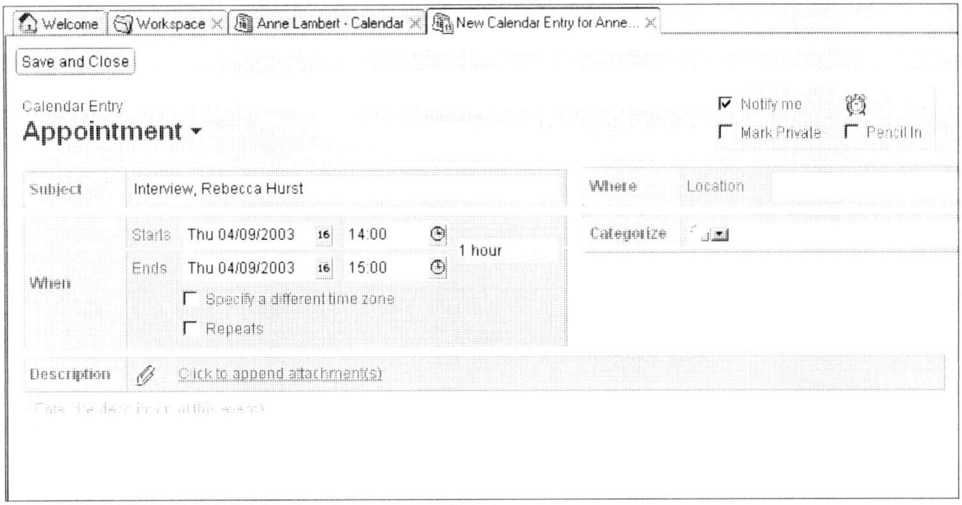

Notice that the event's duration (an appointment in this example) is calculated from the specified days and times.

***All Day Event** and **Anniversary** entries do not have time fields.*

- If you want the event to recur, tick the **Repeats** option and give the recurrence settings in the **Repeat Options** dialog box then confirm with **OK**.

  *By default the **Repeats** option is active for Anniversary type entries, which will repeat each year.*

  *To change the repeat options, use the **Repeats** button.*

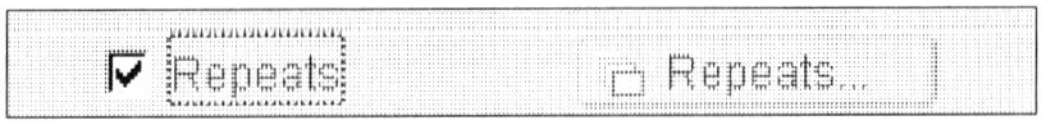

- In the **Location** field, enter a site reference (for example, a geographical location).
- To assign the new item to a category, use the **Categorize** field.
- To hide the entry from other users who may have access to your Calendar, tick the **Mark Private** option.

  If you do so, users can see the dates and times of the event but not its contents.

- To keep the time free should another event crop up, tick the **Pencil In** option.

- If you want to receive a text or sound alarm before the event occurs, tick the **Notify me** option and set the alarm options in the **Alarm Notification Options** dialog box.

  For further details about alarms, see the Managing alarms on Calendar entries section.

- If you wish to add a document, a file, a picture or so on to the entry, use the **Click to append attachment(s)** link then select the item(s) you wish to attach in the **Create Attachment(s)** dialog box and confirm your action with the **Create** button.

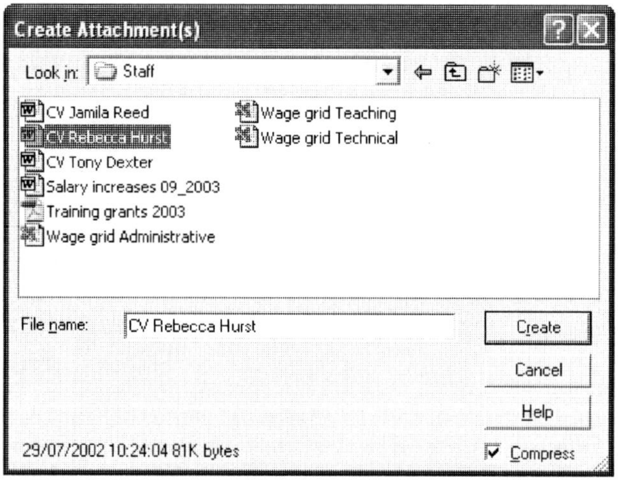

- To enter extra information about the event, click the **Enter the description of this event** link and give the required description.

- Click the **Save and Close** button to confirm the Calendar entry.

  An object appears in the Calendar for the new entry, preceded by a symbol that varies for each type of entry:

	Anniversary		Appointment
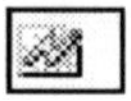	*All - Day Event*	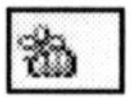	*Reminder*

- To change the event type while you are still creating the entry, click the arrow next to the **Calendar Entry** header and activate the type of entry required in the **Change Calendar Entry Type** dialog box.

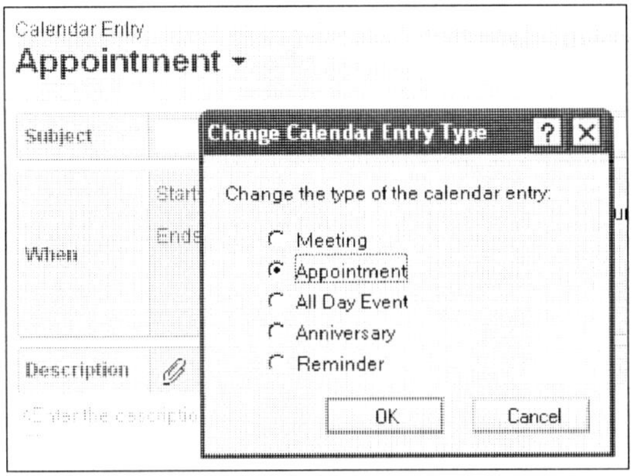

You can also create a Calendar entry by clicking the tool button and choosing **New Calendar Entry**. If necessary, change the type of entry.

A Calendar entry can also be made by double-clicking a time slot or date in the Calendar. A form immediately opens, which you can use to set the type of entry.

By default, appointments are given a length of one hour. To change this value, use the **Actions - Tools - Preferences** command, click the **Calendar & To Do** tab and the **Basics** subtab, then enter the new duration in minutes in the **Duration of a new Appointment or Meeting** field.

You can only make an entry a repeating event while you are still creating it.

Creating a Calendar entry from a message

- Select the e-mail in question then open it.
- **Actions**
  Copy Into New
  New Calendar Entry

  The message's subject becomes the entry's subject and its contents become the description.
- If required, change the type of entry using the **Calendar Entry** drop-down list.
- Create the Calendar entry as usual.

Creating a Calendar entry from a To Do

- Open, or select, the To Do you want to make into a Calendar entry.
- **Actions**
  Copy Into New
  New Calendar Entry
- If required, change the type of entry using the **Calendar Entry** drop-down list.
- Create the Calendar entry as usual.

Deleting recurring entries

- Select the recurring entry.
- **Edit** Del
  Delete

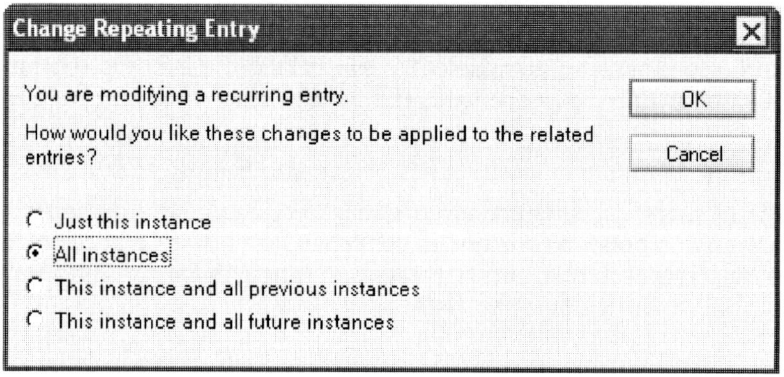

- Activate one of the four options given, as required.
- Click **OK** to confirm and close the **Change Repeating Entry** dialog box.

Managing alarms on Calendar entries

- Start creating or editing the entry.
- Tick the **Notify me** option (this appears only once you have entered a date in the **Ends** field).

  *The **Alarm Notification Options** dialog box opens:*

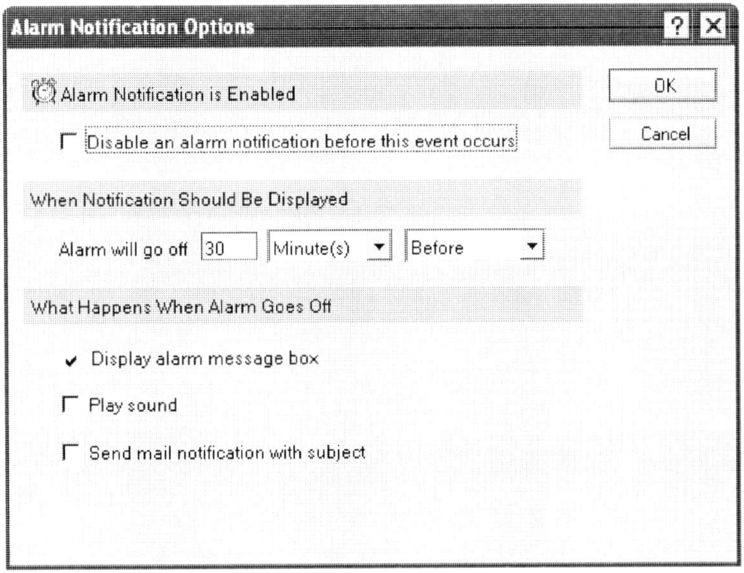

- Tick the **Disable an alarm notification before this event occurs** option to turn off the alarm on the entry.
- Using the options under **When Notification Should Be Displayed**, choose when the alarm should go off: **Before** or **After** the event, using the specified number of **Minute(s)**, **Hour(s)** or **Day(s)**.
- If you want to hear a sound alarm, tick the **Play sound** option and, in the drop-down list that appears, choose the required sound file.

  To test the selected sound, click the  button.

  *Take note that the sound chosen here will replace any sound chosen in the alarm preferences dialog box (for the Calendar or To Dos, for example) produced by **Actions - Tools - Preferences**. If you want to use the sound defined by default in the preferences, leave the **Play sound** field blank.*

- To send an e-mail message when the alarm goes off, tick the **Send mail notification with subject** option. Choose the people who will receive the message: it will have the Calendar entry as its subject.
- Click **OK** to confirm.
- If necessary, finish creating the entry.

To define a default sound for all the alarms, open the Calendar and use the **Actions - Tools - Preferences** command - **Calendar & To Do** tab - **Alarms** subtab. Open the **Default sound** drop-down list and select the required sound file.

In Quick Notes, you can also create a **Quick reminder**, containing simply a heading, a date and a time. Open Quick Notes from the Welcome page, clicking the symbol on the far right.

Cancelling an alarm

- Double-click the entry whose alarm you wish to cancel, to open it.
- Deactivate the **Notify me** option.
- Click the **Save and Close** button to confirm.

Responding to an alarm

When an alarm goes off, Notes displays the following dialog box:

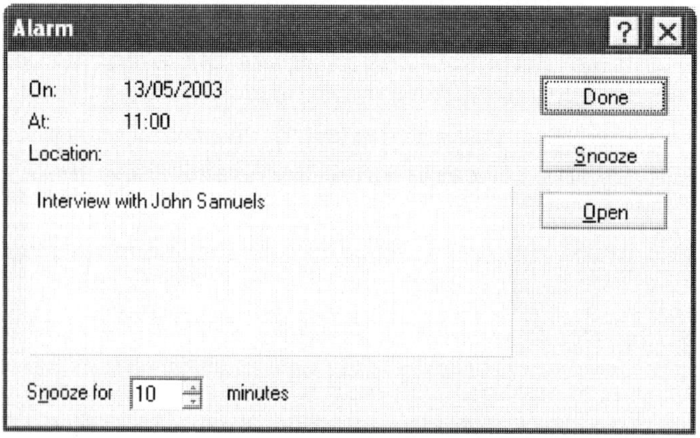

- If you want to alarm to go off again a little later, give a number of **minutes** in the **Snooze for** box and click the **Snooze** button.

The alarm will not sound again if you leave Notes before it is due to play.

- To turn off the alarm, click the **Done** button.
- To open the Calendar entry associated with the alarm, click the **Open** button.

Each time Notes starts, it checks if any alarms should have gone off since you last closed the application. If this is the case, it will ask you whether or not you want to see the skipped alarms; reply with **Yes** or **No**.

Planning a meeting

- Open the Calendar.
- If you wish, choose the date and time the meeting should start, using the date selector or directly in the time schedule.
- Click the **Schedule a Meeting** button.
- Enter the meeting's **Subject**.
- If necessary, change the date and the time the meeting **Starts** and **Ends**, as described previously (cf. Creating a Calendar entry other than a meeting).

  Notes calculates the meeting's duration based on the given days and times.
- If you want the Calendar entry to recur, tick the **Repeats** option then set the recurrence options in the **Repeat Options** dialog box and confirm with **OK.**

Creating the list of participants

- Give the names of the meeting's participants, using these fields:

Required (to)	these people must attend the meeting.
Optional (cc)	these people may attend if they wish.
FYI (bcc)	this sends a meeting notice for information only, but the addressees may add the meeting to their Calendars if they wish. The names entered in this field cannot be seen in the invitations sent to other participants.

Not all the messages received by the participants contain the same reply option buttons: this depends on the type of message.

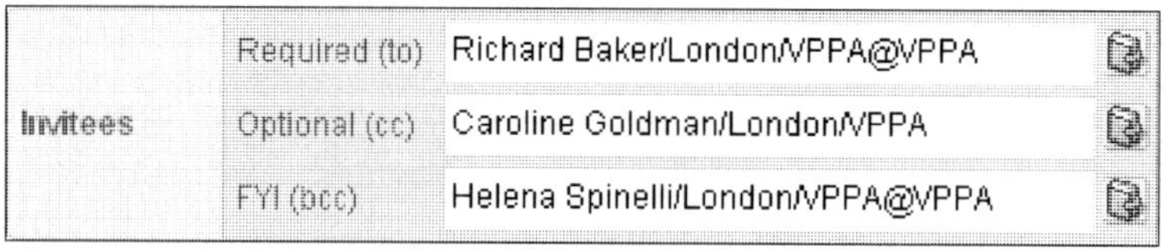

Defining and reserving the meeting's location

- In the **Where** frame, enter a **Location**; this could be a geographical place for example.
- Enter the name of the room you want to reserve using the **Rooms** field, or select the room in an address book using the  button.

***Room** type resources are listed, classified by **Site**; the **Location** entered in the meeting form has no effect on this display.*

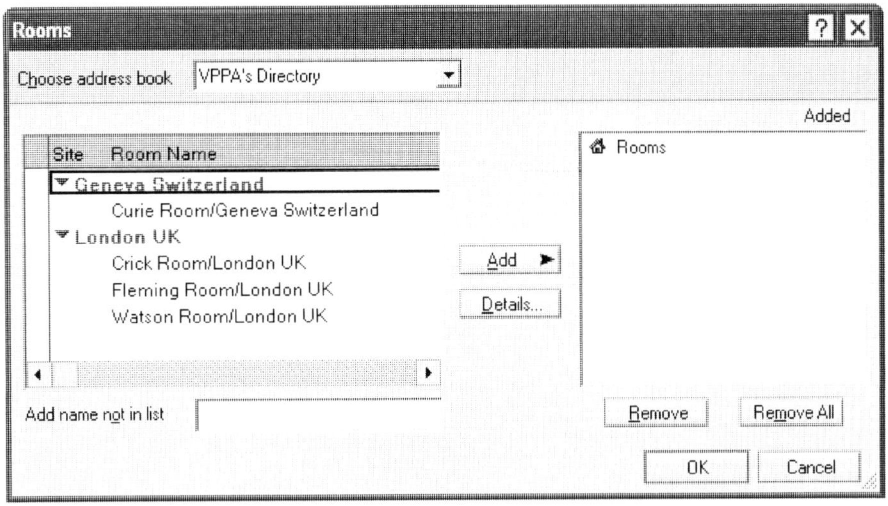

- If necessary, change the address book using the **Choose address book** list.
- Click the name of the room you wish to reserve.
- Click **Add** to put the selected room in the list of reserved rooms.
- When all the rooms have been added to the list, confirm with **OK**.

Reserving resources

- Enter the name(s) of the resource(s) you want to reserve using the **Resources** field, or select from an address book using the  button.
- Use the same selection procedure as described above for rooms.

The complete name, resource plus site, appears:

Setting up an online meeting

- To set up an online meeting, the Sametime 3.0 (or later) application must be installed. Tick the **This is an Online Meeting** option then fill in the extra options related to that:

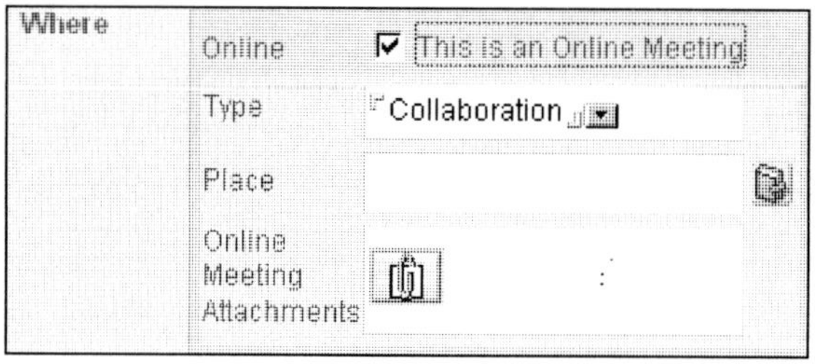

- Give a URL address in the **Place** box or choose an online resource using the button.
- If necessary, click the button on the **Online Meeting Attachments** field to choose any documents you want to add to the invitation.

Categorizing a meeting

- To place this new event in a category, use the **Categorize** field.

Checking the availability of participants and resources

- To see whether participants, rooms and resources are available for a meeting, use the **Scheduler**; to do this, click the associated link or icon:

*By default, Notes displays the schedule of each participant in **Details** mode.*

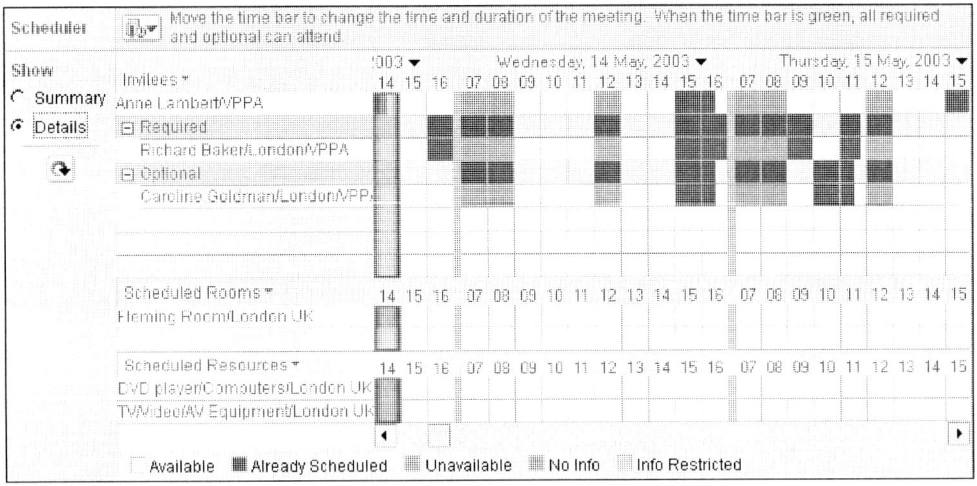

- To change the way each participant's schedule is displayed, choose the **Summary** or **Details** option as required.
- If necessary, click the arrow on the **Invitees** button then choose an option:

All	to see all the participants.
Available	to see only the participants that are available at the time specified on the invitation.
Unavailable	to see only the participants that are not available at the time specified on the invitation.

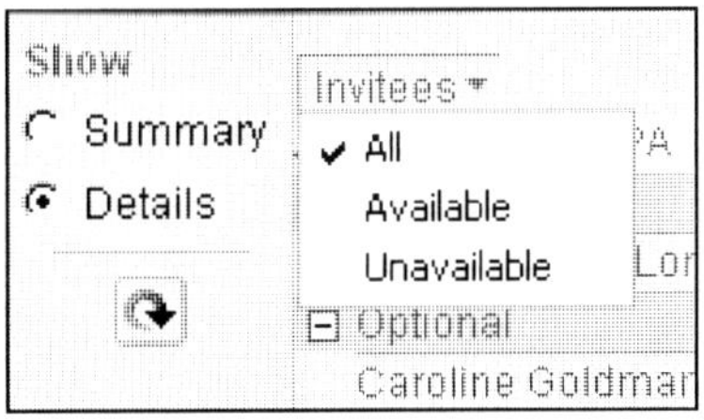

- Proceed in the same way for the **Scheduled Rooms** and/or **Scheduled Resources.**
- To **Check if all required can attend**, go into **Summary** mode and click the corresponding button then click the option of your choice.

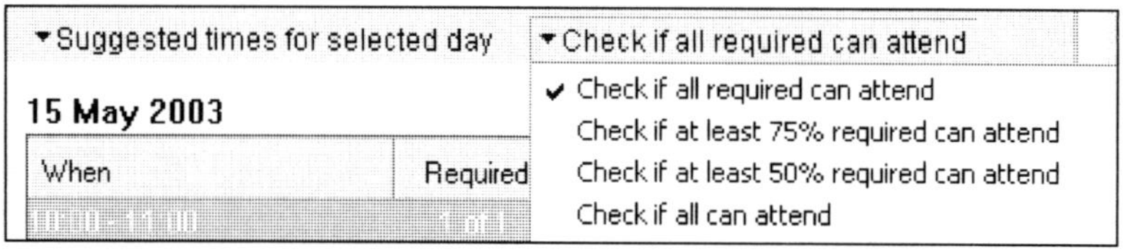

- Use the  button to update the scheduler. Click the  button to hide the **Scheduler**.

Options common to all Calendar entries

- To hide the entry from other users who may have access to your Calendar, tick the **Mark Private** option at the top right of the form.

  If you do so, users can see the dates and times of the event but not its contents.
- To keep the time free should another event crop up, tick the **Pencil In** option.
- If you want to receive a text or sound alarm before the event occurs, tick the **Notify me** option and set the alarm options in the **Alarm Notification Options** dialog box that opens.

  For further details about alarms, see the Managing alarms on Calendar entries section.
- To enter extra information about the meeting, click the **Enter the description of this event** link (if it appears) or click the text box underneath **Description** and give the required description.

Sending the invitations

- To **Save and Send Invitations**, click the corresponding button.

  Notes adds the meeting to your Calendar and sends a message to each person invited.
- If you do not want to send invitations just yet, click the **Save as Draft** button.

  The meeting appears in the Calendar but no invitation is sent. In this case, no free time is booked and you can still change the type of meeting or change a recurring meeting into a single meeting and vice versa.

If you have already sent invitations to a recurring meeting and you do not want the meeting to repeat any more, you are faced with a problem, as you can no longer change the type of the original meeting. What you can do is copy the original entry into a new entry (select the entry and use **Actions - Copy Into New - New Calendar Entry**). All the original information (the participants, the location, the subject, etc.) is copied into a new entry, so you can then change its properties and send invitations again.

Creating an invitation from your personal address book

- Open your personal address book.
- Select the users you want to invite to the meeting.
- Click the **Schedule Meeting** button.
- Proceed as if you were creating an invitation from your Calendar.

Reading a received invitation

- Open the invitation document.

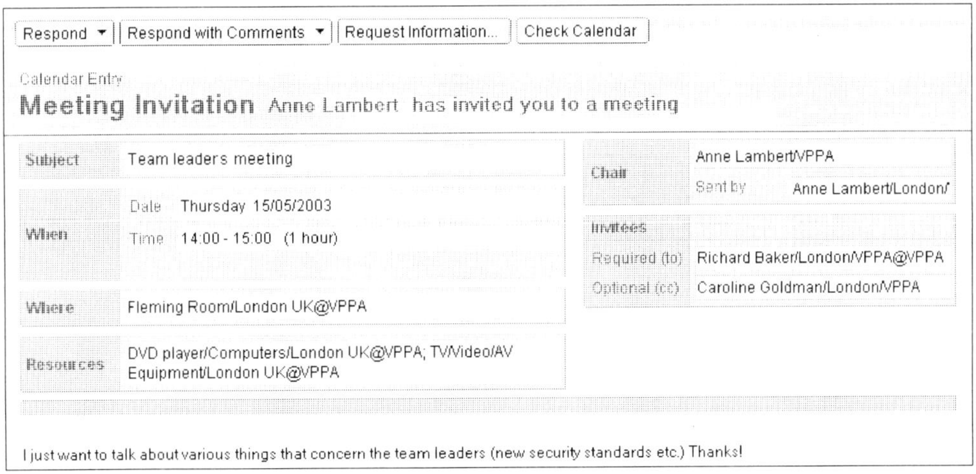

*Notes tells you who sent the message and **When** and **Where** the meeting will take place. You can also see the meeting's **Subject** and who the **Invitees** are.*

Accepting/refusing an invitation

- Open the invitation.
- Click the **Respond** or **Respond with Comments** button.
- Choose one of the options offered:

Accept	Notes adds the meeting entry to your Calendar.
Tentatively Accept	you accept the meeting but the timeslot is not marked as busy.
Decline	you will not be attending the meeting.

- If you clicked **Respond with Comments**, you can enter your **Comments** before clicking the **Send** button.

  There are no options for cancelling your reply and once you leave the form, the comments are sent. If you do not want to send your comments, delete them by dragging to select them and pressing the [Del] *key.*

Accepted invitations carry this symbol while declined ones display this .

Delegating an invitation

- Open the invitation document.
- Click the **Respond** or **Respond with Comments** button.
- Click the **Delegate** option.

*The **Delegate Options** dialog box opens:*

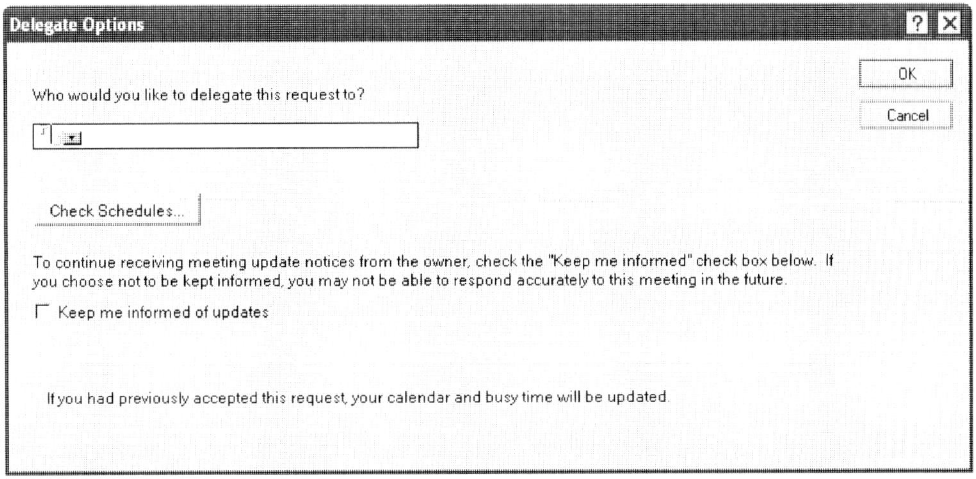

- Click the drop-down button to open the address book and choose the name of the delegate then confirm with **OK**.
- Click the **Check Schedules** button to see the potential delegate's free and busy times. You can change the time slots if necessary. Click **OK** to confirm.
- Click **OK** to confirm the **Delegate Options**.
- If you used the **Respond with Comments** button, enter your comments and click **Send**.

Listing participant replies

- Open the invitation that you sent.
- Click the **Actions** button then the **View Invitee Status** option.

*The **Invitee Status** window opens:*

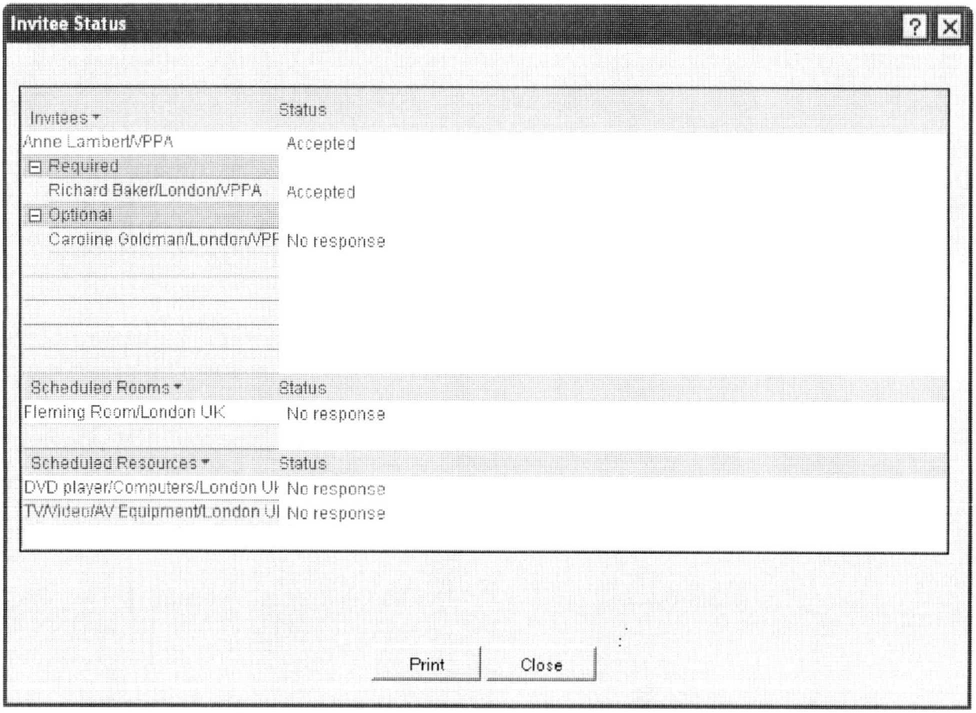

*Notes lists the meeting invitees and the **Status** of each invitation.*

- Click **Close** to shut the window.

Cancelling a meeting

- In your Calendar view, open the invitation that you wish to cancel.
- Click the **Actions** button then the **Cancel** option.

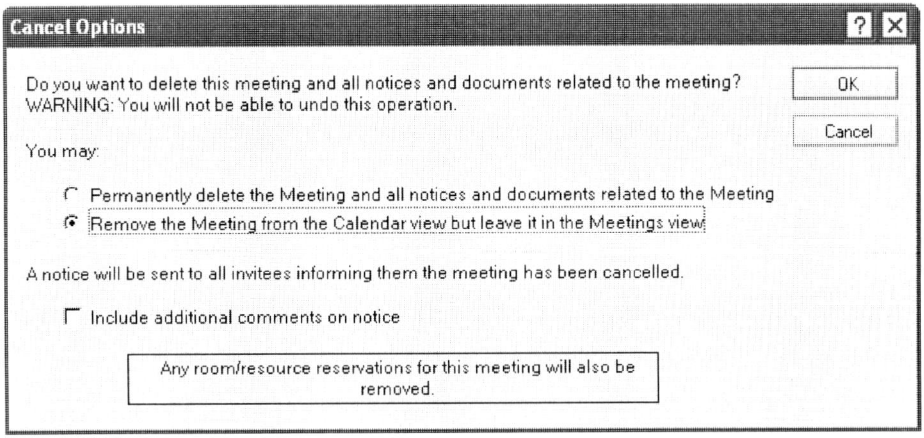

- If necessary, activate the first option so that Notes cancels the request and the replies relating to the cancelled meeting.
  or
  Activate the second option to remove the meeting from the Calendar view.
- If necessary, tick the **Include additional comments on notice** option to add a comment to the notification that will be sent to the participants.
- Click **OK.**
- If you chose to **Include additional comments on notice**, a **Reply Notice** form appears:

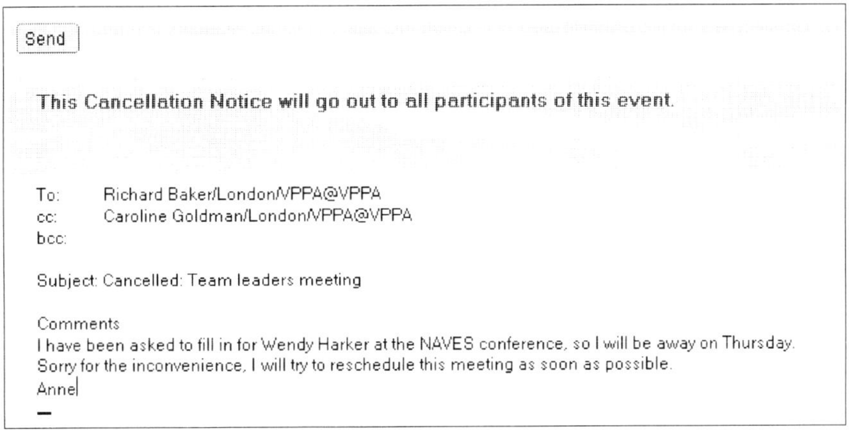

- Enter your text then click the **Send** button.

*Invitees receive a new message preceded by a ☒ symbol and whose subject is **Cancelled**.*

When an invitee opens this message, this notice appears:

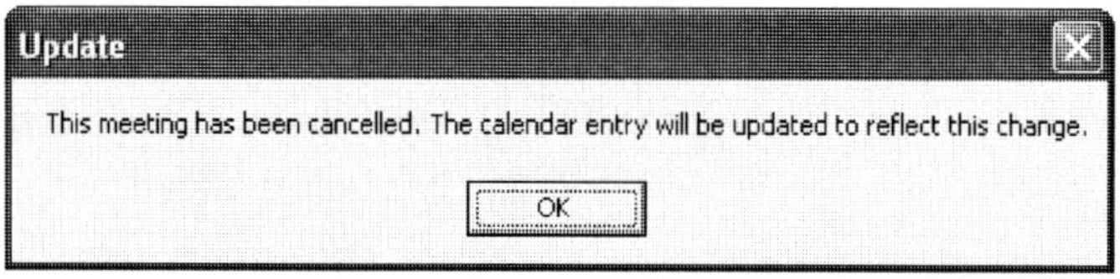

Stopping a repeating meeting

- Open the recurring meeting.
- Click the **Actions** button then the **Cancel** option.
- Fill in the **Cancel Options** dialog box as described in the previous section (cf. Cancelling a meeting) then click **OK.**
- Activate one of the following options:

Just this instance	to cancel just the open occurrence.
All instances	to cancel all the occurrences of the repeating meeting.
This instance and all previous instances	to cancel the open meeting and all the occurrences that come before it.
This instance and all future instances	to cancel the open meeting and all the occurrences that follow it.

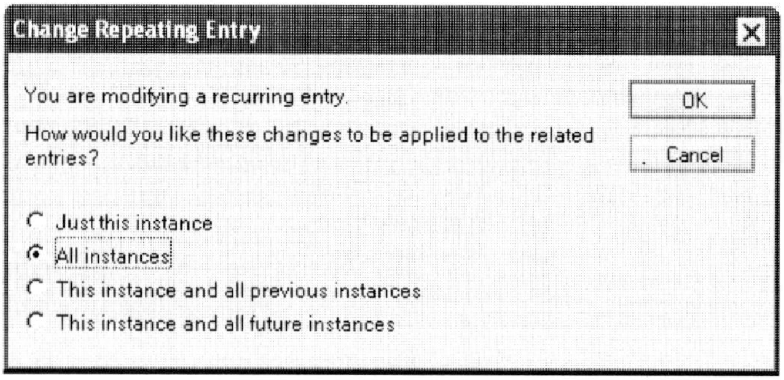

- Click **OK** to confirm.

Setting an alarm for all entries of the same type

- Open your Calendar.
- **Actions**
  Tools
  Preferences
- If necessary activate the **Calendar & To Do** tab then the **Alarms** subtab.
- For each category on which you wish to set an automatic alarm, click the corresponding check box then specify how far in advance the alarm should go off.

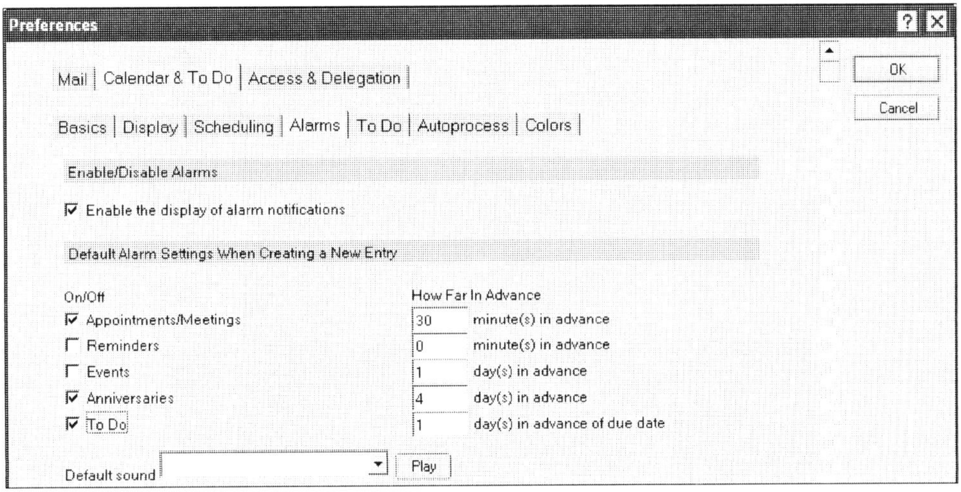

- Click **OK** to confirm.

Allowing access to your Calendar

If you wish, you can let other users see certain information from your schedule. This can be useful when others plan meetings and use the **Scheduler** *to check your availability.*
You can allow other users (people or groups) to not only see what is in your Calendar, but to act on your behalf.
Remember that your administrator may allow other users to check your availability, with a more or less significant amount of detail, and also permit your Calendar entries to be read (again in more or less detail). However you can still keep certain information hidden, even if your administrator has defined that detailed information can be seen by others.

- Open your Calendar.
- **Actions**
  Tools
  Preferences
- Activate the **Access & Delegation** tab then the **Access to Your Schedule** subtab.

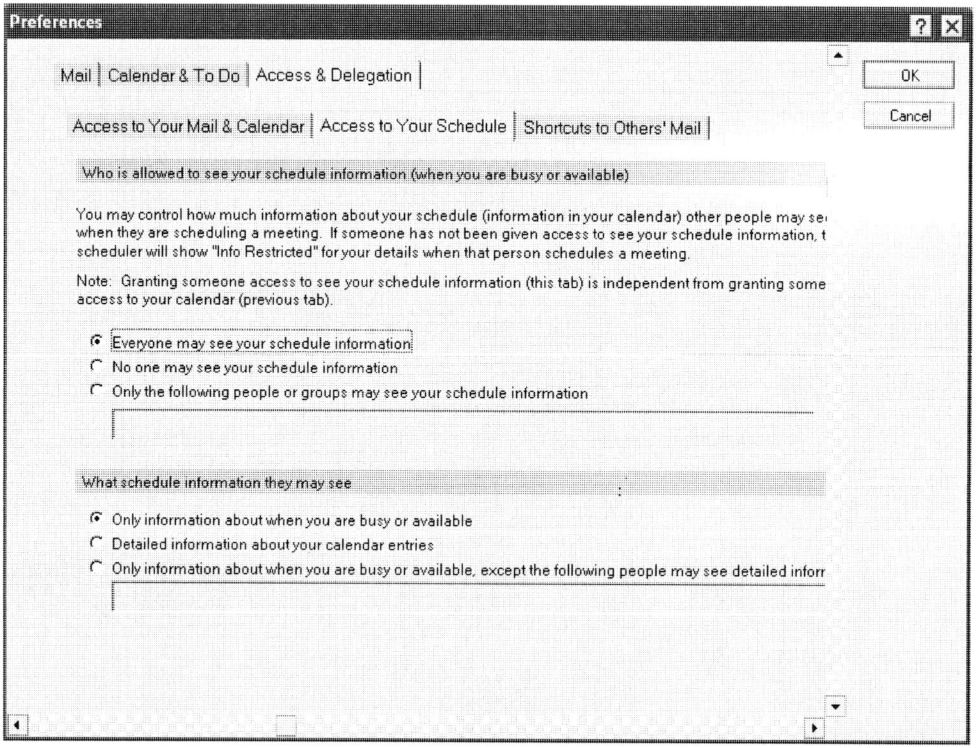

- According to your requirements, specify which people have permission to consult your schedule, using these options: **Everyone may see your schedule information**, **No one may see your schedule information** or **Only the following people or groups may see your schedule information** (for the latter, select the name(s) of the authorised user(s)).
- If you activated an option other than **No one...**, specify to which type of information the selected users or groups will have access. To do this, activate:
  - **Only information about when you are busy or available** so users can see your Calendar entries in the Scheduler, in the form of blocks.

- **Detailed information about your calendar entries** so users can right-click a particular block in the Scheduler to see a dialog box containing information about the corresponding Calendar entry.
- **Only information about when you are busy or available, except the following people may see detailed information**, then use the attached drop-down list to choose those people that can have access to your entries in detail.

To display Calendar entry subjects when a detailed display is used, deactivate the **Do not include the subject of a calendar entry when detailed information is made available** option.

*If you choose the **Only information about when you are busy or available** option, this option does not appear.*

Click **OK**.

Giving management permission

Activate the **Access to Your Mail & Calendar** subtab.

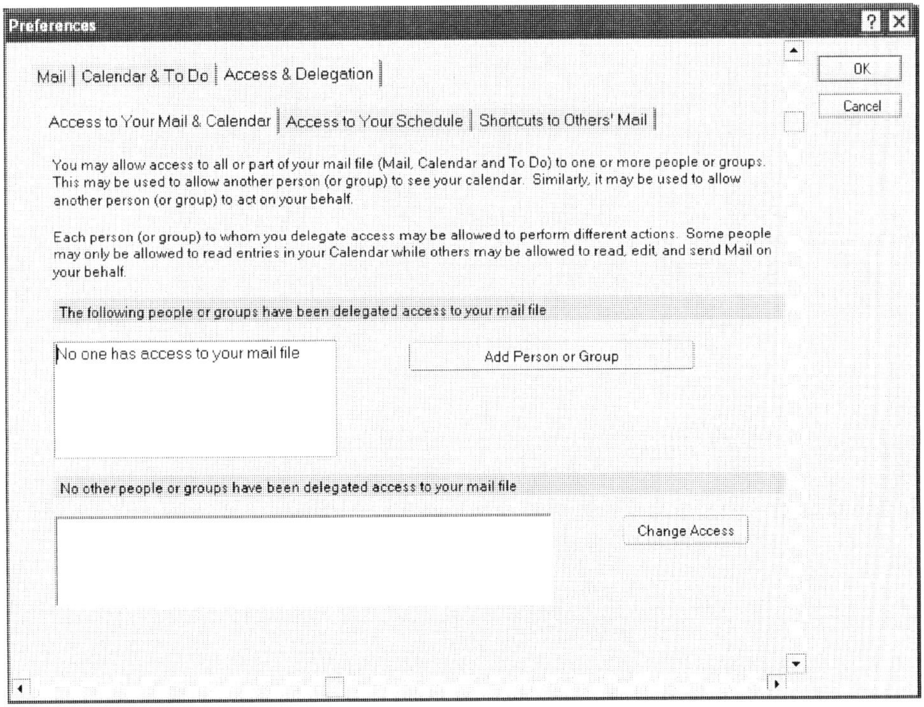

- To fill in the list of people or groups that can access your mail database, click the **Add Person or Group** button to see the **Add People/Groups** dialog box.

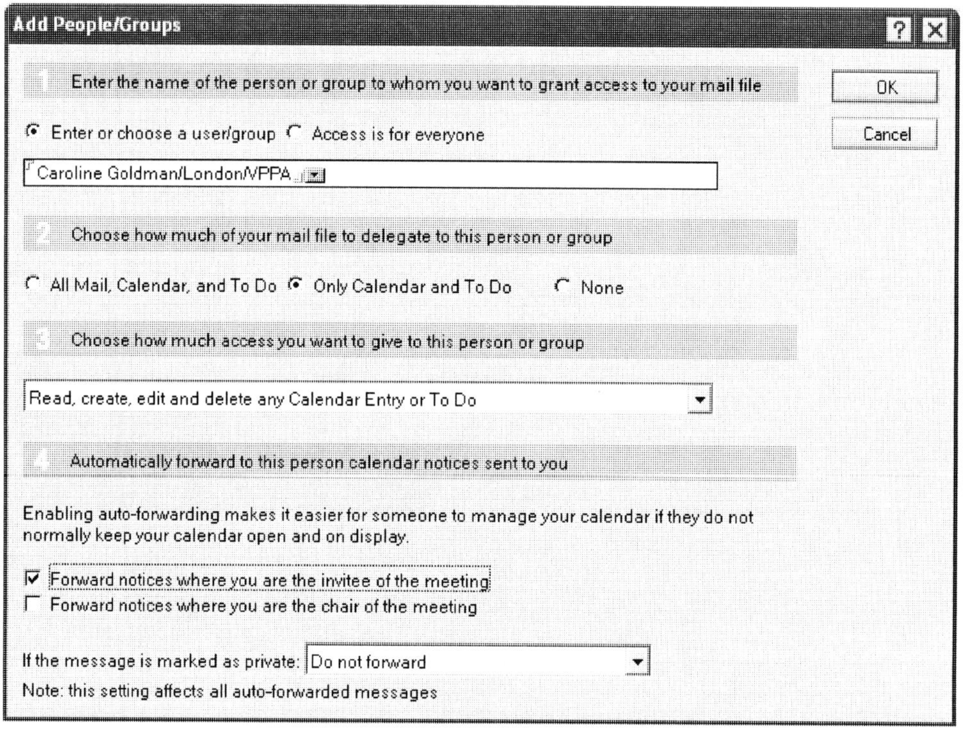

You can see that the options in this dialog box are divided into four numbered sections.

- Using the options given, set the access permissions for your mail, Calendar and/or To Dos.
- Click **OK** to confirm.

The names of the people or groups that have access to your files appear in the first frame. The level of permissions given to the person, or group, selected in the first frame appears in the second frame.

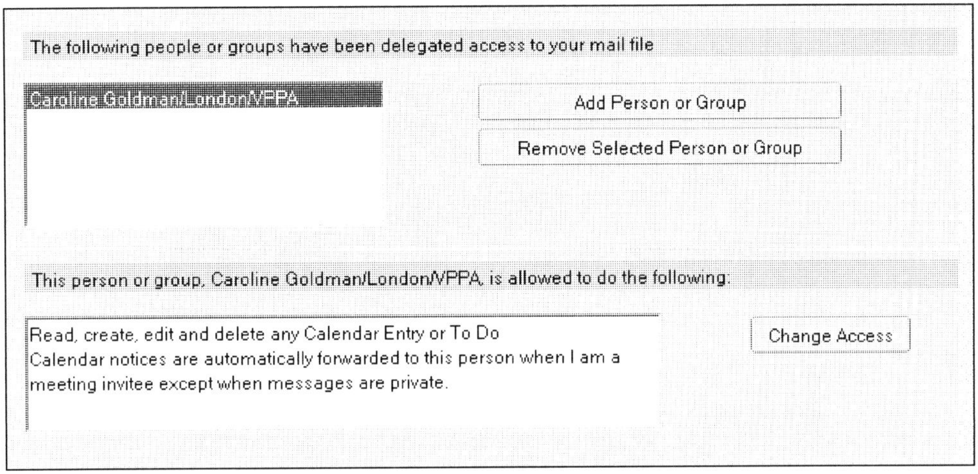

- To change the permissions given to the person (or group) selected in the first frame, click the **Change Access** button. Make the necessary changes in the **Change Access for** dialog box and click **OK** to confirm.
- Click **OK** on the **Preferences** dialog box.

Defining your free time

This time is used when someone checks your availability.

- Open and activate your Calendar.
- Click the **Tools** button then the **Preferences** option.
- Activate the **Calendar & To Do** tab then the **Scheduling** subtab.
- Tick all the check boxes for the days during which you could attend a meeting.
- Set the free time within the days concerned.

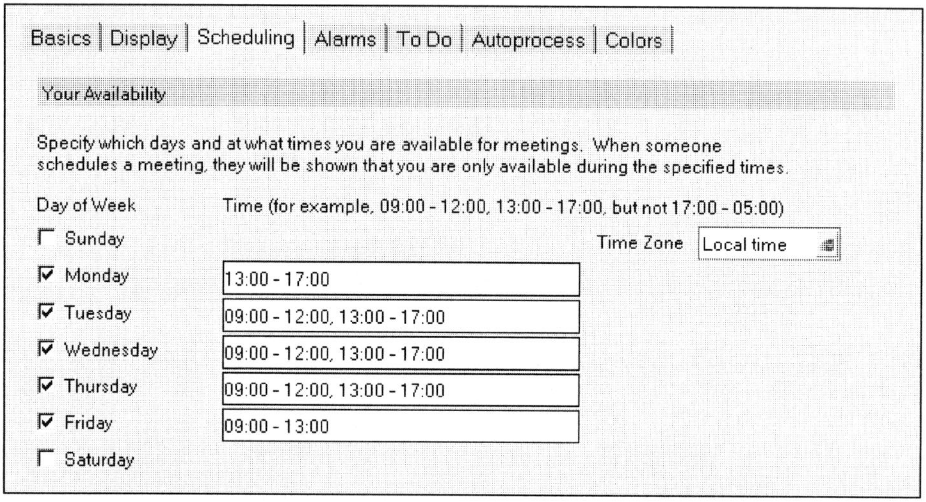

- Click **OK** to confirm.

Informing others that you are absent

- **Actions**
  Tools
  Out Of Office
- In the **Leaving** and **Returning** boxes, under the **Dates** tab, give the start and end dates of your absence.
- If you wish, customise the **Out of Office Message** under the corresponding tab.
- If you want certain users to receive a particular message, activate the **Special Message** tab and select the users in the **To** list, then enter the message in the text box intended for it.

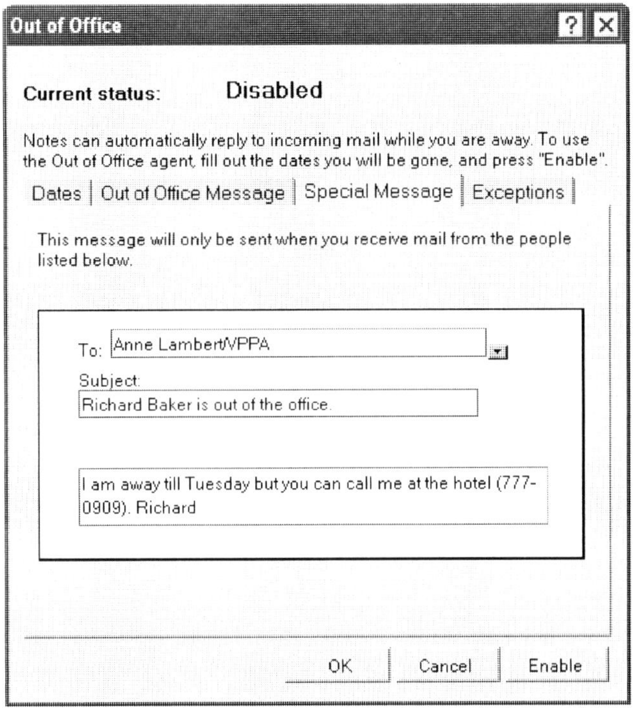

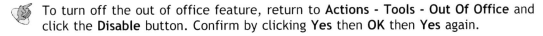

- If certain users should not receive any message at all, activate the **Exceptions** tab and fill in the appropriate text boxes.
- Click the **Enable** button.
- Confirm that you want to activate the out of office feature with the **Yes** button.
- Click **OK** on the message confirming that out of office is active.
- Click **OK** to close the **Out of Office** dialog box.

To turn off the out of office feature, return to **Actions - Tools - Out Of Office** and click the **Disable** button. Confirm by clicking **Yes** then **OK** then **Yes** again.

Other databases

part six

What is a discussion group?

- Discussion groups are also called USENET groups or forums.
- Discussion groups allow several people to swap ideas. Each one can make comments, add remarks, justify a position and so on. In many ways, they resemble electronic boardrooms.
- The base template used for discussion databases is **Discussion - Notes & Web (6)**, with the file name **discsw6.ntf.**
- By default, **Author** permissions are given.

Creating a discussion database

- **File**
  Database
  New Ctrl **N**
- Choose the **Server** on which you want to save the file.
- Give a **Title** for the icon and a **File name.**
- In the **Specify Template for New Database** section, select the **Server** containing the templates.
- Choose the **Discussion - Notes & Web (6)** template.

  *The corresponding file name is **discsw6.ntf**.*
- Click **OK** to confirm.

Joining a discussion group

- On the workspace, double-click the discussion group icon:

Discussion groups have a specific symbol.

You can also open a discussion group by using the **File - Database - Open** command and double-clicking the discussion base name.

Looking at discussion databases

In this type of base, Notes offers various views.

The different views

- The default view is **All Documents**: this displays all the messages with their **Date** and **Topic**. By default, messages are displayed in chronological order.

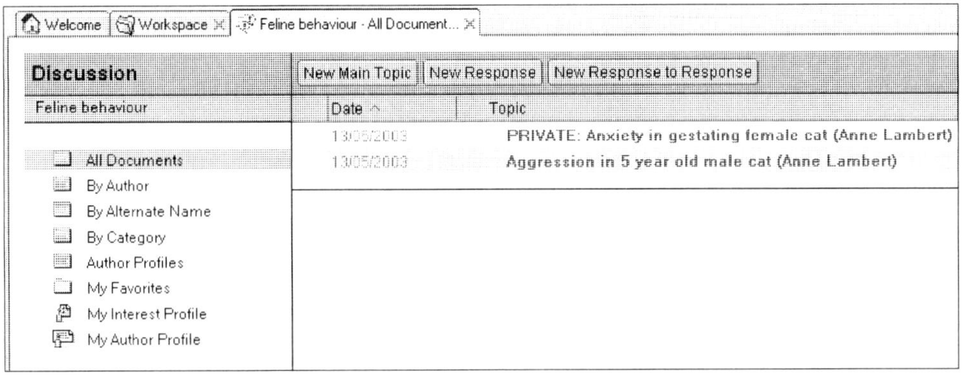

- The **By Author** and **By Alternate Name** views display the list of all the messages created by the same person.
- The **My Favorites** folder contains all the documents that you have set aside as important.
- In the **By Category** view, Notes organises messages by category or section.
- The **Author Profiles**, **My Interest Profile** and **My Author Profile** views provides a way of being known and getting to know other authors through your main interests and the information given in the associated forms.

The view pane

- The number that appears to the left of the original message indicates the number of answers received.

Sending an initial message

- Open the discussion database.
- Click the **New Main Topic** button.
- In the **Subject** frame, give a brief description of the message.

This text becomes the document's title.

- Open the **Category** list, select the category(ies) of your choice or enter a new category using the **New keyword** field.

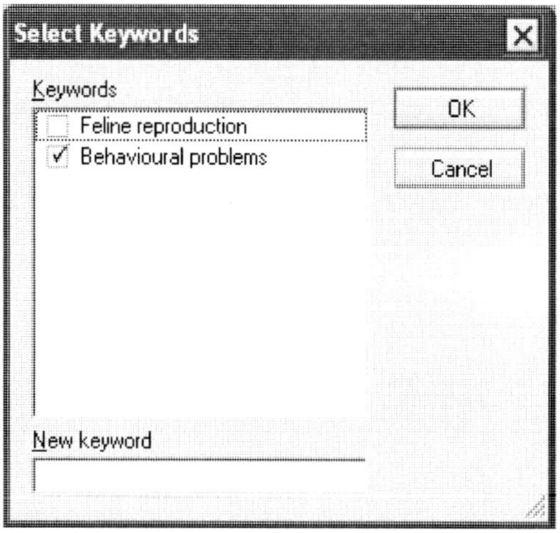

- Click **OK** to confirm.
- Enter the message's **Content** between the field brackets.
- Finish the message by clicking the **Save & Close** button.

Reading a message and replying to it

Before you read a message, you must first open the discussion database.

- Update the database contents with the F9 key.
- Double-click the message you want to read.

Messages are opened automatically in Read mode.

- Click the **New Response** button.
- Enter the **Subject** of the reply message then give the **Content**.
- If you want to display the original message in your reply, activate the **Parent Preview** option in the **View** menu or click the **Parent Preview** button, if it appears.

The window splits into two panes, with your reply in the top pane and the original message in the bottom one.

- Finish the message by clicking the **Save & Close** button.
- If necessary, close the original message.

While you are reading a reply, you can click the **New Response to Main** button to make a new reply to the initial message.

Continuing a discussion

- Select or open the message to which you wish to reply.
- Choose to reply to the main message by clicking the **New Response** button or to reply to another reply by clicking the **New Response to Response** button.
- Proceed as you would for a standard reply.

Making a discussion private

As long as you have not yet finished a message or document, you can mark it as private, so no-one else can read it.

- Start creating or editing the document.
- Click the **Mark Private** button.

The word PRIVATE precedes the document's topic in the list.

- Save and close the message.

Date ^	Topic
13/05/2003	PRIVATE: **Anxiety in gestating female cat (Anne Lambert)**
13/05/2003	**Aggression in 5 year old male cat (Anne Lambert)**

In this example, the message referring to cat anxiety has been marked as private.

To make a private document accessible to other readers, open it and click the **Edit Document** button then click the **Mark Public** button.

Sending an anonymous reply

- Open the document to which you wish to reply anonymously.
- **Create**
  Other
- Select **Anonymous Response** or **Anonymous Response to Response.**
- Click **OK** to confirm.

What is the Resource Reservations database?

This base is designed to help you schedule and reserve physical resources such as rooms or material.

- Before you start, make sure your administrator has created a resource database using the **Resource Reservations (6)** template.
- Before you can create resources, a site profile has to be created. A site profile can be a geographical location or owner to which the resource can be attached.

Displaying the Resource Reservations database

- **File - Database - Open** then select the resource database and click the **Open** button.

Apart from the items specific to resources, you can also access the Calendar from here.

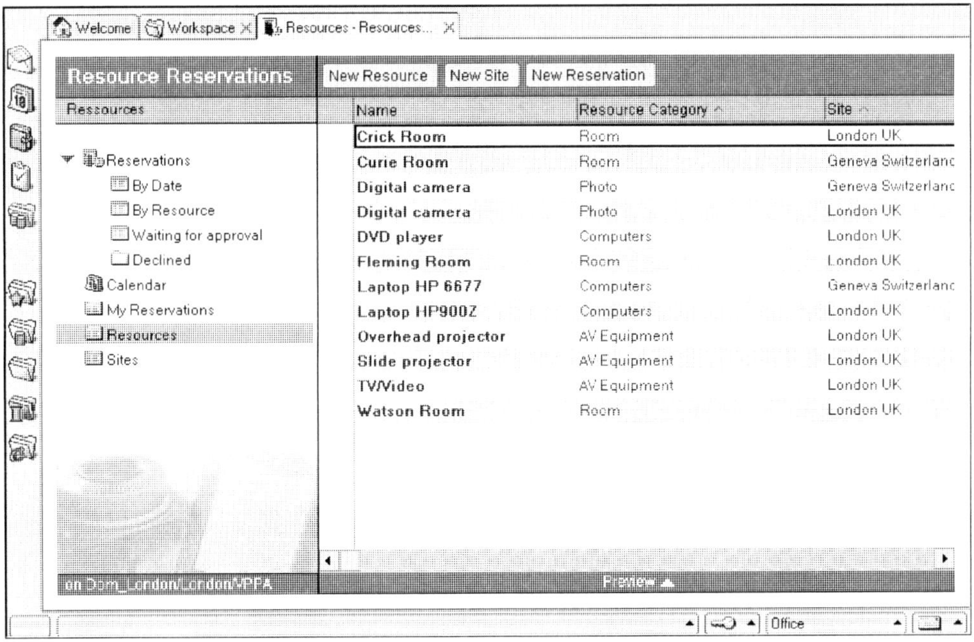

Creating a site

A site can be a place or an owner, for example, and each resource must be tied to a particular site.

- Open the resource reservation database.
- Select any view apart from **Calendar**, **My Reservations** or **Reservations - Waiting for approval.**
- **Create - Site Profile** or click the **New Site** button
- Enter the **Site name** in the corresponding box.

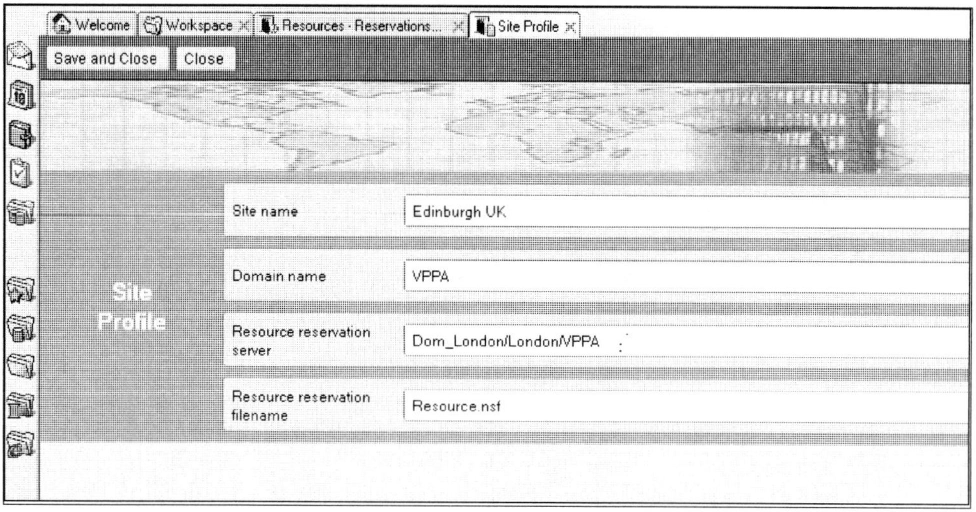

- Check the **Domain name** and the **Resource reservation server** on which the new site will be stored.
- If necessary, change the **Resource reservation filename.**
- Click the **Save and Close** button.

To check that the new site has been correctly created, click the **Sites** view in the navigation pane of the corresponding reservations database.

Creating a resource

- Open the resource reservations database.
- Before creating any resources, make sure that you have been assigned a **Create-Resource** role in the resource base's access control list (**File - Database - Access Control**).

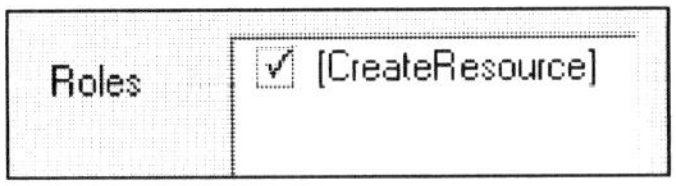

Creating a room resource

- **Create**
  Resource
  or
  Click the **New Resource** button.

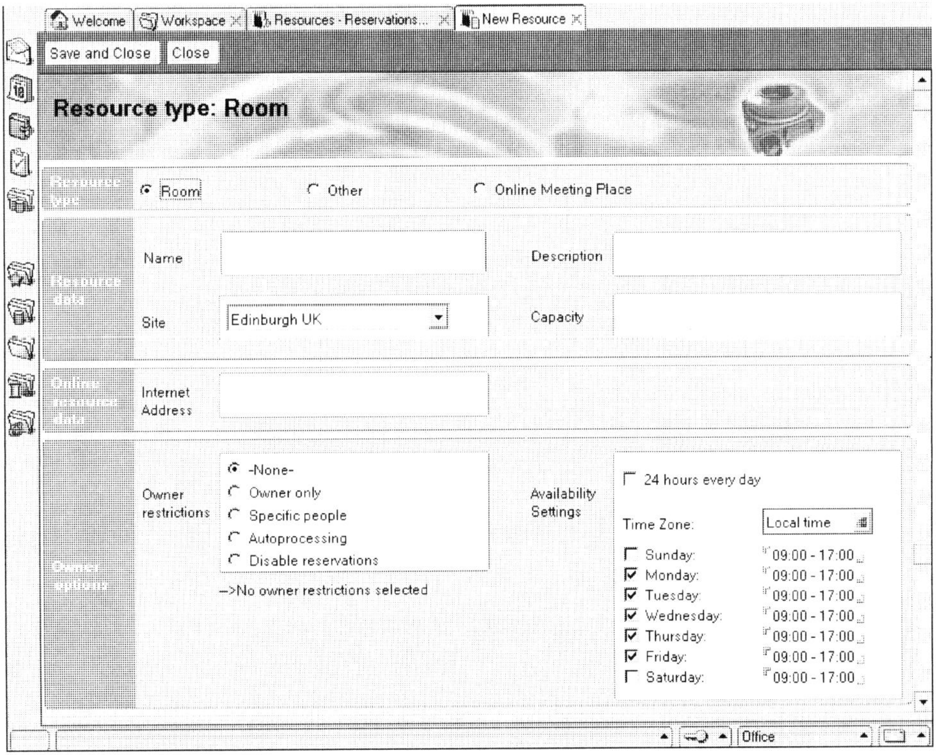

- Keep the **Room** option active in the **Resource type** field.
- In the **Resource data** frame, enter the resource's **Name**, its **Capacity** as a number of people and a **Description** if you wish. Select the resource's **Site** from the corresponding list, if necessary.
- If necessary, use the appropriate options to set the **Owner restrictions**:

None	to set no restriction.
Owner only	only the resource's owner can control it. If you use this option, choose or enter the **Owner's Name**. An owner can be an individual or a group.
Specific people	only those people chosen or entered in the **List of names** can control that resource.
Autoprocessing	only those people chosen or entered in the **List of names** can control that resource. Others must seek approval from the owner specified in the **Owner's Name** field.
Disable reservations	this prevents the resource from being reserved.

- In the **Availability Settings** frame, give the days and times when the resource is available.
- Confirm with the **Save and Close** button.

If Notes accepts the new resource, it displays this message:

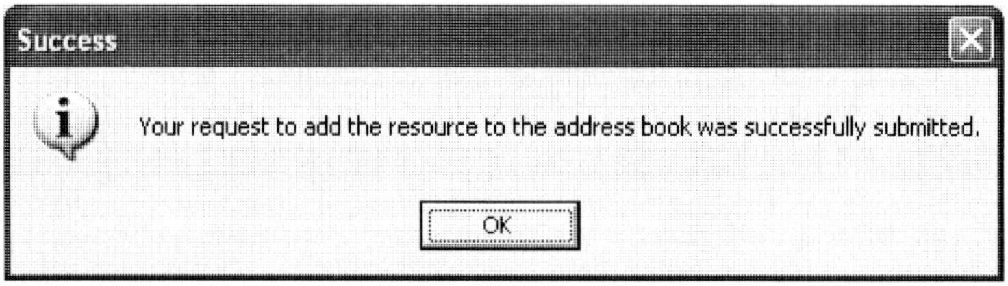

Creating another type of resource

- Open the resource reservation database.
- **Create - Resource** or click the **New Resource** button.
- Activate the **Other** option in the **Resource type** frame.

- In the **Resource data** frame, enter the resource's **Name**, select the **Site** to which the resource belongs then click the arrow on the **Category** field. If you are making a new category, enter its name; otherwise select the category in the list.

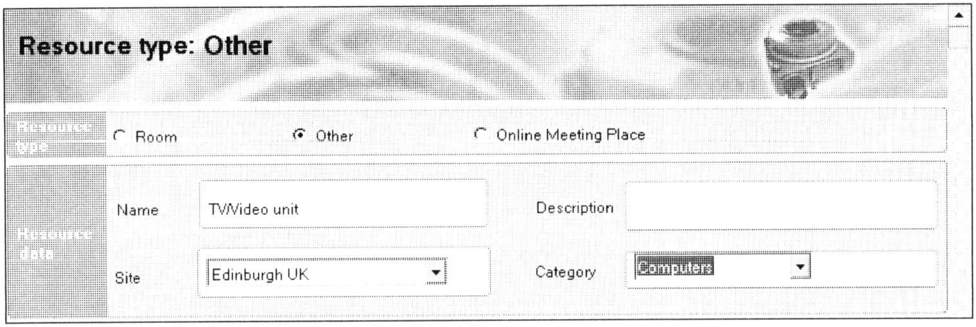

- Define the **Availability Settings.**
- If required, set any **Owner restrictions** as described in the previous section.
- Confirm the new entry with the **Save and Close** button.

Be careful as you create the resource, as the only fields you can change via the **Edit Resource** button are the **Availability Settings** and the **Description** and **Other comments** fields.

Creating an online meeting place resource

Users that want to make online meetings must have the Sametime 3.0 application and Domino 6.

- Open the resource reservation database.
- Use the **Create - Resource** command or click the **New Resource** button.
- Activate the **Online Meeting Place** option in the **Resource type** frame.

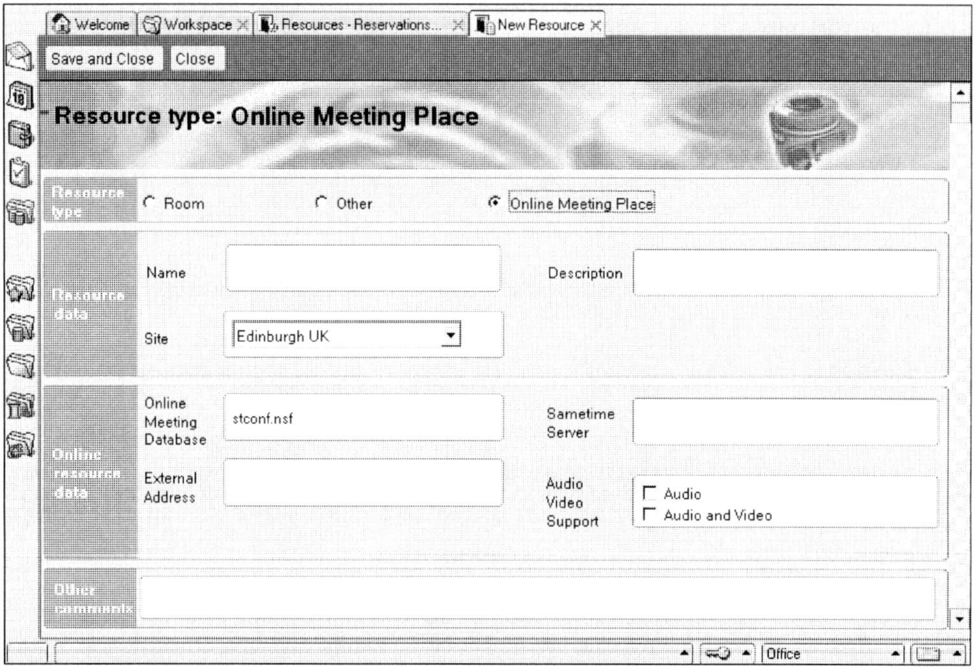

- Give the new resource's **Name** and a **Description** of it.
- Link the resource to a **Site**.

  You can see that the ***Online Meeting Database*** *field automatically contains the name* ***stconf.nsf****.*

- Fill in the **External Address** field with the name of the messaging base on the Sametime server.
- Give the name of the **Sametime Server.**
- Tick the **Audio** and/or **Audio and Video** options as required.
- Confirm with the **Save and Close** button.

Deleting a resource

- Double-click the resource to open it.
- **Actions - Delete Resource** or click the **Delete Resource** button.
- Confirm with the **Yes** button.

- Reply **OK** to the delete confirmation.

Reserving a resource

- Open the resource reservation database.
- Use the **Create - New Reservation** command or click the **New Reservation** button.
- Enter a **Reservation description** in the corresponding field.
- Choose whether to keep the **Reserve a room** option active or activate the **Reserve a resource** option.

  What follows depends on the choice you make.

Reserving according to the required time

- Make sure the **find a room at a specific time** option is active.
- Specify what is the **Site to search** and how many people will be there (**# of attendees**) for a room, or give the **Category** for other types of resource.
- In the **When** frame, specify when you will need the resource.

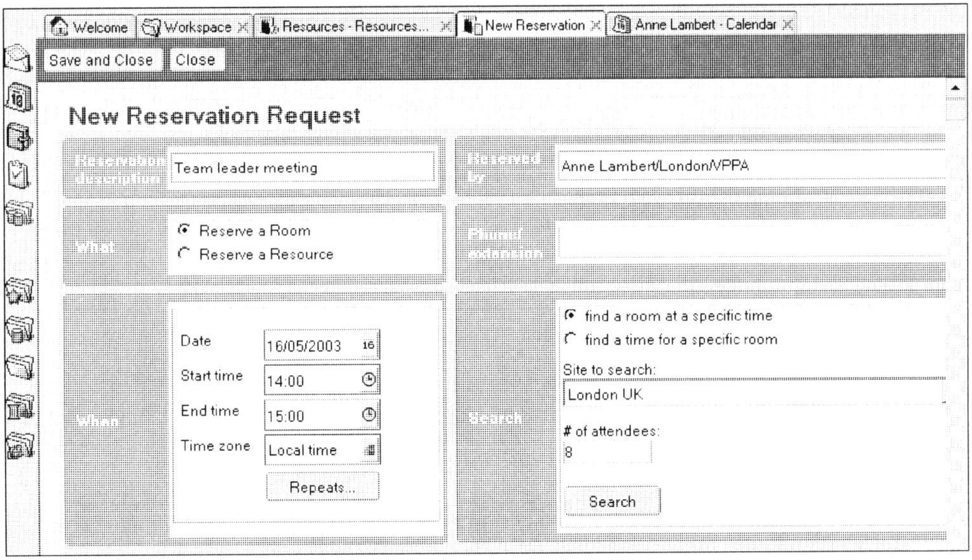

- Click the **Search** button to start the search.

If no room (or resource) meets your criteria, Notes will tell you in the results frame; if several sites could be suitable, Notes will ask you to choose one:

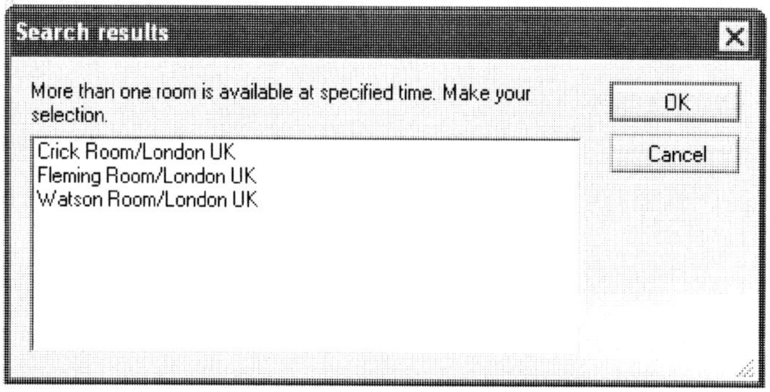

Reserving according to a specific room or resource

- Activate the **find a time for a specific room** option.
- In the **When** frame, specify when you will need the resource.
- Open the **Select room** list to choose a specific room.
- Select the room (or resource) that you wish to use.

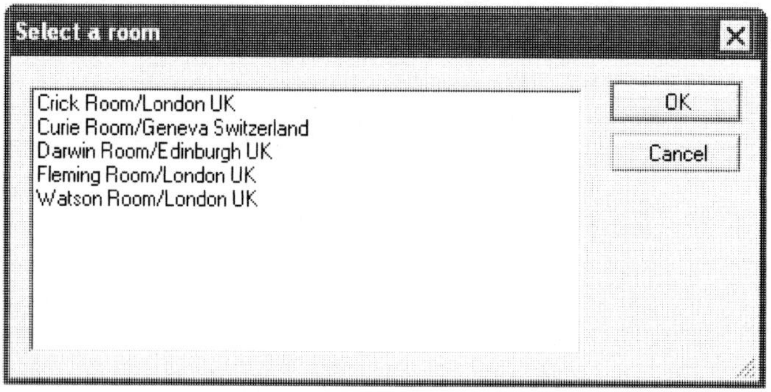

- Click **OK** to confirm.

  *In the **Scheduler** frame, Notes displays a calendar showing the free and busy times for the chosen room.*

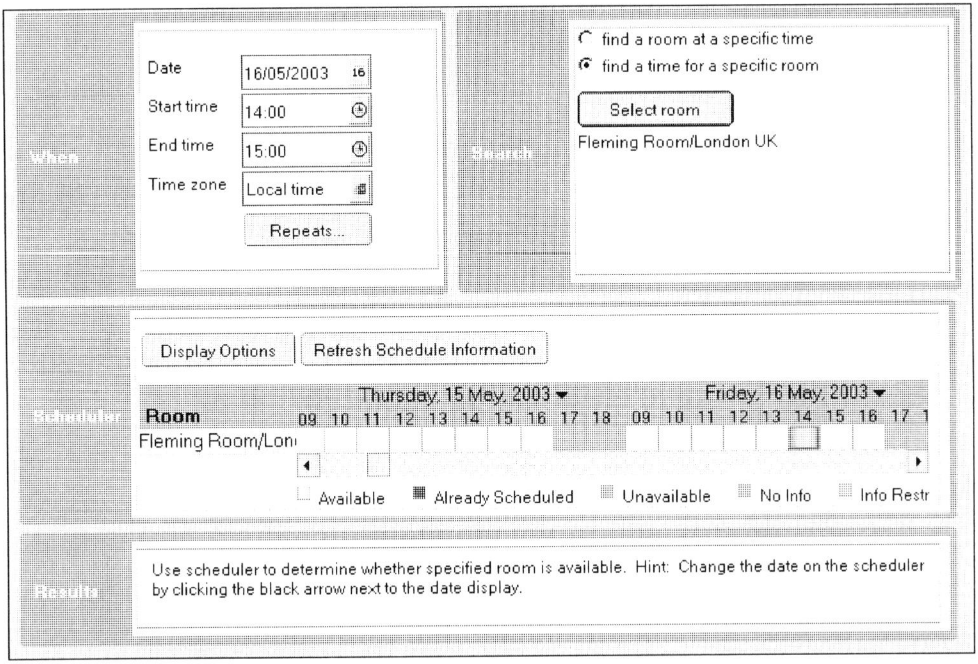

*The times you requested in the **When** frame are highlighted by a black rectangle in the **Scheduler** frame.*

- If necessary, change the reservation times in the **When** frame.
- Click the **Save and Close** button.

Reserving a resource for a meeting

- Open the meeting entry.
- Click the **Find Room or Resource** button then the **Find Room(s)** or **Find Resource(s)** option as required.
- Check and complete the options given in the **Scheduler** dialog box.

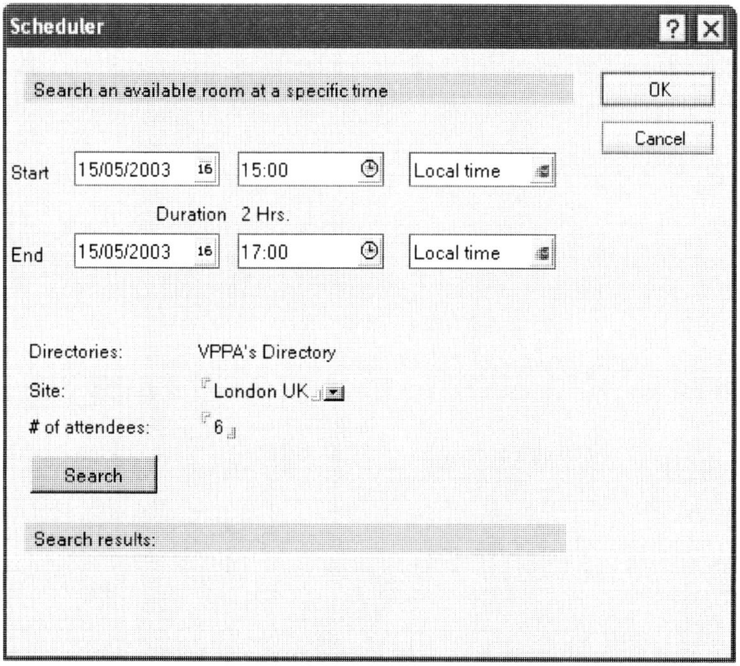

- Click the **Search** button in the **Scheduler** to check the availability of a room or resource.
- Click **OK** to confirm.

You can also choose a room and/or resources when you first plan a meeting (cf. Calendar - Meetings - Planning a meeting).

Seeing the reservations

- In the resource reservations database, activate the **Reservations - By Date** view,
  or
  Activate the **Reservations - By Resource** view.

  These two views list all the reservations regardless of who made them.
- To filter out your own reservations, activate the **My Reservations** view.

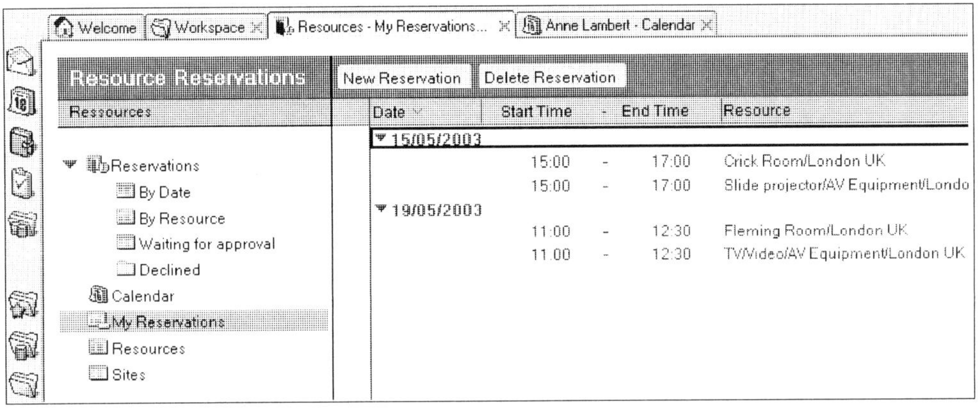

Cancelling a reservation

- Open the resource reservations database, then select the reservation you want to cancel.
- **Actions - Delete Reservation** or click the **Delete Reservation** button.
- Confirm the cancellation with the **Yes** button.

What is the Personal Journal?

- This database holds your confidential documents, whether they be notes or draft documents.
- The Personal Journal database contains two types of document:

Journal Entry	made up of a text box and title that can be printed.
Clean Sheet	made up of a text box and a title that can be neither seen nor printed.

Creating a Personal Journal database

- **File**
  Database
  New Ctrl N
- Fill in the **Server**, **Title** and **File name.**
- Select the **Personal Journal (R6)** template, usually in the **Local** templates.
- Click **OK** to confirm.

The Personal Journal view is immediately active:

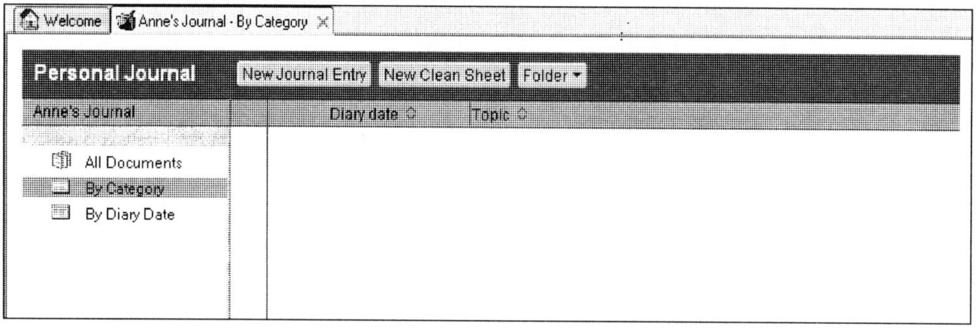

On the workspace, your Personal Journal has an icon like this:

Opening your Personal Journal base

- From the Welcome page, click the 

icon,
  or
  From the workspace, click the corresponding icon: 

,
  or
  Use the **File - Database - Open** menu command and select the database concerned and confirm with **Open**.

Creating a journal entry

- Activate the **All Documents** view in your Personal Journal and click the **New Journal Entry** button.
- Give the entry's **Title**.
- Assign the entry to a **Category** if required.
- By default, the current date is given in the **Diary date** field; change this if need be.
- Click between the field brackets in the lower half of the window then enter the content.

  *The content field is a **Rich text** field.*
- Confirm with the **Save & Close** button.

To create a journal entry without opening the corresponding database, you can use the **Journal entry** button in Quick Notes (accessible from the Welcome page).

Creating a clean sheet

- In the **All Documents** view, click the **New Clean Sheet** button.
- Enter your text between the field brackets.
- Click the **Title/Category** button if you want to enter a **Title** and/or link a **Category** and **Diary date** to the new document.
- Click the **Save & Close** button to confirm.

- If necessary, use the **Folder** button then one of these options: **Create Folder**, **Move To Folder** or **Remove From Folder.**

Editing a journal entry or clean sheet

- In the **All Documents** view, select and open the entry or document in question.
- Click the **Edit Document** button.
- Make your required changes.
- Click the **Save & Close** button to close the window and save your changes.

Documents

part seven

What is a document?

- A **document** is any item in a database containing some kind of information: this could be a mail memo, a discussion group message, a clean sheet etc. The size and type is extremely variable.
- When you create a document, Notes puts it in Edit mode so you can enter information in the fields, usually shown as field brackets or text boxes.

The actions described below work on most documents, bar a few exceptions.

Creating a document

*The type of document varies according to the design of the database in which you want to create it. For example, in the **Mail** database, you can create memos, To Dos, Calendar entries, bookmarks or electronic mails while in a discussion base you can create memos, To Dos, main threads, responses, and so on.*

*To add a document to a database, you must have at least **Author** or **Depositor** access.*

- Open the database appropriate to the type of document you wish to create.
- Open the **Create** menu and click the type of document you want to create.

You can also use the creation buttons given. These vary depending on the type of database used. Here, for example, are the buttons from the Mail database:

The new window instantly opens.

- Enter the contents of the new document.

The items you might enter depend on the nature of the document.

If one of the documents in the database in which you are working is selected as you create a new document, this new document may "borrow" the properties of the selected document. To avoid this, make sure that no document is currently selected or hold down the Ctrl key as you choose the document type in the **Create** menu.

Opening a document

- Open the database that contains the document you wish to open.
- Activate the folder or view containing the document.
- Double-click the document to open it.

Depending on the type of document, it may open in Read mode (for example, discussion group messages), or in Edit mode (mail messages, for example).

Editing a document

Make sure that you have the correct permissions to edit the document. If it is one of your documents, you must have at least Author access to the database. To modify other documents, you need to have Editor access or higher.

- Open or select the document you wish to modify.
- Use **Actions - Edit** or Ctrl **E** or ,

  or
  Click the text of the open document twice.

  This activates Edit mode, so you can start modifying the document.
- Press Ctrl **E** to return to Read mode or click the tool button again.
- Save then close the document as required.

Saving a document

- **File**
  Save Ctrl **S**

  The save procedure may be more elaborate for certain types of document.

Saving a new version

If a database's designer has authorised the manual creation of new versions, you can save several versions of the same document.

- **File**
  Save As New Version

Most databases are set up to save new versions automatically when you use the **File - Save** command.

Closing a document

To avoid a cluttered workscreen, remember to close documents that you have finished editing or reading.

- **File**
  Close

Ctrl W

- If you have made changes that have not been saved, Notes will offer to save the document. Reply as required.

The close button displayed depends on the document (it does not always appear).

Selecting documents

You may wish to select several documents to print them, delete them, and so on.

- Open the database containing the documents you wish to select and activate the view or folder concerned.

Selecting non-adjacent documents

- In the view pane, click the selection margin next to each required document.

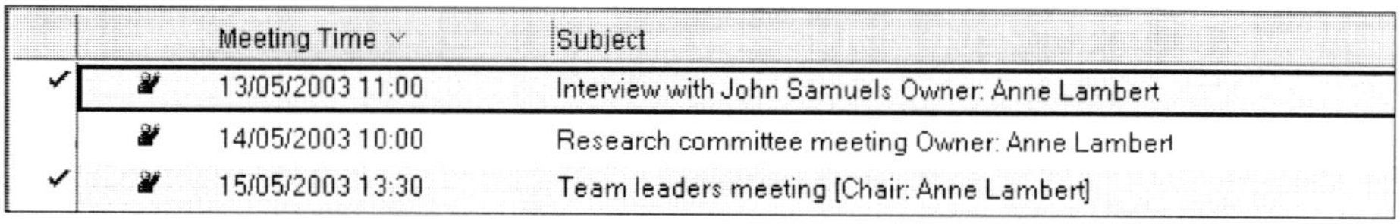
Meeting Time
Subject
13/05/2003 11:00
Interview with John Samuels Owner: Anne Lambert
14/05/2003 10:00
Research committee meeting Owner: Anne Lambert
15/05/2003 13:30
Team leaders meeting [Chair: Anne Lambert]

A tick represents a selected item.

Selecting adjacent documents

- In the view pane, click the selection margin next to the first document required.
- Drag the mouse pointer up or down.

Selecting all the documents

- **Edit**
  Select All — Ctrl A

To cancel a selection of several documents, repeat the technique used to select them. If all the documents have been selected, cancel the selection with **Edit - Deselect All.**

Looking for text in document titles

- Activate the view or folder in which you want to search.
- **Edit**
  Find/Replace — Ctrl F
- Enter the required text in the **Find** box.
- Click **Find Options** to see the various search options available.
- If necessary, tick these options:

Case sensitive	to distinguish between upper and lower case letters.
Accent sensitive	to look for accented characters during the search.
Whole words	to look for a complete word and not a string of characters.

- Use one of the options in the **Direction** list to define in which direction the search should be carried out.

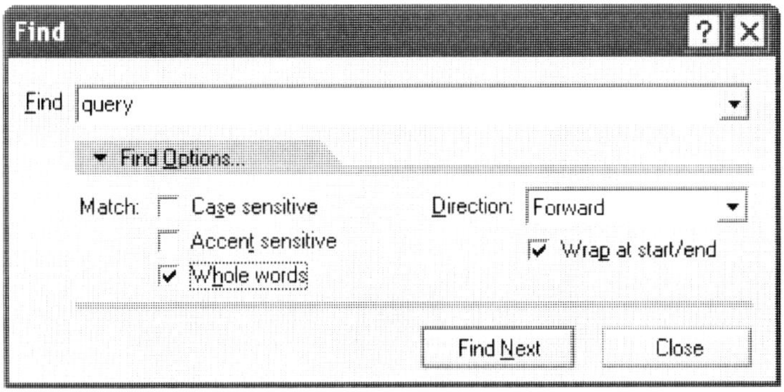

- Click **Find Next** to start the search.
- When you have finished searching, click **Close**.

Looking for documents containing specific text

Unlike the search described above, this type looks in the contents of documents.

Displaying the search feature

- **View**
  Search This View  then **Search This View**

The search feature opens at the top of the view pane.

- To start an initial search, enter the word(s) you wish to find in the **Search for** box then click the **Search** button.

This technique selects all the documents that contain the search text and displays only those:

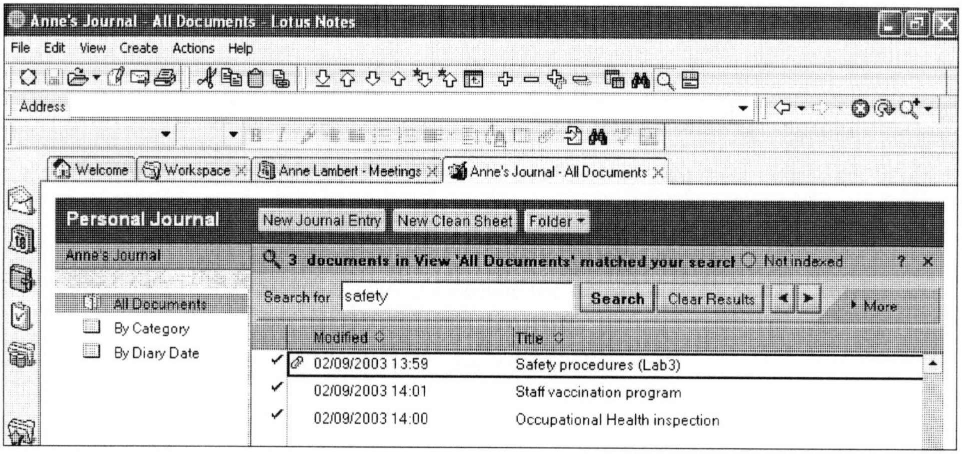

*Above the **Search for** field, Notes indicates the number of documents it has found.*

Saving a frequently-used search

- In the search feature, make the search that you wish to save.
- Click the  button.
- Click the **Save search** button.
- Give the search an easily-recognisable name.

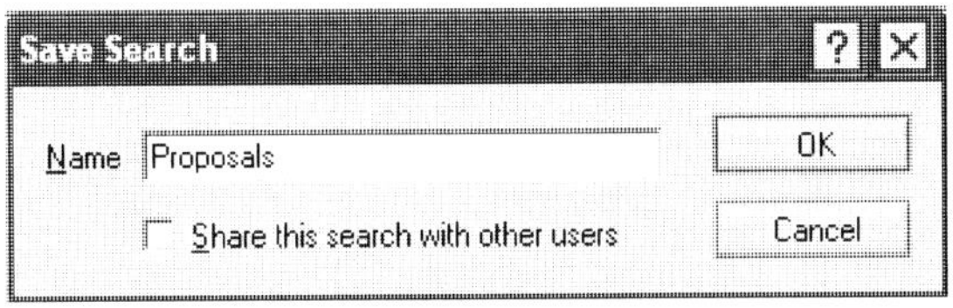

- Click **OK** to confirm.

To retrieve these search criteri a, click the  button then the **Load search** button:

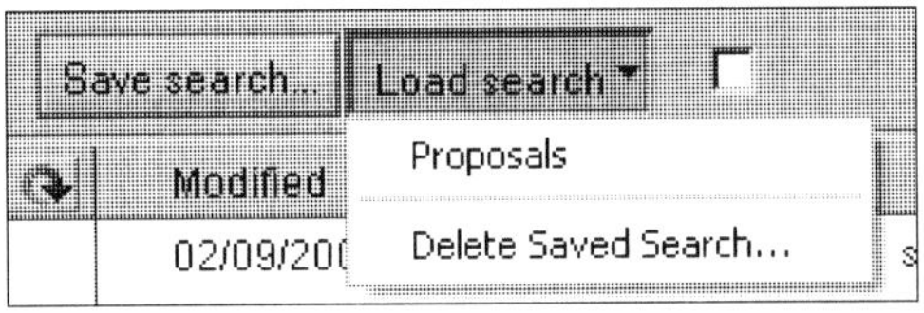

Deleting documents

The deletion procedure occurs in two stages: firstly, documents are marked for deletion, then they are permanently deleted. When they are deleted, documents are sometimes sent to a trash bin (depending on the type of database). Even if a document has actually been deleted, Notes can let you recover it (but only in some cases and according to certain conditions).

Before you delete a document, make sure you have appropriate permissions to do so. If it is one of your documents, you need to have at least Author access to the database. To delete other documents, Editor access or above is required for the database in question.

Deleting documents

- Select the document(s) you want to delete.
- **Edit**
  Delete  

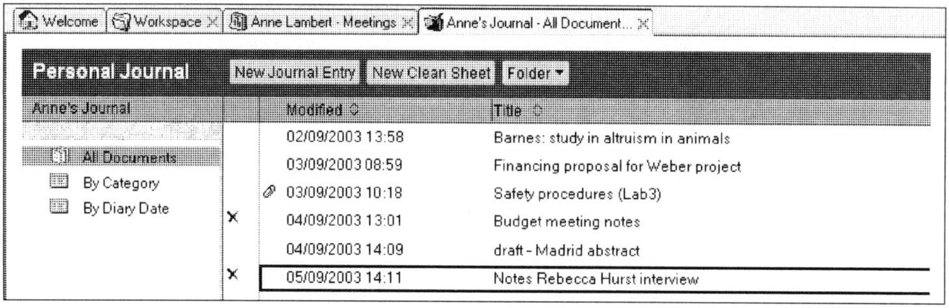

The documents ready for deletion (two in this example) are marked with a cross.

- To remove a deletion mark from a document, taking it out of the deletion process, select it and use **Edit - Delete** again or press Del once more.
- To permanently delete all the marked documents, close the database or use the **View - Refresh** command or F9; Notes will remove all the marked documents from all the views and folders of that base. If required, confirm the deletion the **Yes** button.

Some databases (such as Mail) have a Trash bin, in which deleted documents are stored. It can be possible to restore, or retrieve, a document that has been deleted.

Here is an example of documents deleted but still stored in the Trash:

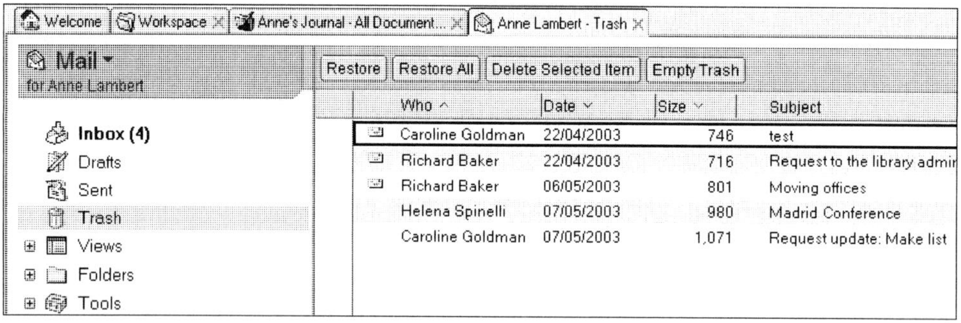

Restoring a file from the Trash

- Activate the **Trash** view.
- If necessary, select the document(s) that you want to restore.
- Click the **Restore** button to recover the selected document(s) or the **Restore All** button to recover all the documents currently in the Trash.

Documents retrieved from the Trash in this way are returned to the initial location.

The **Empty Trash** button definitively removes all the items in the Trash view, generally making it impossible to recover the deleted items. However, Notes allows for a time lapse in the permanent deletion process (known as soft deletion) during which you can sometimes recover deleted documents *in extremis* (cf. Managing documents - Recovering permanently deleted documents).

Recovering permanently deleted documents

In databases with a Trash view, Notes gives you the option of still being able to recover permanently deleted documents, within a certain time lapse, but only if you have taken the following precaution.

- Open the database then use the **File - Database - Properties** command.
- Click the **Advanced** tab.

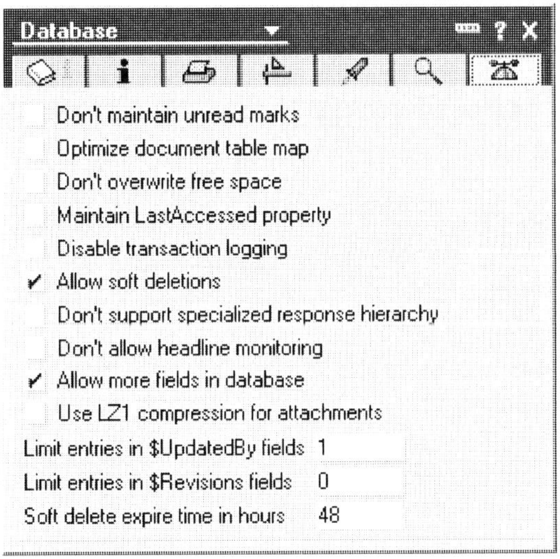

- Tick the **Allow soft deletions** option.
- Give the **Soft delete expire time in hours**; this is the length of time during which items deleted from the Trash can still be recovered.
- Click to close the properties box, confirming your changes.

- You must now set up a view to contain the "soft-deleted" items. Do this with **Create - View**, in the database concerned by the soft deletion setting.

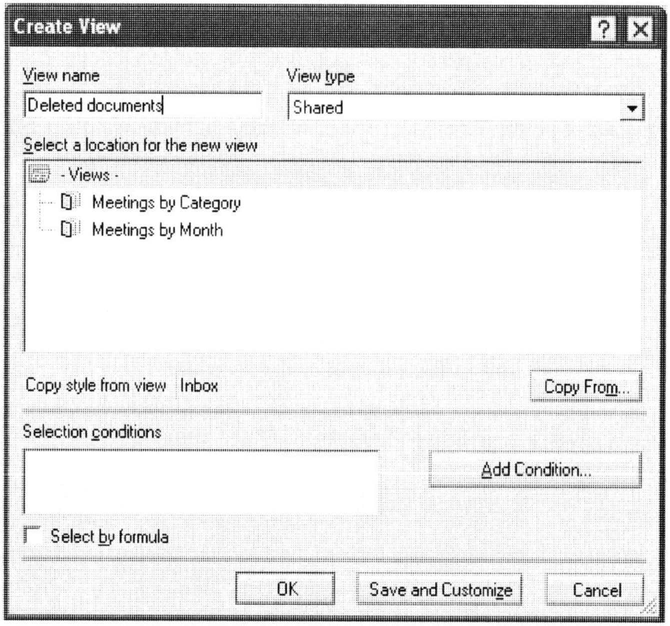

- Give a new **View name**, then select the required **View type**, which can be **Shared** or **Shared, contains documents not in any folders** or **Private.**
- Select a location for the new view in the appropriate area.
- Click **OK** to confirm.

Permanently deleted documents will appear in this view until the end of the specified soft deletion period.

Marking a document as read or unread

- Select the documents you wish to mark.
- **Edit**
  Unread Marks
  Mark Selected Read or **Mark Selected Unread**

Remember that unread documents are symbolised by a red star, and their text colour is different.

Previewing documents

- In the navigation pane, click the documents you wish to preview.
- **View**
  Document Preview
  Show Preview

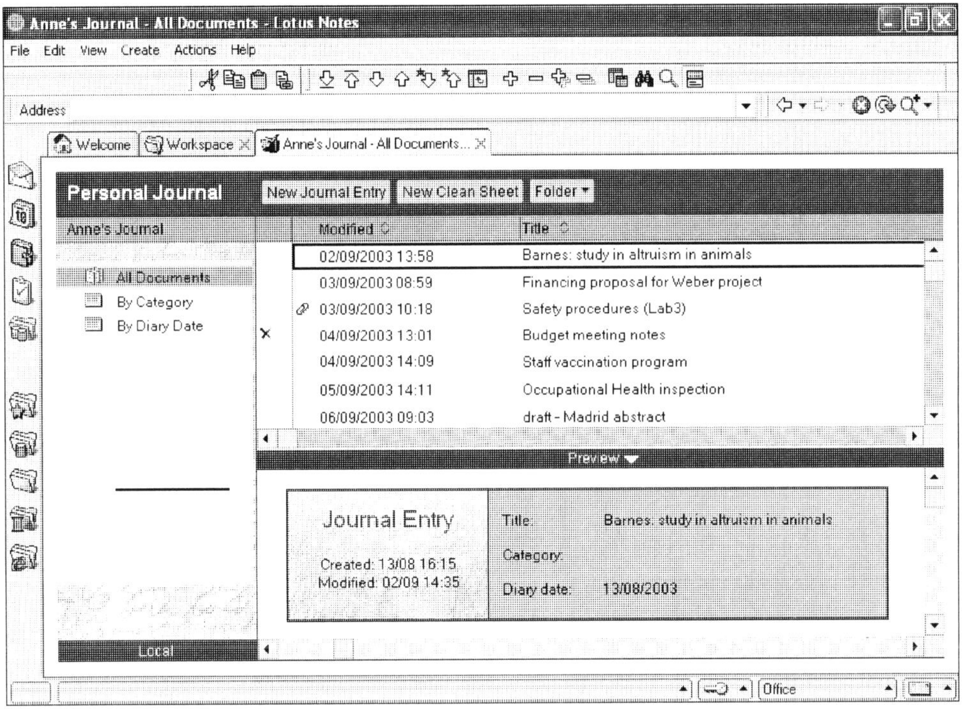

*The **Preview** pane appears.*

- To change the height of the **Preview** pane, drag from the **Preview** bar.
- To hide or display the **Preview** pane, click the arrow on the pane bar.
- To preview the next document, select it in the top part of the window.

  This displays the document in Read mode.

To return to a standard window, deactivate the **Show Preview** option in the **View - Document Preview** menu.

Browsing the unread documents in several databases

- Select the databases concerned on a workspace page.
- **Edit**
  Unread Marks
  Scan Unread

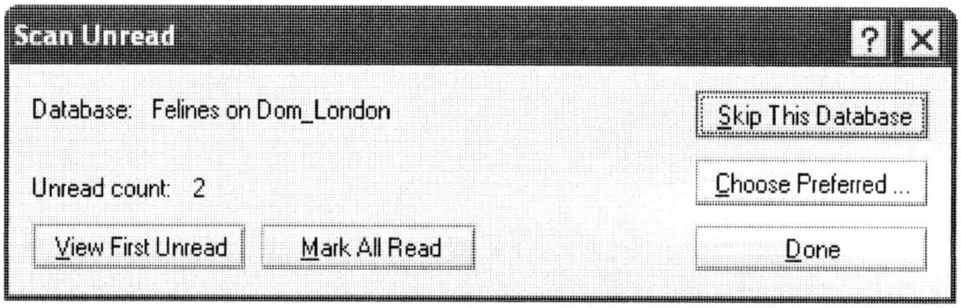

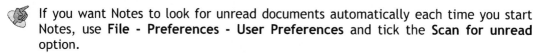

- To display the first unread document in the database, click the **View First Unread** button then browse back and forth through the other unread documents in the base with the  and  buttons.
- To go on to the next database, ignoring the unread documents in the current database, click the **Skip This Database** button.
- To finish looking for unread documents, click the **Done** button.

If you want Notes to look for unread documents automatically each time you start Notes, use **File - Preferences - User Preferences** and tick the **Scan for unread** option.

Creating a new folder

Folders are used to store various documents so you can find them more easily.

Knowing the required access permissions

- To create a private folder, you need at least **Reader** access for the database.
- To create a shared folder, you need to have **Editor** access and the **Create shared folders/views** option needs to be active in the access control list.

Creating a folder

- Select or open the database in which you want to create the folder.
- **Create**
  Folder
- Enter the **Folder name** (up to 60 characters).
- If you wish, **Select a location for the new folder** using the hierarchy given.

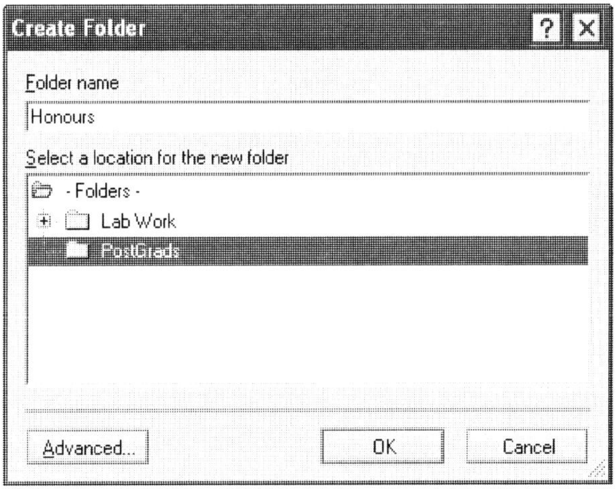

- To apply the default view or folder design from the current database to the new folder, click **OK**.

To modify the type or style for the new folder, click the **Advanced** button:

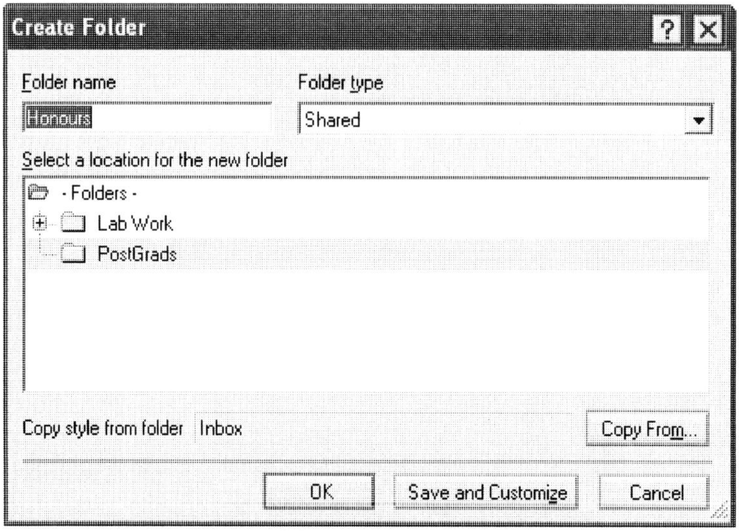

- If required, change the **Folder type** (**Shared** or **Private**).
- Click the **Copy From** button to use the style of an existing folder (in this case, you can use the **Blanks** option to copy no other style). Confirm your choice with **OK**.

  *The **Save and Customize** button can be used to create a customised folder with the help of Lotus Domino Designer 6.*

Renaming a folder

- Select the folder or subfolder concerned.
- **Actions**
  Folder Options
  Rename
- Enter the new name for the folder.

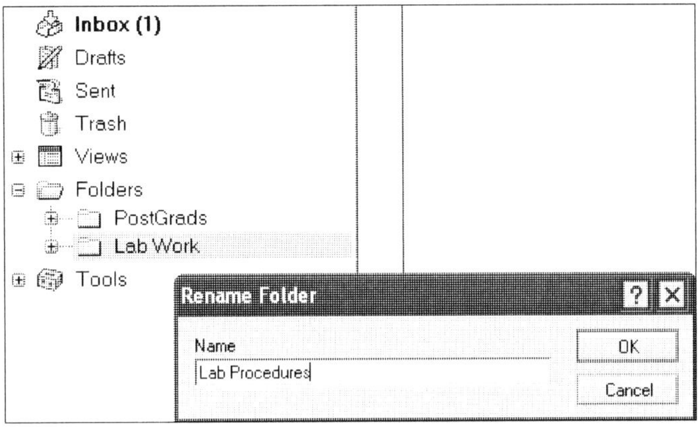

- Click **OK** to confirm.

Deleting a folder

- Select the folder or subfolder you want to delete.
- **Actions**
  Folder Options
  Remove Folder
- Confirm the deletion by clicking **Yes**.

Deleting a folder does not delete the documents previously placed in it, but it does delete any subfolders present.

Moving a folder

- Select the folder or subfolder concerned.
- **Actions**
  Folder Options
  Move
- Click the folder or subfolder into which you want to place the selected folder.

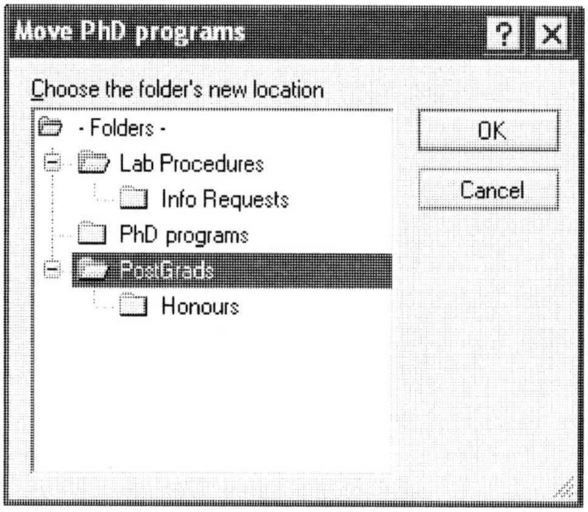

- Click **OK** to confirm.

Putting documents in a folder

Once you have created or received documents, storing them correctly will make it easier to find them at a later time.

- In the view pane, select all the documents that you want to put in the same folder.
- **Actions**
  Folder
  Move To Folder

  You can also click the ***Folder*** *button and choose the* ***Move To Folder*** *option.*
- In the dialog box, **Select a folder** from the list.

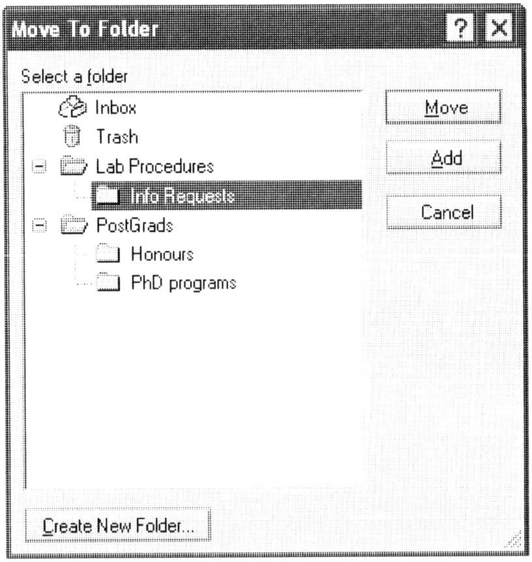

- Click **Move** to move the selected documents into the folder or click **Add** to move a copy of them only.

The **Move** option is accessible only when the documents selected are already in a folder.

Removing documents from a folder

- Display the navigation pane.
- Activate the folder containing the document(s) you wish to remove.
- Select the documents you wish to take out.
- **Actions**
  Folder
  Remove From Folder

  This takes the documents out of that folder but does not delete them from the database or its views. They remain in any view in which they were originally placed, plus the All Documents view.

Copying a document from one base to another

- Select the document.
- **Edit** Ctrl C
  Copy
- Open the destination database for the copied document.
- **Edit** Ctrl V
  Paste

  The document is pasted into the other database, where it is marked as unread.

Assigning a category to a document

__Categories__ are subject areas in which you can class your documents (cf. Views - Managing categories).

- Select the documents that you want to place in the same category(ies).
- **Actions**
  Categorize

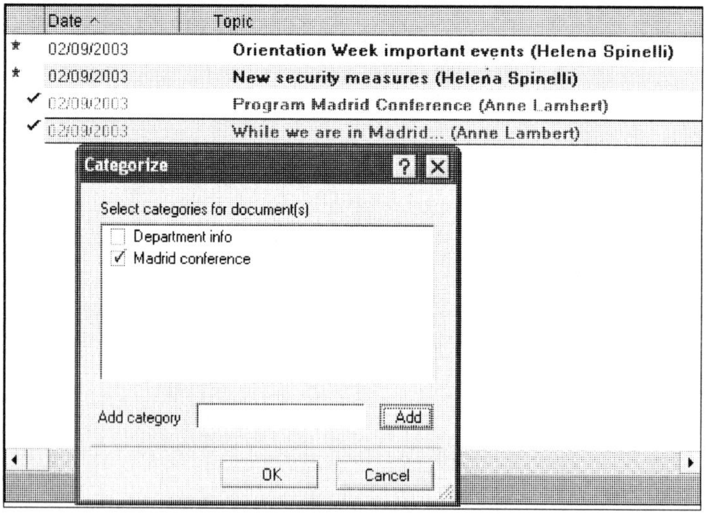

A window appears, listing the various existing categories.

- Tick the category(ies) that interest you and make sure the others are not ticked.
- Click **OK** to confirm.

If none of the current categories are suitable, create a new category by entering its name in the **Add category** box (cf. Views - Managing categories).

Creating page headers/footers

Page headers and footers are texts that appear in the top and bottom margins of a document, respectively.

- **File**
  Document Properties
- Activate the **Printing** tab .
- Specify whether you require a **Header** or **Footer** by choosing the corresponding option.

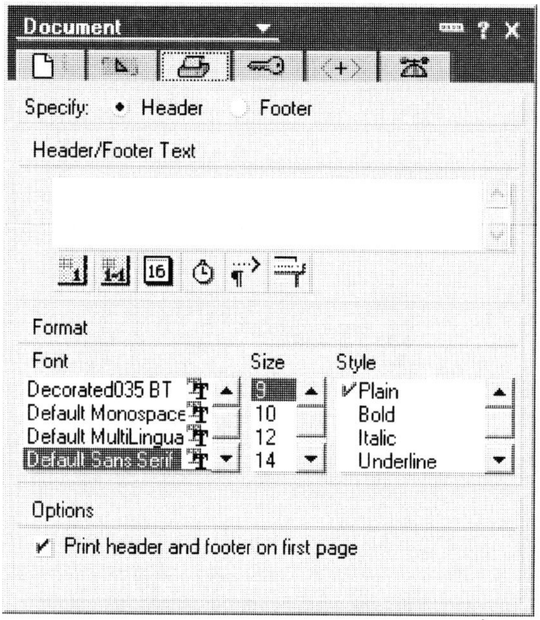

- If you want to enter certain predefined contents, use these tools:

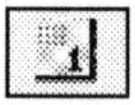 the page number

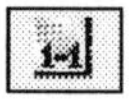 the total number of pages

 the control date

 the control time

 a tab stop

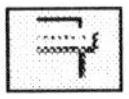 the document's title

- If necessary, change the **Font**, the font **Size**, or the font **Style.**
- Indicate whether or not the header and/or footer should appear on the first page by activating or deactivating the **Print header and footer on first page** option.

Headers and footers are printed in the top and bottom margins; you can change their position in the margins using **File - Page Setup** and changing the values **Above header** and **Below footer** in the **Page Margins** frame.

Defining a document's page setup

- Select or open the document.
- **File**
  Page Setup
- Set the margins in the specified measurement unit, using the **Above header/body** and **Below body/footer** options:

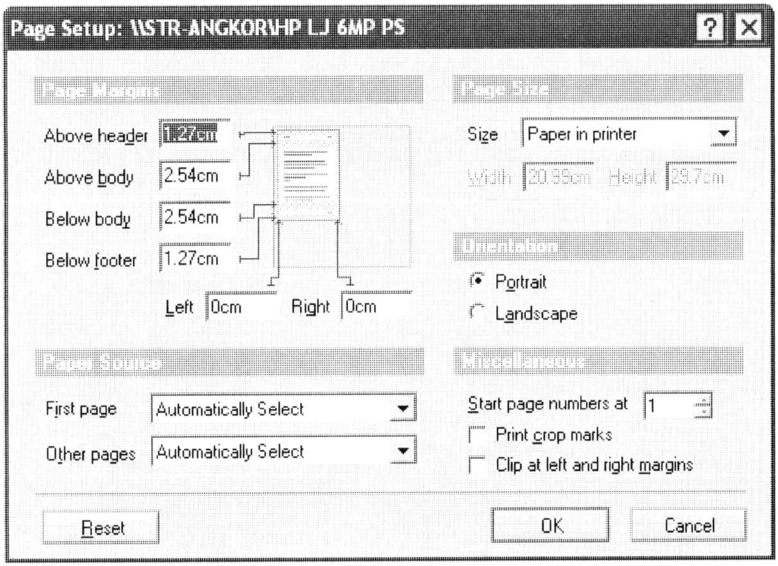

- Set the **Left** and **Right** margins.

- In the **Orientation** section, choose whether the page should be printed in **Landscape** (horizontal) orientation or in **Portrait** (vertical) orientation.
- Click **OK** to confirm.

The page setup options can also be filled in from the **Print Document** dialog box - **Page Setup** tab.

Managing page breaks

Options are available to prevent badly-placed page breaks, either by creating forced breaks or forbidding breaks in certain places.

- Open the document in Edit mode (double-click its name then click the **Edit Document** button).
- Click the paragraph concerned.
- **File**
  Document Properties
- Display the **Text** properties then activate the **Paragraph Margins** tab.

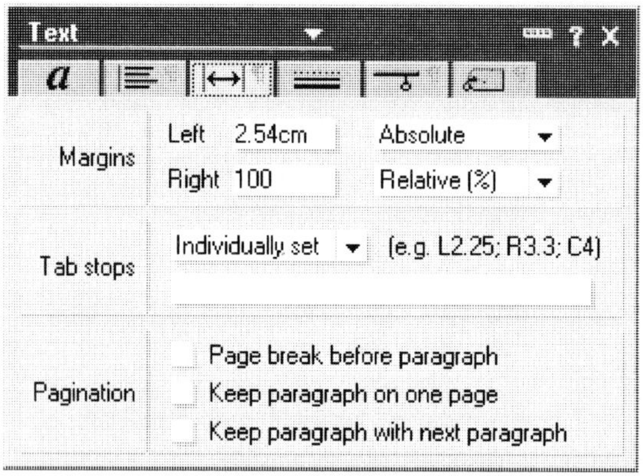

- As required, use the options in the **Pagination** frame:

Page break before paragraph	forces an automatic page break before the active paragraph.
Keep paragraph on one page	prevents any page break appearing in the paragraph.
Keep paragraph with next paragraph	forbids any page breaks between the active paragraph and the one that follows it.

Forcing a page break

- Open the document in Edit mode (double-click its name then click the **Edit Document** button).
- Place the insertion point where the page break should appear.
- **Create**
  Page Break

To cancel a forced page break, bring the insertion point back into the paragraph that follows the break and use the **Create - Page Break** command again.

Printing a document

- Open the document you wish to print.
- **File** [Ctrl] **P**
  Print

  *The **Print Document** dialog box appears, which contains two pages:*

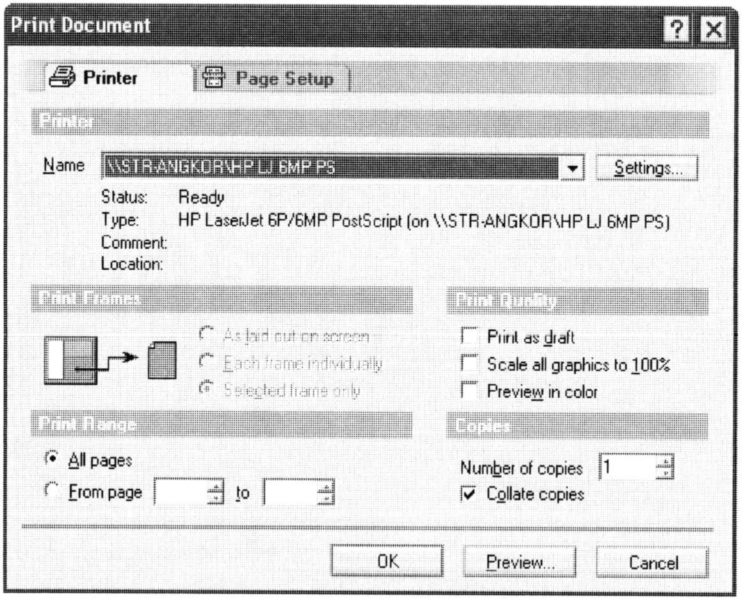

*The option on the **Page Setup** tab are described in the Defining a document's page setup section.*

- To print a group of pages, give the starting page number in **From page** then the number of the last page in the **to** box, in the **Print Range** section.
- To make a fast printout, tick the **Print as draft** option in the **Print Quality** section.
- To print all pictures at their original size, tick the **Scale all graphics to 100%** option.
- To print several copies, give the **Number of copies** in the corresponding box.
- Click the **Preview** button to see how the document will appear once printed.
- Click **OK** to start printing.

Printing several documents

- In the view pane, select the documents you wish to print.
- **File** Ctrl P
  Print

  *The **Print View** dialog box appears, containing three pages:*

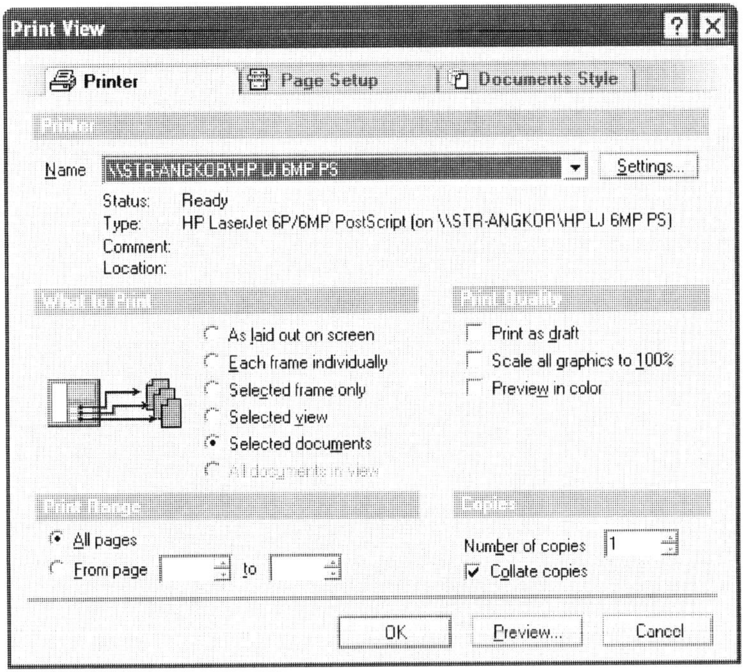

- Depending on the settings you want to change, activate one of the tabs:

Printer	to select or set up the printer of your choice and choose what you want to print and the print quality.
Page Setup	to set the margins and the print orientation.
Documents Style	to choose a print mode or page numbering.

- Click the **Preview** button to see how the document will appear once printed.
- Click **OK** to start printing.

Document text

part eight

Displaying the Text properties box

This box contains all the necessary tools for text formatting. The various options are grouped by page, which you can access by clicking the corresponding tab. Remember that changes made in properties boxes take effect immediately.

- Open the document in Edit mode.
- **Text**
  Text Properties

*The **Text** properties box appears:*

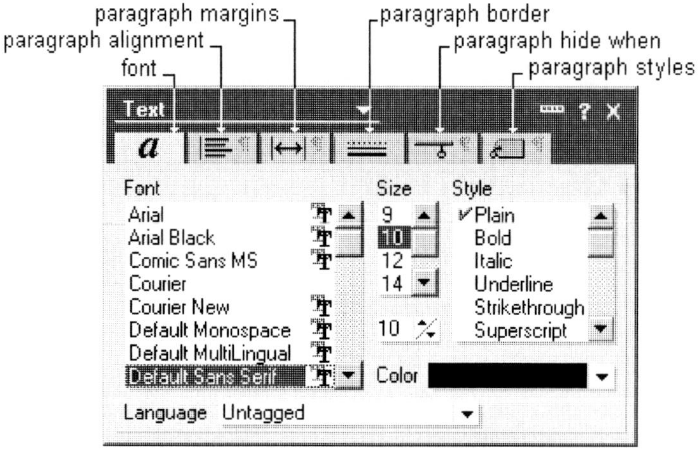

You can also display this box with shortcut keys: the Ctrl K or Alt Enter keys open the **Font** page and Ctrl J opens the **Paragraph Alignment** page.

Changing the working mode

There are two modes you can use when working with documents: Edit mode and Read mode.

- To go into Edit mode, double-click inside the document or click the tool button.
- To go into Read mode, click again or use the Ctrl **E** shortcut.

Seeing the right edge of pages

As documents are generally designed for electronic mail, no indication is made for the right edges of printed pages. This can cause problems when you actually want to print the document.

- **View**
  Show
  Page Breaks

If the ruler is visible, the right indent markers become available in certain databases.

Showing/hiding the nonprinting characters

When you show the nonprinting characters, you can see where all the items such as ends of paragraphs or tab stops are placed.

- Open the document in Edit mode.
- **View**
  Show
  Hidden Characters

Where you have used the [Enter] *key, the ¶ symbol appears; use of the* [⇄] *key appears as a >> symbol and spaces are shown as dots.*

Showing/hiding field help

By default, Lotus Notes displays a brief description of the current field at the bottom of the document window.

- Open the document in Edit mode.
- **View**
  Show
  Field Help

Cancelling the last action

Notes often keeps your last action in memory, so it can cancel it if need be.

Edit
Undo — Ctrl Z

If the action cannot be undone, this option is unavailable.

Looking at the different field types

When you work in memos, messages, documents and so on, text is entered in fields. These are indicated by field brackets or boxes.
Several types of field may be available:

Text	These can contain letters, punctuation, spaces and any number as long as there is no calculation.
Rich Text	These can be used to enter and format text, import images and charts, attach files and integrated objects.
Keywords	Here you can enter only predefined texts.
Date/Time	These are used to define the time and date. In general, these fields are filled in automatically by Notes, and they cannot always be modified.
Number	A field used for entering numbers, such as currency values or quantities.
Authors	The field containing the name of the document's author.
Readers	The field containing the list of people authorised to read the document.
Names	The field displaying the list of user names and servers (but which does not give them access rights).

Most of the actions described in this chapter refer to Rich Text fields.

Editing text

- Correct text as you type using the following keys:

Del	to delete the next character.
←	to delete the previous character.
Ctrl ←	to delete the previous word.

Moving the insertion point

You can move the insertion point with the mouse, but as you type, you may find it quicker to use the keyboard.

- Use the following keyboard combinations:

Ctrl Home	Start of the document.
Ctrl End	End of the document.
Ctrl →	Next word.
Ctrl ←	Previous word.
Home	Start of the current line.
End	End of the current line.
Pg Dn	Next screen page.
Pg Up	Previous screen page.

Selecting text

The techniques to use depend on the text you are selecting.

A word

- Double-click the word.

A portion of text

- Drag the mouse from the beginning of the required text over to the end.
  or
  Click in front of the first character you want to select, point just after the last character, hold down the [Shift] key and click.

An entire field

- Click in the field you want to select.
- **Edit**
  Select All — [Ctrl] **A**

Moving/copying text

In everyday usage, moving text is often called "cut and paste", while duplicating text is described as "copy and paste".

- Select the text you wish to move or copy.
- To cut text, use:
  Edit
  Cut  [Ctrl] **X**

  The selection disappears and is placed in the clipboard.
- To copy text, use:
  Edit
  Copy  [Ctrl] **C**
- Once you have cut or copied your selection, put it in its new position: place the insertion point where the text should now appear and use:
  Edit
  Paste  [Ctrl] **V**

  The selection is still in the clipboard, so you can paste it again, if required.

Replacing text

Notes can quickly replace one text by another, wherever it occurs in the document.

- **Edit**
  Find/Replace — [Ctrl] **F**

- Enter the text that you want to **Find.**
- Enter the replacement text in the **Replace with** box.
- If necessary, show the **Find Options** by clicking the corresponding arrow then set these options:

Case sensitive	Tick this option to look for the search text, taking into account the combination of upper and lower case letters used.
Accent sensitive	Tick this option to look for a text containing the specified accented characters.
Whole words	Tick this option if you want to look for the search text as a complete word (preceded and followed by a space). Otherwise, the text is considered as a string of characters, which could occur within another word.

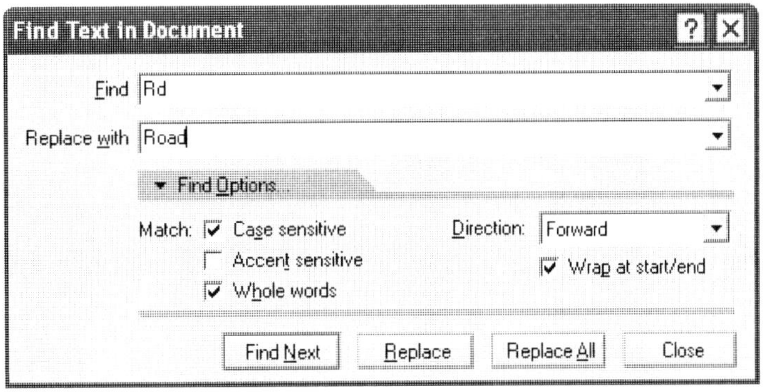

- Click **Find Next** to start searching.
- Click the following :

Replace All	to replace the text every time it occurs.
Replace	to replace the selected occurrence.
Find Next	to skip this occurrence and look for the next one.

- If necessary, finish all the replacements and click the **Close** button.

Checking spelling

What is the spell checker?

- The spell checker looks for misspelled words using two dictionaries, namely the main dictionary and a user dictionary, which can be customized.
- As well as unknown words, the spell checker will point out repeated words, such as Bora Bora.
- It does not check single letter words (such as "I"), nor those containing numbers, nor those with more than 64 characters.

Starting the spell check

- If you want to check only a part of the document, select that portion, otherwise, click anywhere in the document.
- **Edit**
  Spell Check or **Check Spelling**

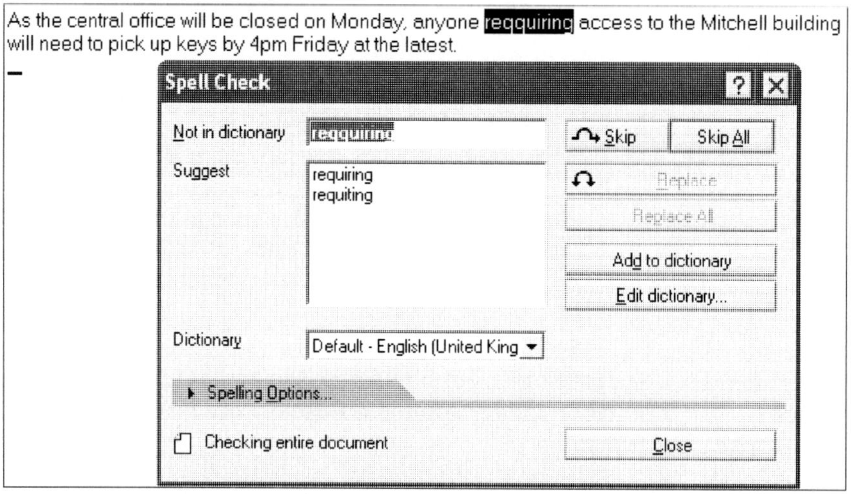

Notes stops on the first unknown or repeated word.

*The language of the main dictionary appears in the **Dictionary** list.*

- To continue the check without changing the current word, click the **Skip** button, or **Skip All** to skip all occurrences of that word.

- To continue checking and add the word to the user dictionary, click the **Add to dictionary** button.
- To correct the word, choose the correct spelling in the **Suggest** list and click the **Replace** button, or enter the correct word in the **Not in dictionary** box and press Enter to confirm.
- To stop the check before the end, click the **Close** button.
- To leave the spell checker when the spell check is complete, click **OK** on the message that appears:

If you find that you need other dictionaries than those listed, you can always install more. To do this, use the **File - Preferences - User Preferences** command, click the **International** tab then the **Spell Check** tab. Click the **Install Dictionary** button then choose the required languages from the **Languages** list, confirming with **OK**. Use the button next to the **Dictionary** field to locate the dictionary in question on the Notes CD-ROM or on your hard disk il all the languages have already been installed from the CD-ROM.

Editing the user dictionary

- **File**
  Preferences
  User Preferences
- Activate the **International** page then click the **Spell Check** page.
- Click the **Edit User Dictionary** button.

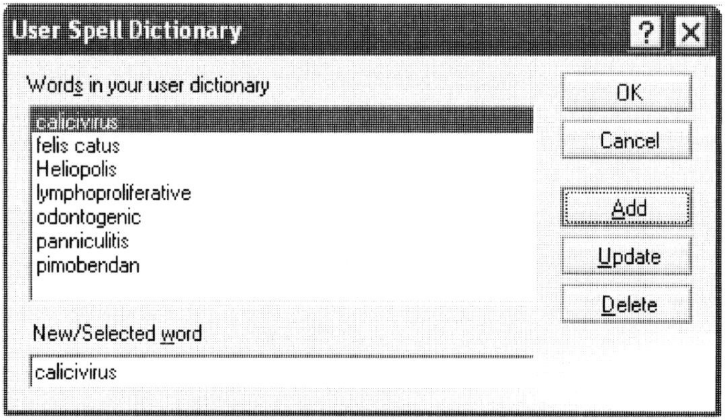

The list of all the words added to the dictionary appears.

- To add a word, enter it in the **New/Selected word** box and click the **Add** button.
- To remove a word from the list, select it and click the **Delete** button.
- To change the spelling of a word, select it in the list, make the correction in the **New/Selected word** box and click the **Update** button.
- Click **OK** to confirm.

Formatting characters

You can apply various character styles such as bold or italic type.

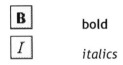

- If the text has already been entered, select it.
- To apply or remove bold or italics, use the corresponding buttons:

bold

italics

- To change the font or the font size, click the corresponding buttons on the status bar:

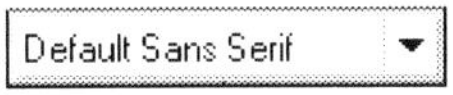

font

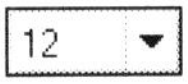

font size

- Apply formatting with the options in the **Text** menu:

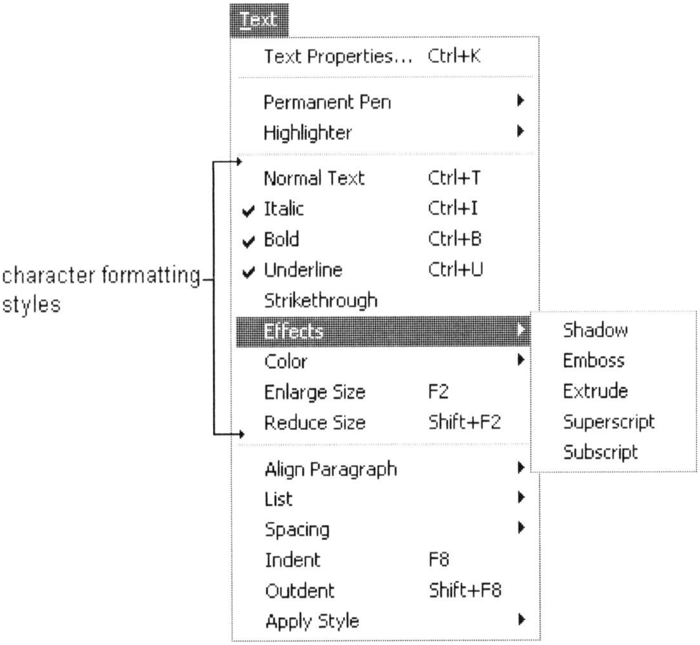

Those options that are ticked are active.

- Use the following shortcut keys:

Ctrl B	**Bold**
Ctrl I	*Italic*
Ctrl U	Underlined
F2	Increase font size
Shift F2	*Decrease font size.*

You can also use the **Font** tab *a* on the **Text** properties box.

To remove all character formatting, select the text concerned and use the **Text - Normal Text** command or Ctrl T.

Highlighting text

This can make your text stand out more clearly.

- Open the document concerned in Edit mode.

Activating highlighting

- Activate highlighting with the **Text - Highlighter** command then click the colour of your choice: **Use Yellow/Pink/Blue Highlighter**.
- Drag from left to right over the text you want to highlight.
- To deactivate highlighting, use the **Text - Highlighter** command again and click the active colour (the one which is ticked).

Removing highlighting

- To clear highlighting from text, use the **Text - Highlighter** command and click the highlighting colour that you want to clear.
- Drag from right to left over the highlighted text.
- To deactivate highlighting, use the **Text - Highlighter** command again and click the active colour (the one which is ticked).

You can also use the **Permanent Pen** feature to make text stand out (cf. Other document contents - Permanent Pen text).

Changing paragraph alignment

- If you want to align several paragraphs, select them. Otherwise, just click the paragraph concerned.
- Use the **Alignment** options in the **Text** properties box, **Paragraph Alignment** tab:

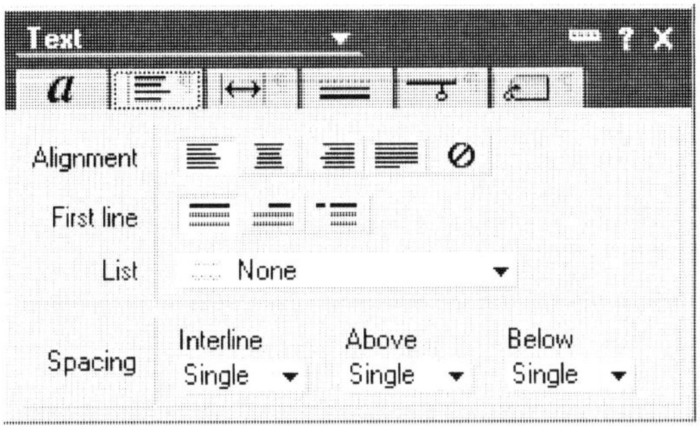

- You can also click the arrow on the tool button on the **Text Properties** toolbar. Take the option of your choice:

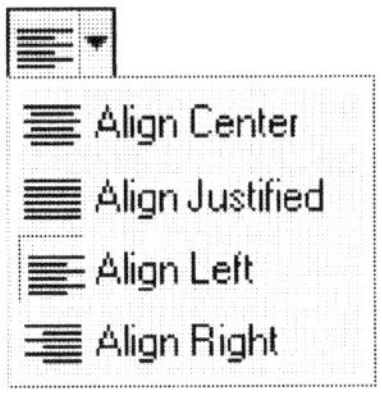

- **Text**
  Align Paragraph
  Left or **Right** or **Centre** or **Full**

Creating lists

Lists in Notes can be preceded by bullets or numbers.

- Select the paragraphs concerned, if they are already in the text.
- Apply one of these presentations, using the **Bullets** or **Numbers** tool button, or using the **Paragraph Alignment** tab on the **Text** properties box:

  Bulleted list (marked with a dot).

Numbered list (1. 2. 3. etc.).

To cancel these formats, click the same tool button again.

If an intermediate paragraph should not take a bullet or number, make a line break at the end of the previous paragraph, instead of a new paragraph. Line breaks are made with Shift Enter.

Adding a horizontal line

Horizontal lines can be placed in a document to separate sections or to improve presentation.

- To add a line, go into Edit mode ( ), click the place where the line should appear then use the **Create - Horizontal Line** command.
- To change the presentation of a selected line, show its properties with the tool button, then change the line's **Width** or **Height** with the corresponding options in the **Size** frame. Click the validation button to confirm.
- If necessary, open the **Color** list and choose the one you want to apply.
- You can give a gradient style to a horizontal line. To do this, click the tool button in the **Fill** frame then open the **To** list to choose the gradient colour.

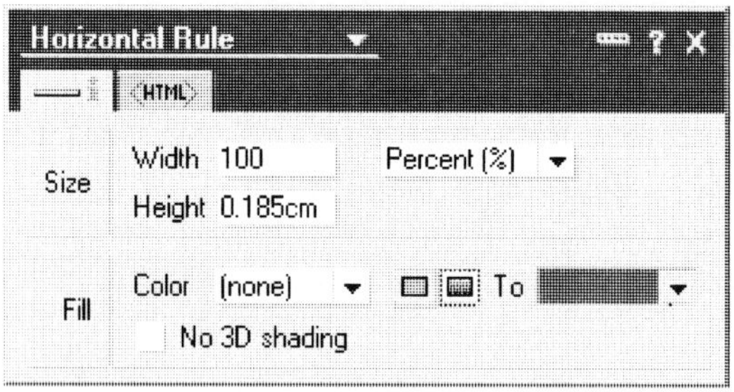

Colouring a document's background

- Open the document in Edit mode.
- **File**
  Document Properties

- Activate the **Background** tab ( ) then open the **Color** list and choose the required colour.

To return to the original background colour, use the **Reset to form color** button on the **Background** page in the **Document** properties box.

Using named styles

Named styles store formatting elements that you can subsequently apply to other paragraphs.

Creating a named style

- Select the paragraph whose formatting you wish to save as a style.
- In the **Text** properties box, activate the **Paragraph Styles** tab ( ).
- Click the **Create Style** button then enter the **Style name**.

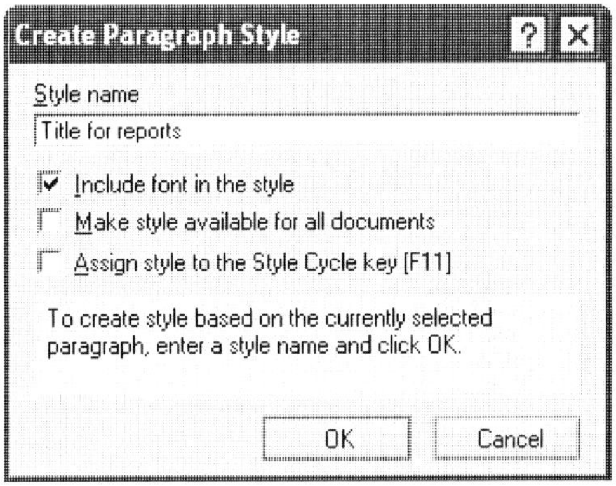

- Click **OK** to confirm.

The created style now appears in the list of existing styles.

Applying a style

- Select the paragraphs to which you wish to apply the style's formatting.
- Open the **Text** properties box, activate the **Paragraph Styles** tab and click the style you wish to apply.

Other document contents

part nine

The actions described in this chapter apply to Rich Text fields, with Edit mode active.

Defining the look of Permanent Pen text

*You can use the **Permanent Pen** feature to add comments to a document. This can be a help in distinguishing between questions and answers in a document.*

- In the **Text** properties box, activate the **Font** tab (a).
- Set the formatting you want to apply using the **Font**, **Size** and **Style** options.
- Open the **Color** list and choose the required hue.

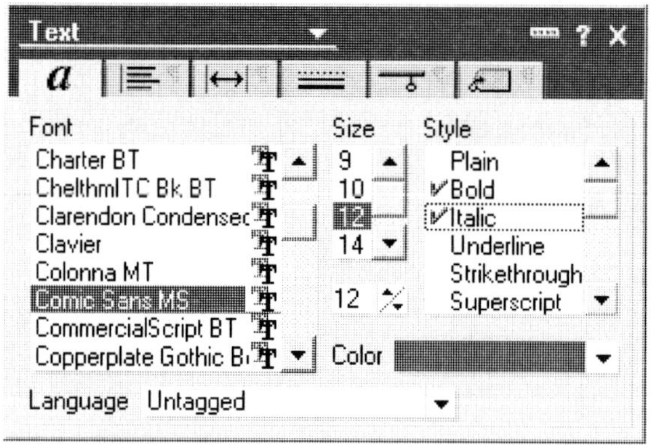

- Close the **Text** properties box.
- **Text**
  Permanent Pen
  Set Permanent Pen Style

Once you define the Permanent Pen font, Notes activates the pen automatically.

Entering Permanent Pen text

- To activate the Permanent Pen, use the **Text - Permanent Pen - Use Permanent Pen** command.

  *The words **Permanent pen enabled** appear on the status bar.*
- Enter the extra information.

- Return to entering normal text by deactivating the **Use Permanent Pen** option in the **Text - Permanent Pen** menu.

  *The words **Permanent pen disabled** now appear on the status bar.*

You can also use the highlighter to make your text more noticeable (cf. Text presentation - Highlighting text).

Inserting a table

- Place the insertion point where the table should appear.
- **Create**
  Table

- Enter values to indicate the **Number of rows** and the **Number of columns** to create in the table (you can also use the increment buttons).

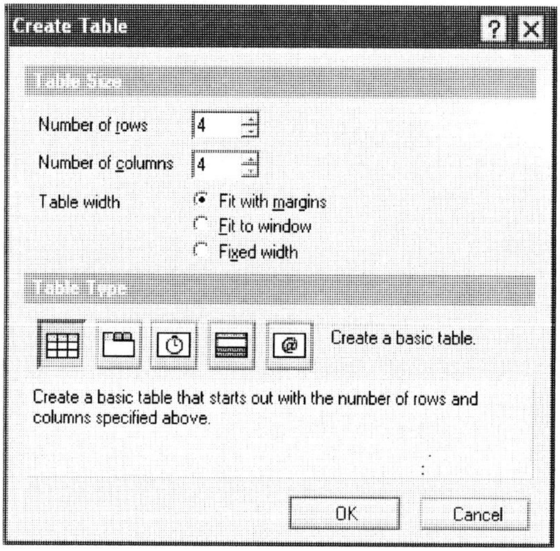

- Set the **Table width** by activating the appropriate option.
- Choose a **Table Type:**

 Standard table.

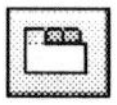 Tabbed table. Each row appears with a tab.

 Animated table. Each line appears for 2 seconds.

 Caption table.

 Programmed table. The row appears according to a field value.

- Click **OK** to confirm.

*The table's outline appears, and a **Table** menu can be seen on the menu bar. In this example, a Standard table has been created.*

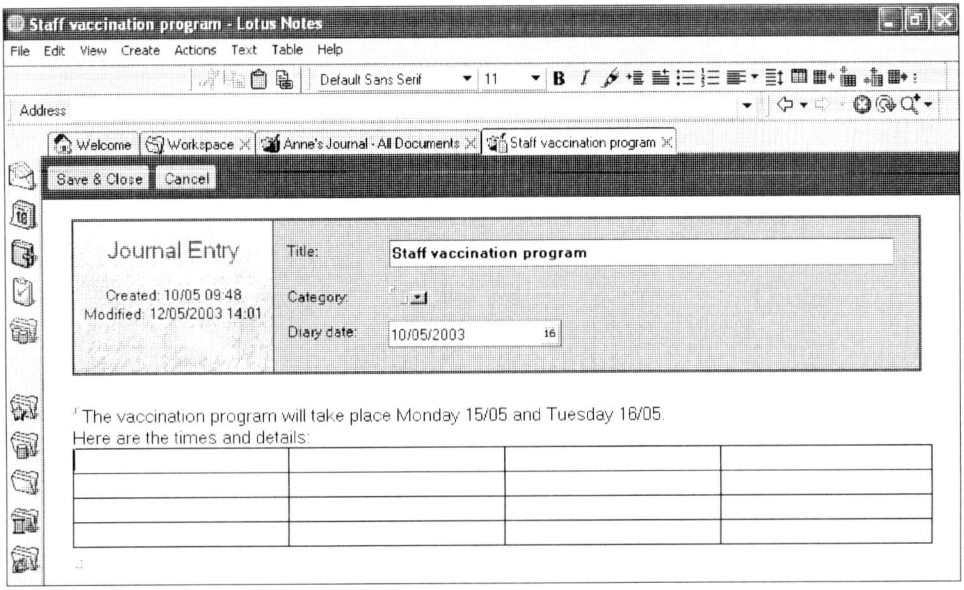

Each box in a table is called a **cell**. The **active cell** is the one in which the vertical line (or insertion point) flashes.

Column width depends on the number of columns created and the width of the sheet.

Entering data in a table

- To bring the insertion point into the required cell, click that cell or use the keyboard:

  [Tab] to go to the next cell.

  [Shift] [Tab] to go to the previous cell.

- Enter the contents like an ordinary paragraph.
- Go to the next cell and continue entering your data.

Inserting rows/columns

- To insert a row or column, click in the row or column before which the new one should appear and use the **Table - Insert Row** or **Insert Column** command.
- To insert several rows or columns, click in the row or column before which the new ones will appear then use the **Table - Insert Special** command.

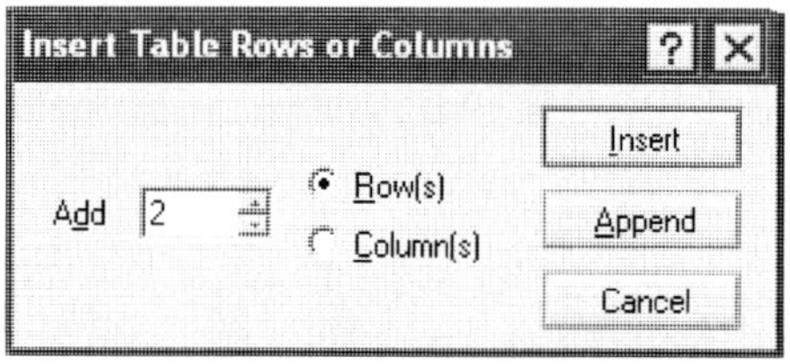

- Give the number of columns or rows that you want to **Add.**
- Specify whether you want to insert **Row(s)** or **Column(s)** with the corresponding option.
- Click the **Insert** button to add the new items <u>before</u> the insertion point or click **Append** to add them to the end of the table.

You can also insert a new row at the end of a table by clicking in the last cell of the table and pressing the ⇆ key.

Deleting rows/columns

- Select the rows or columns you want to delete by dragging over them.
- **Table**
  Delete Selected Row(s) or **Column(s)**
- Confirm with the **Yes** button.

The **Table - Delete Special** command can be used to specify how many rows or columns to delete.

Displaying the Table properties box

- Right-click one of the cells in the table and activate the **Table Properties** option.

You can also click one of the cells in the table then the tool button.

Formatting cell contents

- Proceed as for any document text, either by changing formatting (with the keyboard, toolbars, menus or the **Text** properties box) or by applying named styles.

Resizing a table

By default, columns share an identical width and tables are spread across the whole available width.

- Click one of the cells in the column you want to modify.
- Display the **Table** properties box and activate the **Table Layout** tab ( ).

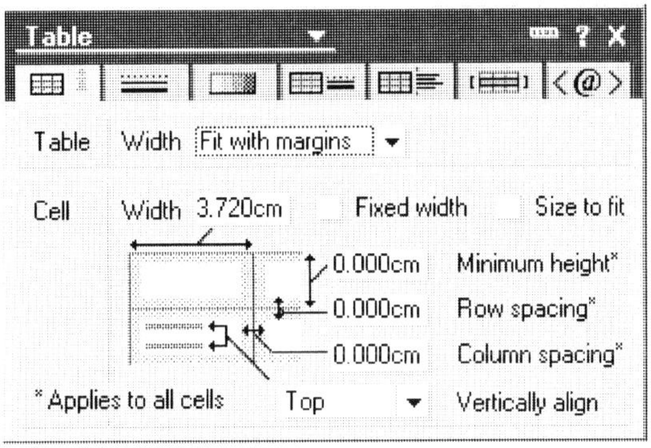

- Open the **Width** list in the **Table** frame then define the table's width by choosing one of these options in the list:

Fit with margins	the table will fill a frame that takes into account the page margins.
Fit to window	the table will completely fill the window from left to right.
Fixed width	the column width is fixed, no matter what the size of the document frame.

- If necessary, give a cell **Width** in the **Cell** frame's text box and click the button to confirm your changes.

- For all the cells, define a **Minimum height**, and the **Row spacing** and **Column spacing** values then click the tick icon to confirm.
- Select how Notes should **Vertically align** the text within the cell (**Top, Center** or **Bottom**).

Positioning a table horizontally

Once a table's width has been changed, the table remains aligned on the left.

- Activate the **Table Margins** tab (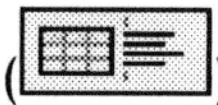) in the **Table** properties box.
- Give the amount by which the table should indent in the **Table Margin - Left** box.
- Confirm your changes with  or press Enter.

Changing a table's borders

- Select the part of the table whose borders you want to customise (this can be a cell or cells, rows, columns or the whole table).
- Activate the **Table Borders** tab (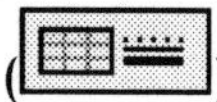) in the **Table** properties box.
- Using the lists, choose a **Border style** and its **Color**.
- If necessary, apply an effect to the border lines using the **Drop shadow** option in the **Border effects** frame.
- Indicate the line **Thickness** using the four corresponding text boxes.

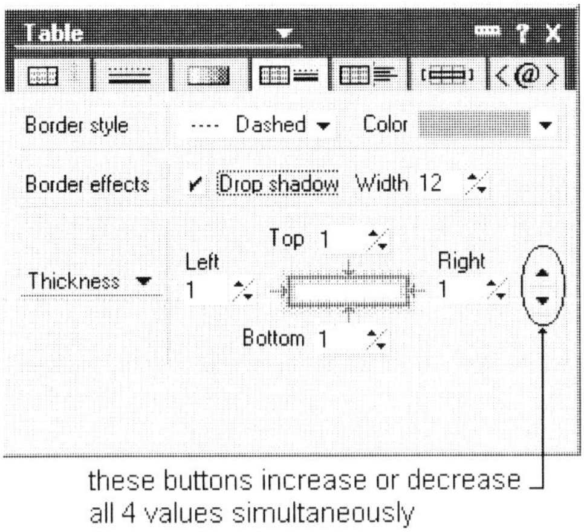

Merging cells

Merging cells groups several cells into one cell.

- Select the cells you wish to merge.
- **Table**
  Merge Cells

To retrieve all the original cells, select the merged cell and use the **Table - Split Cell** command.

Colouring cells

- If necessary, select the cells concerned.
- Activate the **Background** tab () on the **Table** properties box.
- Under **Cell color**, choose the **Color** you want to apply.
- Choose the **Style** you want to apply:

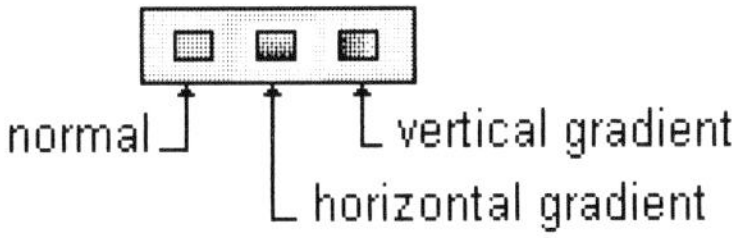

- If you want to apply these settings to all the cells, click the **Apply to All** button.

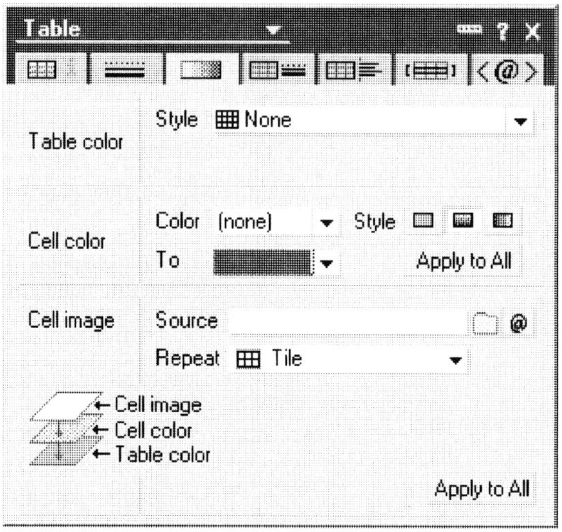
Table
Table color
Style
None
Cell color
Color
(none)
Style
To
Apply to All
Cell image
Source
Repeat
Tile
Cell image
Cell color
Table color
Apply to All

What is a hotspot?

- A hotspot appears as a framed piece of text. In Read mode, pointing to a hotspot makes extra pieces of information appear on the screen in a "pop-up".

<u>An example</u>

Before you point to the area:

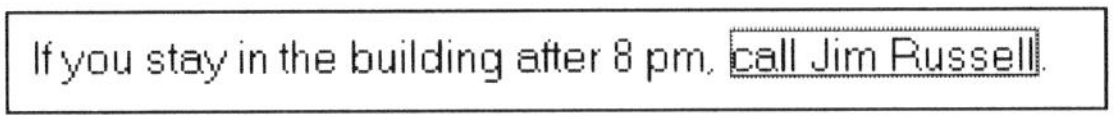
If you stay in the building after 8 pm, call Jim Russell.

When you point to the hotspot:

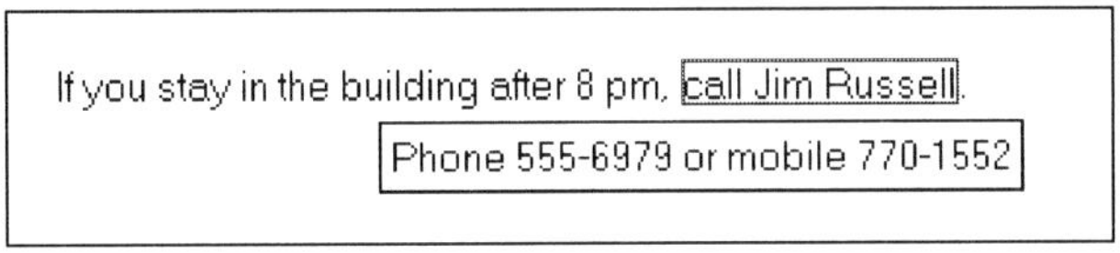
If you stay in the building after 8 pm, call Jim Russell.
Phone 555-6979 or mobile 770-1552

Creating a hotspot

- Select the area that will become a hotspot.

  In the above example, the text "call Jim Russell" has been selected.

- **Create**
  Hotspot
  Text Pop-up

  *The **HotSpot Pop-up** properties box appears.*

- Enter the extra information in the **Popup text** box.

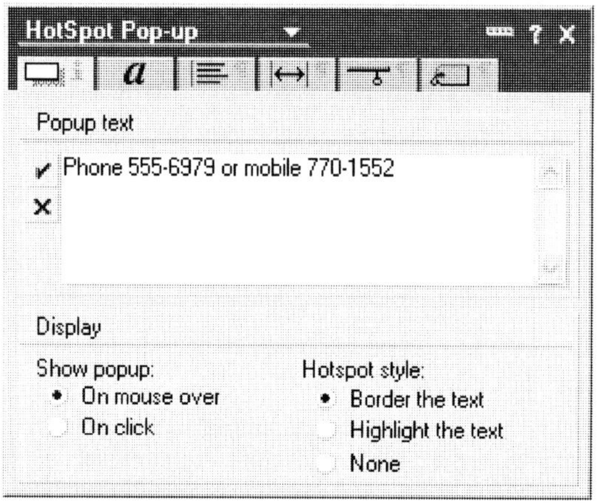

- If necessary, choose the **Display** settings at the bottom of the box.

Before you test your hotspot, do not forget to return to Read mode.

Reading the contents of a hotspot

- Open the document containing the hotspot in Read mode.
- Point to the hotspot.

The extra information instantly appears in a pop-up.

Removing a hotspot

- Open the document containing the hotspot in Edit mode.
- Right-click the hotspot you want to cancel or open the **Hotspot** menu.
- Take the **Remove Hotspot** option.

This action removes the hotspot dynamics and the pop-up text, but not the text that you originally framed with the hotspot.

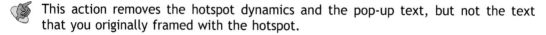

Why link documents?

- It may occur that several documents contain related information. Linking documents makes it easier to access one or other of these documents.
- To do this, you need to insert a link into one document (the **destination** document) that leads you to another document (the **source** document).

Linking documents

- Go to the correct view in the database containing the source document and select that document in the view pane.
- **Edit**
  Copy As Link
  Document Link
- Open the destination document in Edit mode.
- Place the insertion point at the spot where the link should appear.

  In the example below, the insertion point is placed after the text "To see the dosage table, click here:".
- **Edit**
  Paste Ctrl V

  A small page icon symbolises the link:

  To see the dosage table, click here:
- Save the document.

Reading a linked document

- Open the document containing the link in Read mode.
- Click the link icon.

  The linked document instantly opens.
- Once you have read the linked document, close it with the **File - Close** command.

  The starting document once again appears in the foreground.

Removing a document link

- Open the document containing the link in Edit mode.
- Select the link icon.
- Press the [Del] key or use the **Edit - Delete** command.

Naturally, this removes the link but does not delete the linked document.

Inserting external data

With this technique, you can import information from other applications, such as spreadsheets, word processors, drawing programs and so on.

- Start the source application.
- Select the data you want to transfer then the use the **Edit - Copy** command in the source application.
- If necessary, return to Notes. Open the destination document for the imported data in Edit mode and place the insertion point where the data should appear.
- **Edit**
  Paste Special
- Activate the **Paste** option to make a simple copy of the item(s) or **Paste link to source** if you want to be able to activate the source application and file from the copied item(s).
- Using the **As** list, select the type of data that you want to retrieve in your Notes document.

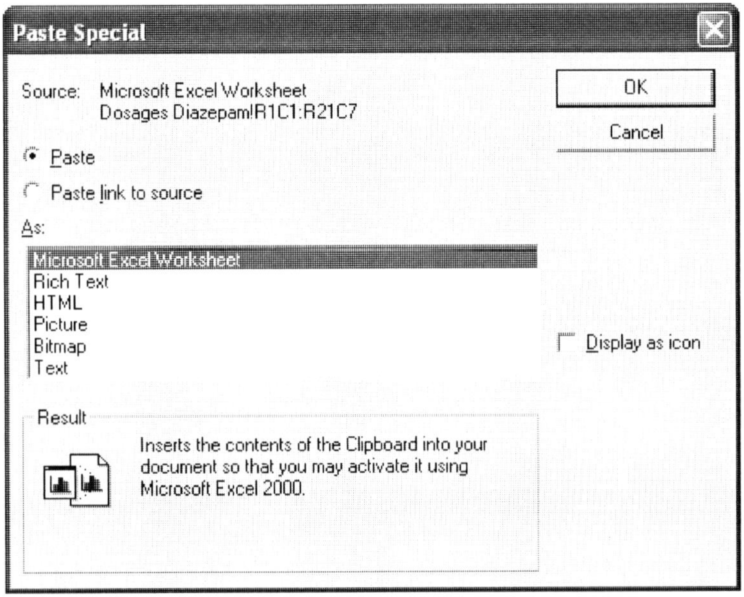

- Click **OK** to confirm.

  The icon of the source program may briefly appear, but it is then replaced by the pasted data.

Attaching files to a message

You can add various items to a Notes message, such as word processing documents, spreadsheet workbooks, drawings from graphics programs and so on.

- Open the message concerned.
- **File**
  Attach

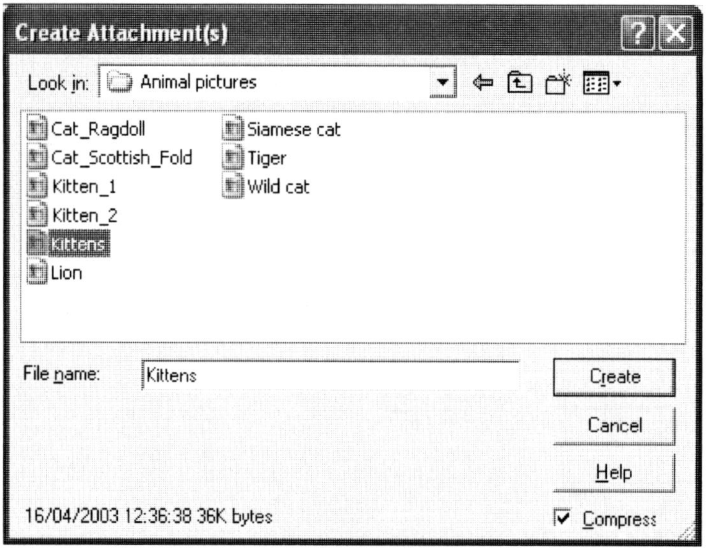

- In the **Look in** list, select the drive and the folder where the file is located.
- Next, select the name of the file you want to attach.
- By default the **Compress** option is ticked, to make the attached file as light as possible to speed up delivery time. If you do not want to compress the attached file, deactivate this option.
- Click **Create** to confirm.

The attachment appears in the document as an icon:

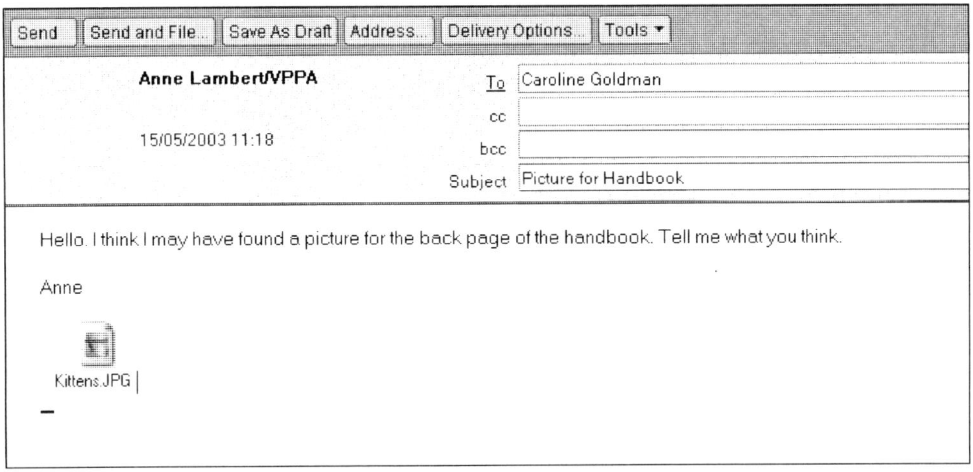

On a Mail document, an attachment appears in the view as a paperclip symbol:

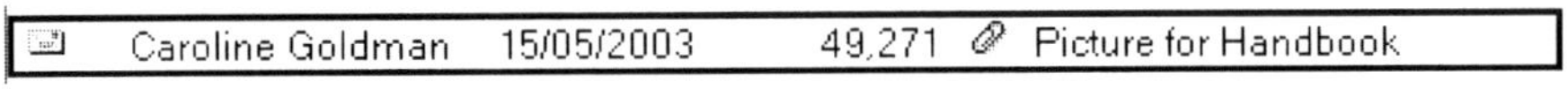

Replication

part ten

Looking at replication

In Notes, making a duplicate of a database is called creating a replica. A replica is another copy of the same file. Unlike a simple copy of the base (**File - Database - New Copy**), a replica carries the same identification number as the original file (this is the replica ID). This allows Notes to find and compare all the replicas of the same base.

You can create a local replica on your own computer of each database that you use. The local replica of a database remains identical to its original as any changes made to the base appear in both places at the same time. Replication is the process of making two replicas identical.

Types of replica

There are two types of replica, complete replicas and partial replicas.

A **complete replica** contains all the documents and design elements of a database, while a **partial replica** contains only previously selected documents and/or shortened documents, summaries, or specified parts of documents. This type of replica has various advantages, such as using less disk space or reducing replication time over remote connections (thus reducing cost).

Why and when to use replication?

Replication is useful when, for example, you are not connected to your company network. In this case, working on a local replica is much faster than constantly exchanging data over a remote connection.

Replication is also used when several users are on several networks in different locations, so they can share the same information contained in a database.

An example of using a replica

Let's take the example of your Mail database; each time the base is replicated, Notes brings new messages from the server replica into your local replica and sends any outgoing mail to the server. Notes will also take into account any changes made to your base.

How?

Depending on the type of connection used to access Notes, replication automation may differ. If you connect to Notes over a phone line, Notes can, if you wish, connect automatically to each server with which you want to replicate.

If you connect to Notes via a relaying server or a remote LAN server, Notes can call a single number and replicate all the local bases in one go, even if they are on different servers. Settings for the various options are usually carried out the Domino administrator.

If you use Notes on several computers, your Domino administrator has probably given you a roaming user status. In this case, you can use the same preferences and settings on all your machines; you can also let Notes manage replications between the different computers.

Setting replication preferences

To apply certain settings by default to all your replicas, you can set your user preferences.

- **File**
  Preferences
  User Preferences
- Activate the **Replication** page.

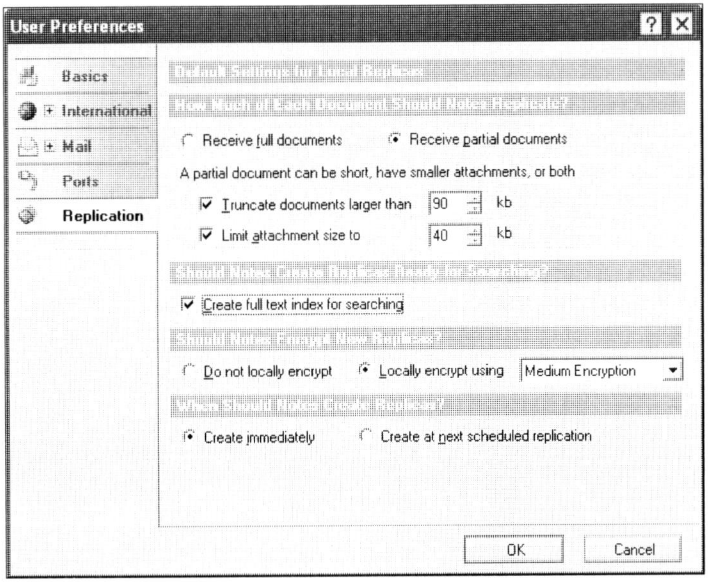

- To limit the maximum size of documents you receive, activate the **Receive partial documents** option then tick the **Truncate documents larger than** option and in the **kb** box, indicate the maximum size. Documents over this limit will be truncated.
- To limit the maximum size of attachments received, activate the **Receive partial documents** option, if necessary, then tick the **Limit attachment size to** option and in the **kb** box, indicate the maximum size.
- If required, tick the **Create full text index for searching** option for faster searches in the new replicas.

  This type of index will take up between a tenth and a quarter more disk space than the database alone.
- To change the default encryption mode for all new replicas, open the **Locally encrypt using** list then choose the required mode. To turn off any encryption, activate the **Do not locally encrypt** option.
- In reply to **When Should Notes Create Replicas?**, activate one of the two options offered. By default, Notes creates a complete replica when you use the **File - Replication - New Replica** command, but you can also set it up to take the planned replications into account (**Create at next scheduled replication**).
- Click **OK** to confirm.

If you modify the **Replication Settings** for a particular local replica, Notes will no longer refer to its **Default Settings** set for all databases, especially for the document size reduction options (cf. Replication - Customising a local replica).

You should use the **Default Settings** to reduce documents in the same way for all replicas, but use the **Replication Setting** if you want to apply reductions only to certain local replicas.

Creating a complete replica

- Drag the bookmark of the database you want to replicate onto the **Replication**  icon on the Bookmark bar,

  or

  Open the database you want to replicate, and use **File - Replication - New Replica**,

or
Right-click the bookmark of the database you want to replicate and select the **Copy Bookmark to Clipboard** option. Click the **Replication** icon on the Bookmark bar to open the **Replication** page then use **Edit - Paste**.

*Depending on whether the database you are replicating is on a server or on your hard disk (a local database), the dialog box you see may differ. If the database being replicated is on a server, Notes opens the **Create Replica For Database [name]** dialog box.*

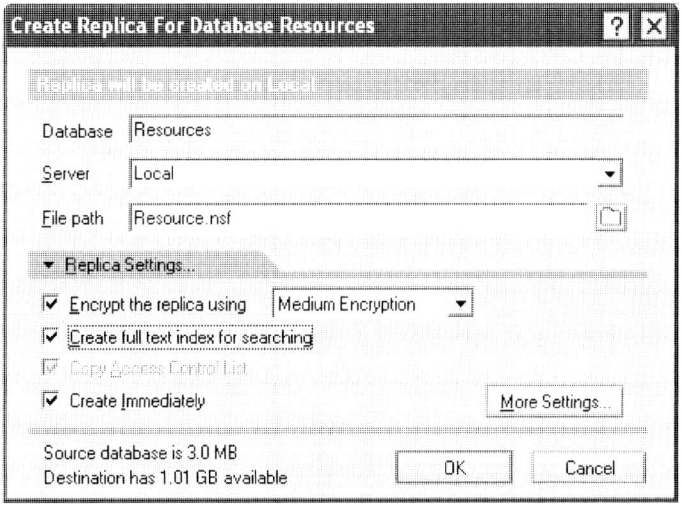

*If the database being replicated is on your hard disk (a local base), Notes opens the **Overwrite Replica For Database [name]** dialog box:*

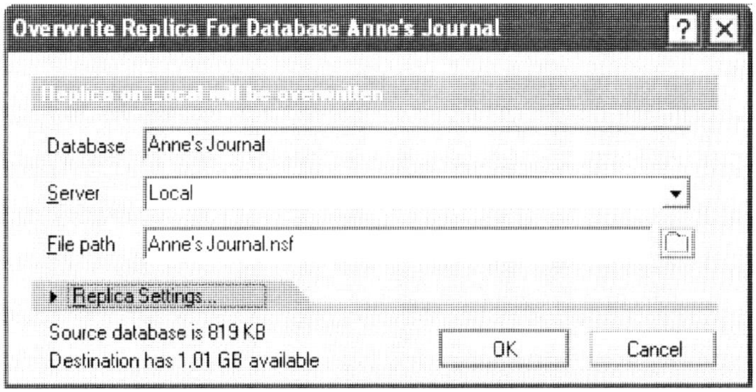

- If you want to create a replica on a server, open the **Server** list, select the name of the server concerned by the replica. In this case, the title of the dialog box will be **Create Replica for Database [name]**.
- If you want to create a local replica, keep the **Local** option in the **Server** field.
- If required, change the file name in the **File path** field. Changing the file name will stop the original database being overwritten, if it is locally stored.

  To check or specify the folder (and/or subfolder) into which the replica will be saved, you can use the button.

  *Be careful: if you create a replica of your Mail database, make sure you give the new replica the same file name and path as those indicated in the **Mail file** field on the **Mail** page of your current site document.*
- If necessary, click the **Replica Settings** arrow and set the parameters as required.

  By default, the settings offered are those that were defined in the user preferences (cf. Replication - Setting replication preferences).

  *The **Copy Access Control List** option is available only when you are not the database manager and the manager does not impose a consistent access control list on all its replicas.*
- Click **OK** to start replicating.

  *For each local replica made, Notes instantly adds a bookmark in the **History** folder and a database entry on the **Replication** page.*

Creating a partial replica from selected documents

There are several potential types of partial replica: for the purposes of this book, the example used will be a replica of selected documents in a base. This procedure can be useful if for example you frequently work with just a few documents that are in a large database located on a server. In this case, by making a replica of only those few documents locally, you avoid storing the entire database on your hard disk.

Creating a partial replica of certain documents is carried out in more or less the same way as a complete replica; the main difference is that you must select the required documents before you make the replica.

- To create a partial replica that contains only documents, start by opening the base you want to replicate.
- In the view, select the documents that you want to replicate, clicking the column to the left of each document.

A document is selected when a tick appears next to its name.

- Drag one of the selected documents onto the **Replication** icon , releasing the mouse button when the pointer becomes an arrow with a plus sign.

*Depending on whether the original database is located on a server or locally, Notes opens the **Create Replica For Database [name]** or **Overwrite Replica For Database [name]** dialog box.*

If the original database is on a server

Remember that if the database is on a server, this dialog box will open:

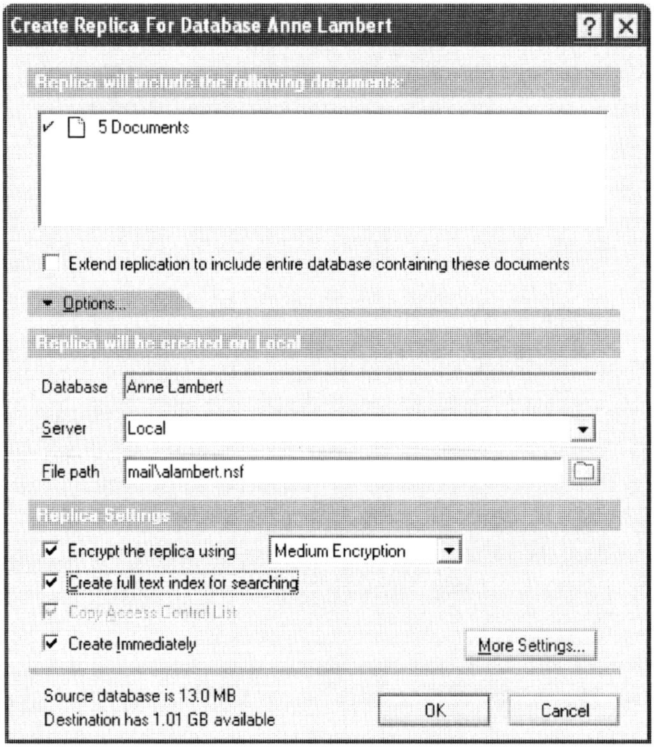

The number of documents previously selected appears in the first frame of the dialog box (5 in this example).

- Define where the replica will be created using the options in the **Replica will be created on [name]** section. By default, Notes offers to create the replica on your hard disk (**Local**).
- If required, modify the **Replica Settings**.

  *Remember that if you do not have much space on your hard disk, you are advised to deactivate the **Create full text index for searching** option, as an index can sometimes double the size of the document you are creating.*
- Click **OK**.

Notes tells you how the current replication is progressing:

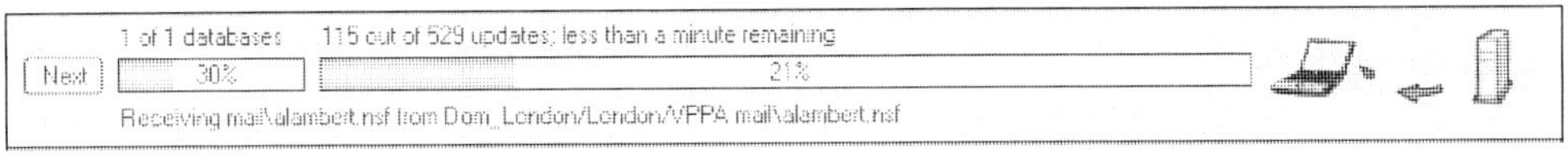

Once the replica is created, Notes adds a bookmark in the ***History*** *folder and a database entry on the* ***Replication*** *page:*

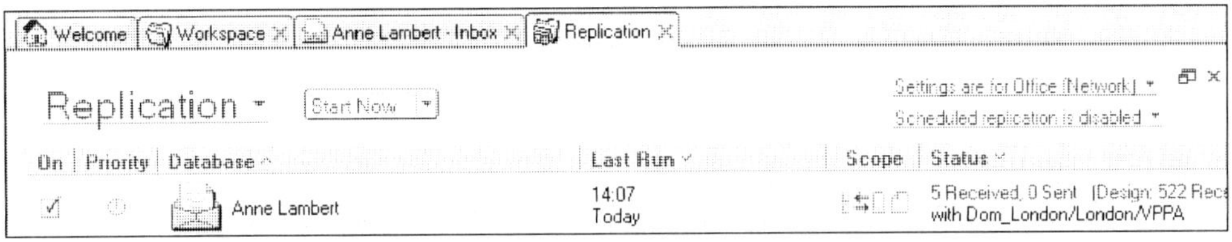

If the original database is stored locally

Remember that if the database is on your local disk, this dialog box will open:

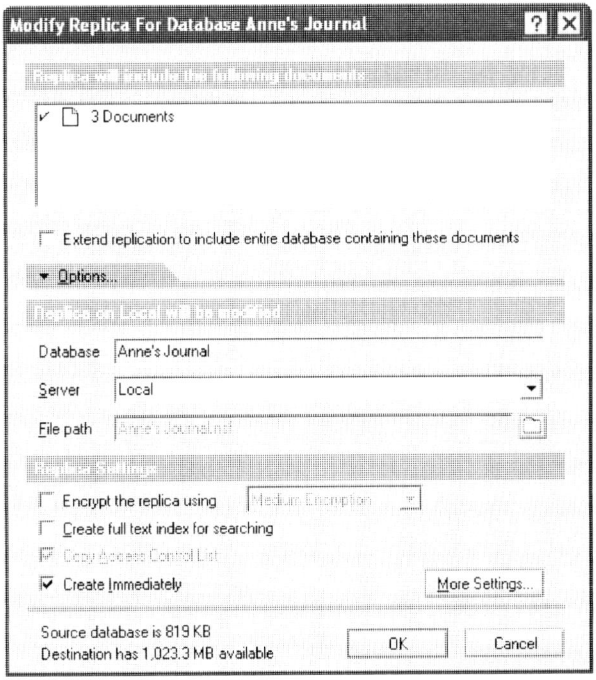

The number of documents previously selected appears in the first frame.

- Define where the replica will be created using the options in the **Replica on Local will be modified** section. By default, Notes offers to create the replica on your local hard disk.

  If you choose a **Server** other than **Local**, the section header changes to **Replica will be created on [name].**
- If necessary, change the **Replica Settings.**

  Remember that if you do not have much space on your hard disk, you are advised to deactivate the ***Create full text index for searching*** *option, as an index can sometimes double the size of the document you are creating.*
- Click **OK.**

Customising a local replica

- Activate the **Replication** page.
- Open the database you want to modify by double-clicking the corresponding database entry.
- **File**
  Replication
  Settings
- Choose one of the five categories of options depending on the changes you want to make:

Basics	The options in this category are used to customise a single local replica. This gives you the opportunity of choosing whether or not to apply new settings to all the sites or to only the current site.
Space Savers	The options in this category are used to change a replica's size, for example, by removing old documents or receiving summaries instead of whole documents.
Send	The options in this category let you choose whether or not to send deletions, title and catalogue changes and/or security modifications.
Other	The options in this category are for managing replication priorities, replication activation and limitations on incoming documents based on date criteria.

Advanced The options in this category are used to specify replication settings for specific servers or to choose which properties to replicate from incoming database.

- Click **OK** on the **Replication Settings** window to confirm all your changes.

The settings made in the **Replication Settings** dialog box for a particular replica cancel the **Default Settings** set for all databases, especially for the document size reduction options (cf. Replication - Setting replication preferences).

You should use the **Default Settings** to reduce documents in the same way for all replicas, but use the **Replication Settings** if you want to apply reductions only to certain local replicas.

Looking at the replicator

- Click the  bookmark to open the **Replicator** page.

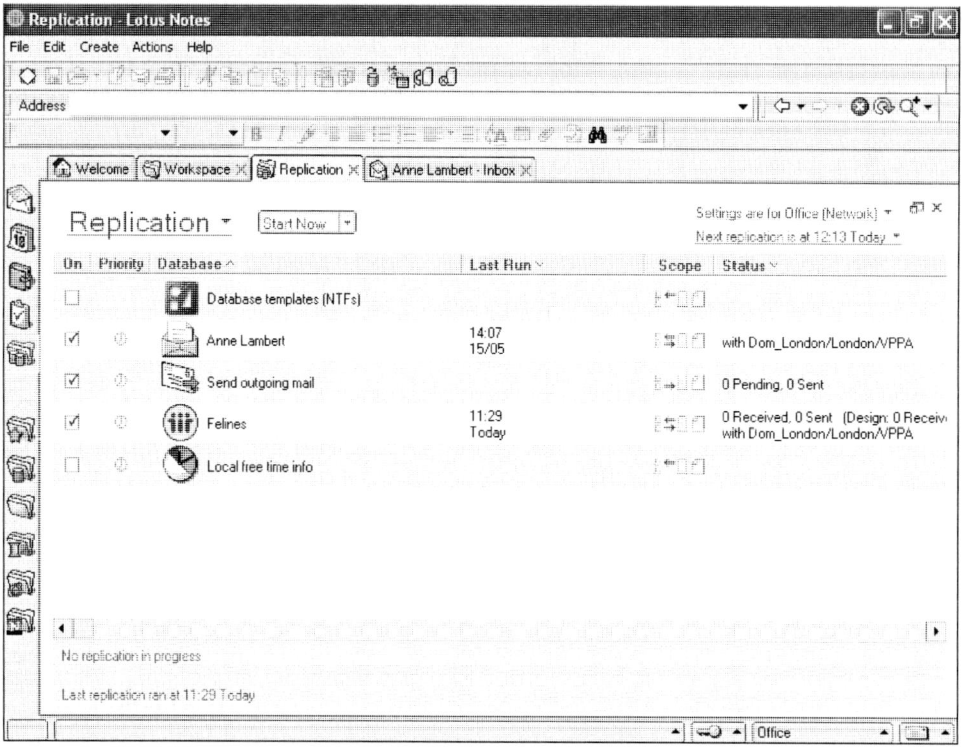

- The **Replicator** page presents one row or entry for each item or group of items being replicated. The order of the entries corresponds to the order in which the databases are replicated.

- The replication settings displayed on the **Replicator** page are applied to only the current site. The site concerned appears at the top right of the page:

*To change the active site, use the **File - Mobile - Choose Current Location** command.*

- When the check box in the **On** column is ticked, this means that replication is active for that entry.

- The symbol located in the **Scope** column indicates whether replication is one- or two-way.
- The **Start Now** button becomes a **Stop** button during replication.
- To move a replicator entry to change the order of the replications, drag the entry concerned to its new position then release the mouse button.
- To remove an entry from the **Replicator**, click the entry you want to delete, press the Del key and click **Yes** to confirm.

  This removes the entry from all sites. If you want to cancel the replication on only one site, deselect the base's entry for the site in question, rather than deleting it.

Changing the Replicator's display

- Click the arrow to the right of the **Replication** heading and choose one of these options:

large Icons, **Medium Icons** or **Small Icons**	to change the icon type.
Display as Slide-Out	to display the Replicator page as a slide-out panel. Return to a whole-page display by clicking .
Display as Page	to display the Replicator page over the entire height and width of the screen.
Display Selected	to display only those entries that are ready for replication.
Display All	to display all the entries.

Creating a call entry

*A call entry created on the **Replicator** page automates server connections when you replicate data from a Notes Direct Dialup site.*

The connection stays online long enough for Notes to go through each entry on the Replicator page and cuts off when Notes reaches either a new call entry or a hangup entry.

- If necessary, choose a Notes Direct Dialup site on the status bar.

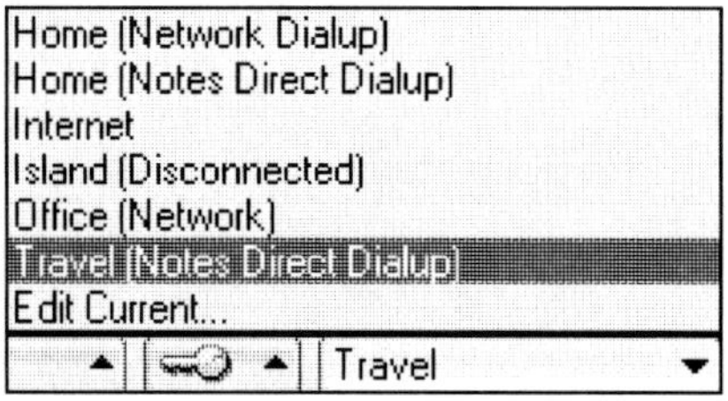

- If you have not already done so, click the bookmark to open the **Replicator** page.
- Click the place where you want to insert the call entry.

  Notes inserts the call entry above the entry you clicked.

- **Create**
  Call Entry

  Notes creates the entry for the default host server.

- If you wish to change the name of the server, click the call entry action button twice ( ), select the server you want to call then click **OK**.

  *Notes displays the servers for which dialling numbers have been set. To add a server to the list or modify the call number, use the **Server Phone Numbers** command in the **File - Mobile** menu.*

When the Replicator calls the server, it stays connected until it reaches either a new call entry or a hangup entry.

Creating a hangup entry

A hangup entry automatically disconnects the server when Notes is replicating over a modem connection.

- Choose a site that connects to the Domino server(s) via a modem.
- Click the **Replication** bookmark.
- **Create**
  Hangup Entry
- If necessary, move the hangup entry by dragging it.

You only need one hangup entry at the end of the list, even if several call entries are defined (as meeting a new call entry also makes Notes hang up).

Deleting an entry

- To delete a database, call or hangup entry, select the entry concerned then right-click it. Click the **Remove** option.

  When you remove a database entry for a site, you also delete it from all the other sites.

Deleting an entry does not affect the associated replica. A replica should be deleted in the same way as a database.

If you do not want to replicate an entry, you do not have to delete it; simply deactivate it by removing the tick from its check box on the Replicator page.

Replicating databases

- Click the **Replication** bookmark to open the **Replicator** page.

A single database

- Select the entry for the base that you want to replicate.
- **Actions**
  Replicate Selected Database
- If you want to stop the replication, click the **Stop** button at the top of the Replicator page.

Only your mail

- Choose the **Send Outgoing Mail** option in the **Actions** menu to replicate your outgoing mail base or choose **Send or Receive Mail** to replicate the whole Mail database.

  Notice that the Calendar and To Dos are replicated at the same time as the mail, as these are also part of the Mail database.

Several databases

- Tick the databases you want to replicate and make sure that you deactivate those that are not to be replicated.
- Click the **Start Now** button.
- During replication, you can click the **Next** button (at the bottom left of the Replicator page) if you want to stop replicating the current base and skip to the next one.
- To stop replication completely, click the **Stop** button (at the top of the Replicator page).

High priority databases

High priority database entries are displayed on the Replicator page with a icon.

- Use the **Actions - Replicate High Priority Databases** command. You can also click the arrow on the **Start Now** button and choose the **Start High Priority Databases Now** option.

To give a base high priority, select the corresponding entry and right-click it, then choose the **High Priority** option.

Scheduling replication

- Activate the site you wish to schedule.
- Click the bookmark to open the **Replicator** page.

Defining scheduling settings

- Open the **Scheduled replication is...** list.

- Click the **Set Replication Schedule** option.

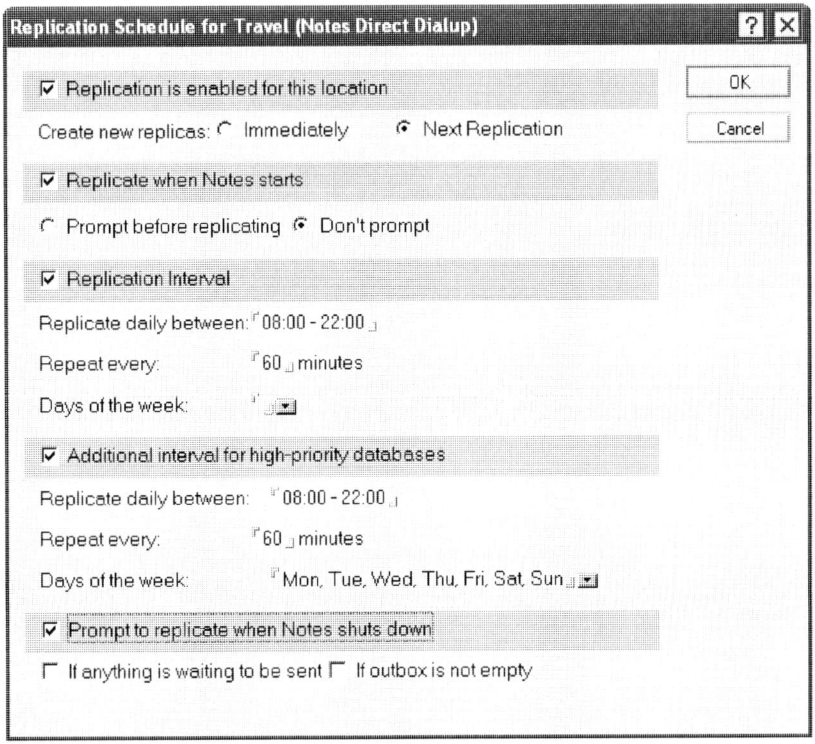

- Set up the replication schedule using the options given.

- Click **OK** to confirm.

Activating the replication schedule

- Open the **Scheduled replication is...** list.
- Click the **Enable Scheduled Replication** option.

Turning off replication temporarily

- Open the database concerned.
- **File**
  Replication
  Settings
- Activate the **Other** page.
- Tick the **Temporarily disable replication for this replica** option.
- Click **OK** to confirm.

You can also open the **Next replication is at...** list on the Replicator page then click the **Disable Scheduled Replication** option.

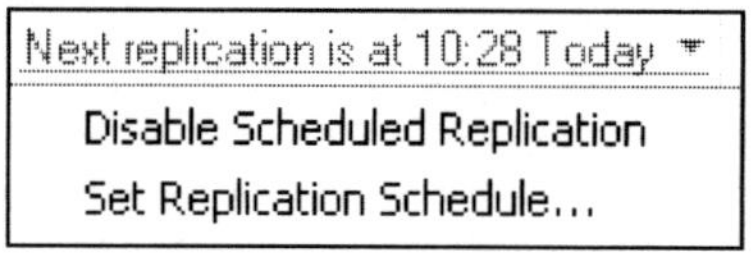

Security

part eleven

How does it work?

If you have ever wondered how your computer knows who you are, here is some (not too technical) theory that may be of interest to you.

To access your Notes data, your network administrator had to create a unique identifier so that your information remains personal and confidential. This is your **user ID.** On a practical level, this is a computer file containing information specific to you, such as:

- your user references (first and last name etc.),
- your password,
- certificates (three of them),
- a period of validity (by default, this is 2 years, which corresponds to the validity of the certificates),
- other miscellaneous information.

Your computer recognises you thanks to this identifier, so it can give you access to various data according to your needs and permissions.

As a user, you can identify yourself to your Lotus server and access your data simply by giving a password. Although you do not see it happening, your computer then retrieves the information necessary for it to work with you.

Certificates and encryption keys

Without going into too much technical detail, the **certificates** integrated into your user ID are like identity cards, with an expiry date (after 2 years by default); these certificates generate **session keys** and also contain your **private** and **public keys.**

The session key is a way of protecting the network communication between your Notes workstation and the Lotus server (Domino) by encryption. This key has a limited lifespan as it is recalculated each time an entity reconnects to the server.

The public and private keys contained in your user ID are used to identify and protect you. These two keys are closely linked. A document encrypted with a public key can only be decrypted with the corresponding private key. When a document protected in this way travels on the Internet, it cannot be intercepted or read by a third party.

Notes offers extra security apart from encrypting e-mail, in the form of digital signatures, which guarantee the sender's authenticity and the message's integrity. This type of protection also uses the sender's private key and indirectly the corresponding public key.

Of course, the user sees none of these processes as they occur behind the scenes!

Some advice

As we said above, the user ID is indispensable for connecting to Notes. The corresponding file is saved in the Notes working folder and carries an **.id** extension (for example jsmith.id).

As this file is similar to a passport or identity card, you must keep it in a safe place. We highly recommend that you keep a safeguard copy on your hard disk or on a floppy disk. A floppy disk is a good idea as you can keep it safe, plus you can take it with you in order to access Notes from other workstations.

Locking Notes during an absence

If you leave your desk, it is a good idea to lock Notes, which means no-one else can access Notes during your absence, but your Notes application and documents remain open in the background.

Press the F5 function key or use the **File - Security - Lock Display** command.

Unlike closing the application, locking it does not mean that you have to close your documents. However you may prefer to close them, especially if you will be away for some time.

*The **Logout Screen** appears:*

- To unlock the connection, click anywhere on the screen to open the password prompt:

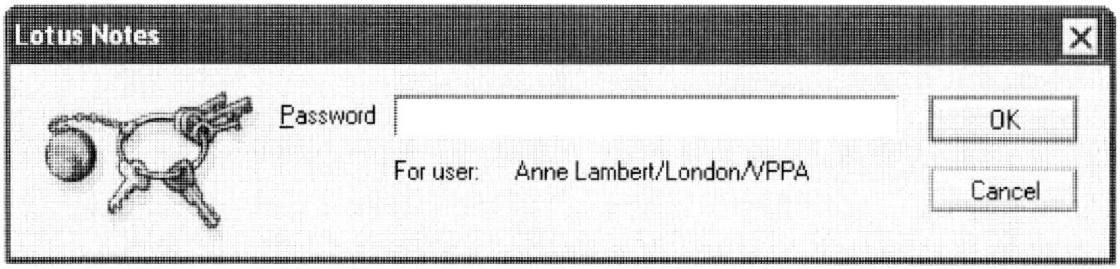

- Enter your password and click **OK** to confirm.

Remember that Notes is case-sensitive so be careful with upper and lower case letters.

Setting automatic locking

If you set your user ID to lock automatically, Lotus Notes will disconnect from servers and ask you your password once the application has been inactive for a certain time.

- **File**
  Preferences
  User Preferences
- Keep the **Basics** page active.
- Tick the **Logout (and lock Notes display) if you haven't used Notes for x minutes** option at the bottom of the screen then give the required period of inactivity in minutes.
- Click **OK** to confirm.

*When it locks automatically, Notes displays the **Logout Screen** (cf. previous title). To reactivate the connection, click anywhere on the **Logout Screen** then enter your **Password**.*

Switching ID

If several users work on the same computer, each needs to activate his/her own ID before starting work.

- **File**
  Security
  Switch ID
- In the **Look in** list, specify where your ID file is located.

  Your ID file can be on a floppy disk, or stored locally on your hard disk or on a Domino server, depending on how your administrator carried out the installation.
- Double-click the name of the file.
- Enter your password and confirm.

Changing the password

Conditions for creating and using passwords

You will only be asked for a password if your administrator has deemed it necessary. When the administrator creates your user ID, he/she decides whether a password is required and the password quality.

Your administrator can decide, for example, how many characters the password must have. He/she may also give the password an expiry date, which means that every so often you must create a new one. Should you find yourself with an expired password, there is no need to panic, simply log in with the old password; you can still use Notes but you will only be able to access local databases, not those on the server. You will have access to the server only when you have changed your password.

There may also be constraints on the password's quality. Its quality refers to how difficult it would be for someone else to guess your password. Quality is measured from 0 to 16 (16 being the hardest to "crack"). If your administrator wants you to use high quality passwords, but you choose a very simple word such as "dodo", Notes may refuse your password. If this occurs, create a more difficult one, for example by mixing upper and lower case letters, or including numbers and punctuation marks.

Changing your Notes password

- **File**
  Security
  User Security
- Enter and confirm your current password.
- If necessary, activate the **Security Basics** page.
- Click the **Change Password** button.
- Enter your current password again then confirm with **OK**.

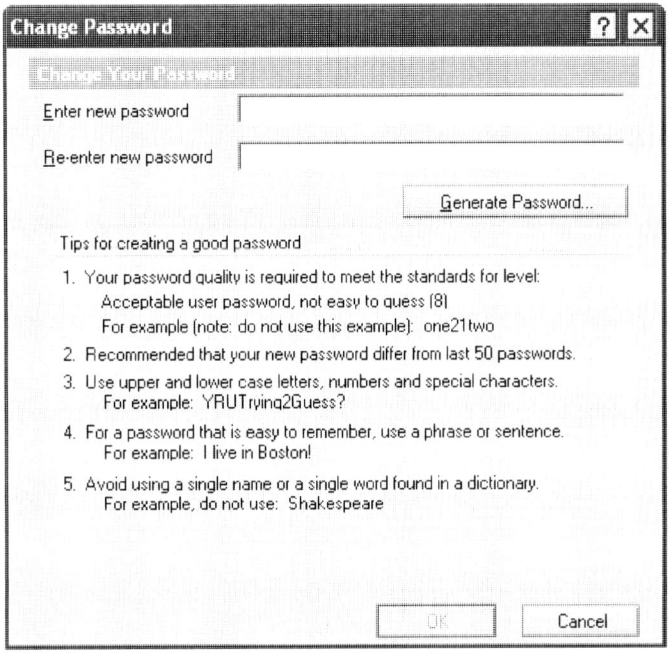

Before giving your new password, read the advice from Notes very carefully. These tips vary depending on the password characteristics used by your administrator. In this example, the password must have 8 characters (tip 1.), it must differ from the last 50 passwords you used, and so on.

- With the password conditions in mind, give the new password in the **Enter new password** box and confirm it in the **Re-enter new password** box.
- Click **OK** to confirm.

Your password is now part of your user ID; you should update any backup copies of the latter.

Generating a new password

If your password is based on quality and not length (cf. Conditions for creating and using passwords, above), Notes can generate your password randomly.

- **File**
  Security
  User Security

- Enter and confirm your current password.
- If necessary, activate the **Security Basics** page.
- Click the **Change Password** button.
- Enter your current password again then confirm with **OK.**
- Click the **Generate Password** button.

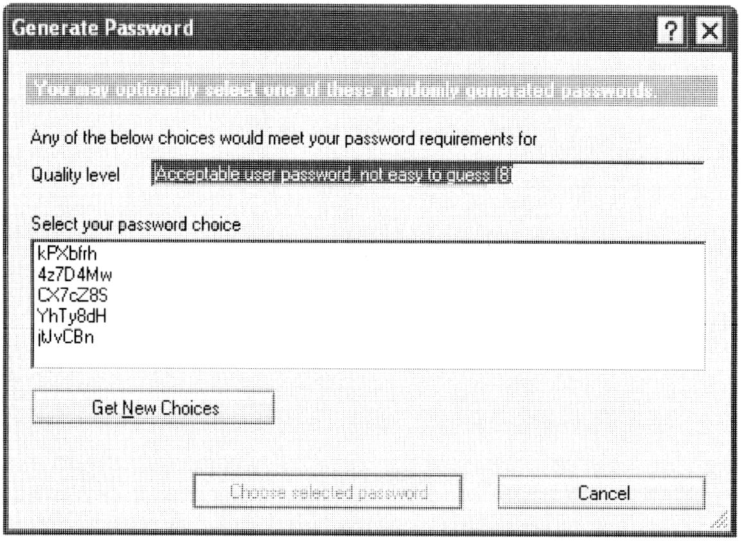

- **Select your password choice** in the corresponding list then click the **Choose selected password** button.

  *The **Get New Choices** button will show you another list of suggestions if required.*
- The **Enter new password** field in the **Change Password** dialog box is filled in automatically; simply confirm the new password by entering it in the **Re-enter new password** box.

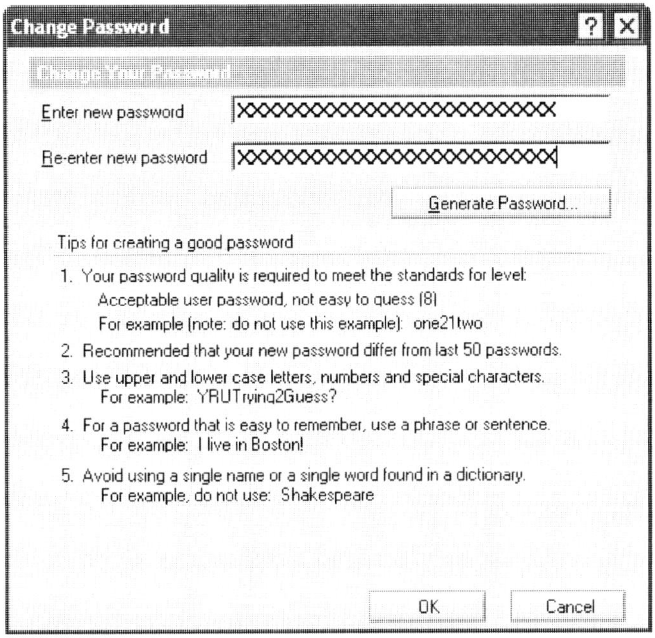

- Click **OK** to confirm the new password.

Looking at the access control list

Notes can let you carry out tasks in a database (editing data, deleting or copying it etc.) but only if you have authorisation to do so. Before letting you work, Notes checks the database's Access Control List (ACL) to determine which rights you (or another user) have over it.

These access levels are given by the Manager of the database in question; some permissions can later be fine-tuned by Designer or Manager level users.

- There are seven access levels:

Manager A manager can carry out any operation in a database, including setting access levels for other users on the network; he/she can also delete databases.
Each Notes database must have at least one manager, but it is a good idea to have two (in case someone is away, falls ill, etc.).

Designer A designer can create, edit or delete documents and also create and edit forms and views.
This level is often given to the person who designed the database or who is responsible for updating its structure once it is in use.

Editor An editor can create documents and edit them even if they were created by another user.

Author An author can create and edit his/her own documents but can only read those by other people.

Reader A reader can only read documents in the database.

Depositor A depositor can only add documents to the database.

No Access This type of access prevents the user from entering the database.

Access levels differ from one database to the next.

Finding out your access level for a database

- On the workspace, select the database for which you want to know your access level, or open the base from a bookmark or with **File - Database - Open**.
- Click the **Security** button (the key icon) on the status bar.
- If necessary, enter the password.

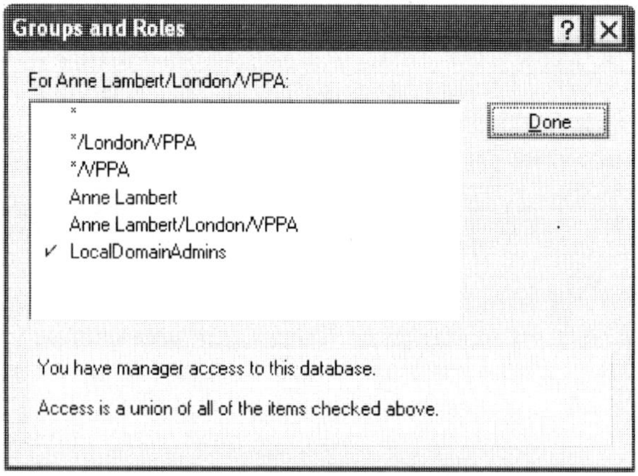

*The **Groups and Roles** dialog box appears: your access level is seen in it.*

- Click the **Done** button to close the dialog box.

If you cannot see the **Security** button, make sure that the **Security** option is ticked in the status bar properties options (cf. Lotus Notes overview - Modifying the status bar preferences).

Defining who is allowed to access a database

Users with Manager status can change the access control list (ACL), while a base's designer or manager can add one or more roles to adjust permissions to certain items in the database (forms, views, sections or fields).

- Select the icon of the database in question, or open it.
- **File**
  Database
  Access Control
- Activate the **Basics** page.

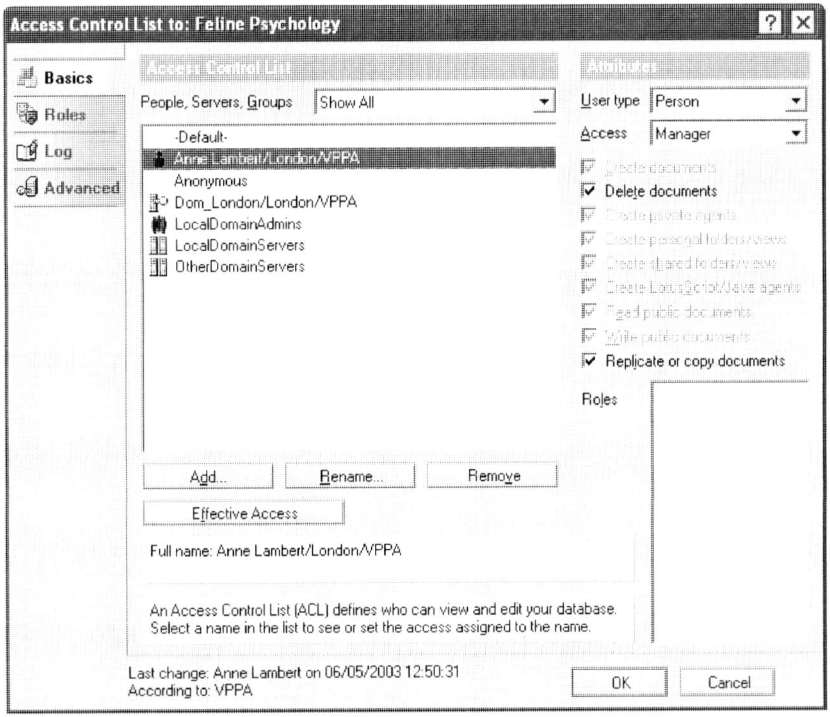

The ACL appears in the dialog box.

*The **Access** list at the top right of the box shows the access level authorised for the selected person, server or group (Anne Lambert in this example).*

- To add a user or server or other in the ACL, click the **Add** button. Click the 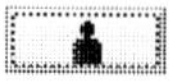 button.

  *The **Select Names** dialog box opens:*

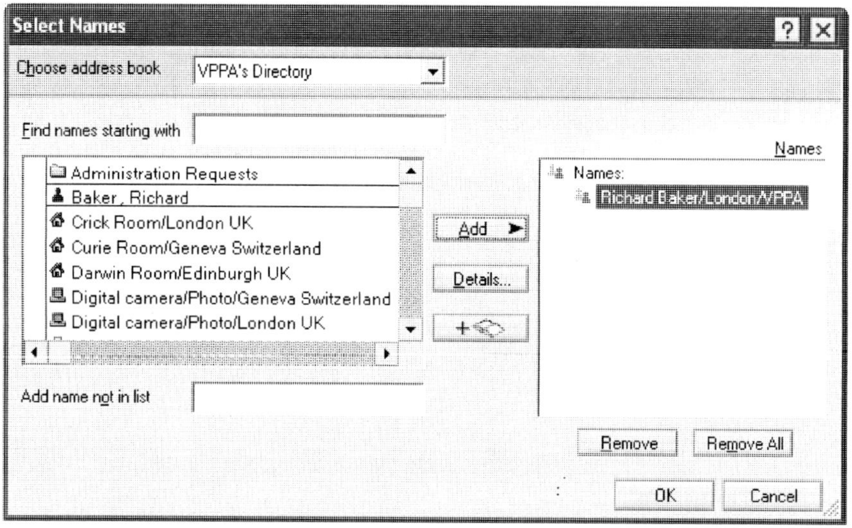

- Pick an address book from the **Choose address book** list then click the name of the user, server or group that you want to add to the list of users authorised to access the database, before clicking **Add.**

  *The **Remove** and **Remove All** buttons can cancel one or all of the additions you have just made.*

  The 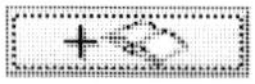 *button inserts the selected name automatically into your Personal Address Book.*

- Once you have added the required names, click the **OK** button.
- To define the **User type**, select the user's name (or the group, etc.) in the **Access Control List** window, open the **User type** list and click the appropriate type.
- To define the access rights, select the name of the user (or group etc.) then open the **Access** list and click the level you want to give.
- If necessary, refine the access rights for this user (or group or server) by activating and deactivating the options as required.

- To remove an item from the list, select its name in the **Access Control List** and click the **Remove** button.

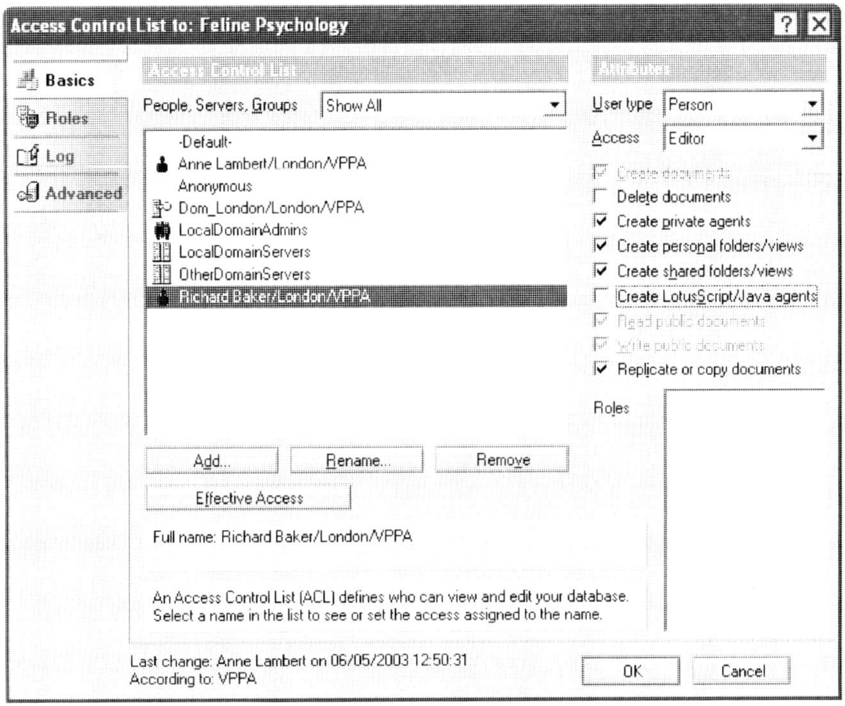

- Click **OK** to confirm.

Remember that all ACLs must contain at least one manager.

Defining who is allowed to read a document

*Unless you change the settings, any user with **Reader** access or higher to a database can read all its documents. However, you can make a specific document more confidential by listing exactly which users, groups or servers can read it.*

- Select the document whose access you wish to restrict.
- **File**
  Document Properties
- Activate the  tab.

- Deactivate the **All readers and above** option.
- Click the button and add all the users, servers or groups that are allowed to read the document. Then click **OK** to confirm.
- Close the properties box by clicking the button.

Hiding a paragraph

- Open the document in Edit mode.
- Click the paragraph that you wish to hide in certain contexts.
- **File**
  Document Properties
- Open the list of options by clicking the triangle to the right of the **Document** header.
- Choose the **Text** option.
- Activate the tab on the **Text** properties box.
- In the **Hide paragraph when document is** frame, tick each option that describes in which circumstances the paragraph should be hidden (for example, during printing).

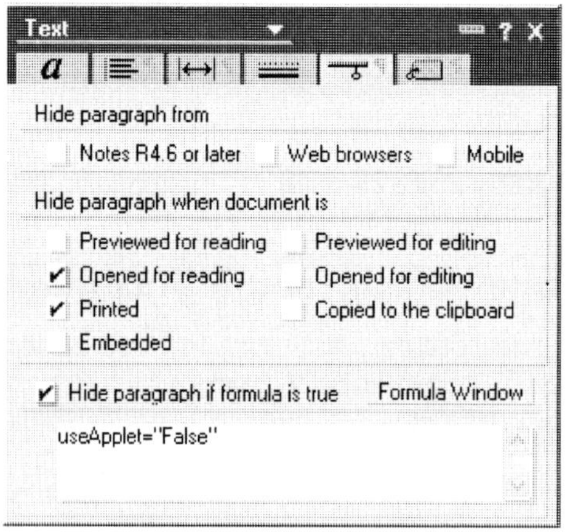

In this example, the paragraph will be hidden whenever the document is open in Read mode and it will not appear during printing.

Encrypting local databases

You have seen in other chapters that you can define who can access a database or document, but you can also protect your data effectively by using encryption. It can be useful (and probably wise) to encrypt local databases or replicas, especially if you use a portable computer or if you share a computer with other users. Remember that encryption means coding data with the help of a key (contained in your personal user ID), so that the data cannot be decrypted unless the same key is used.

A new database

- If you want Notes to encrypt any new database automatically, use the **File - Security - User Security** menu.
- Enter and confirm your password.
- Activate the **Notes Data** page then the **Databases** page.

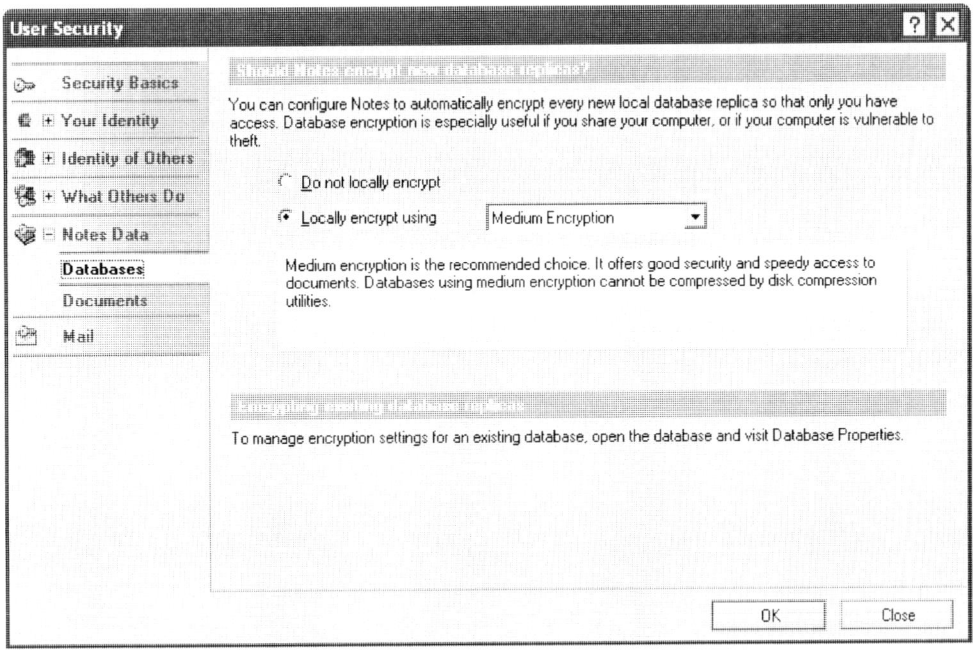

- Activate the **Locally encrypt using** option then choose a level of protection from the associated list:

  Simple Encryption for protection against electronic spying.

  Medium Encryption for protection that combines security, effectiveness and rapid access to the base's data. This is the recommended level of encryption.

  Strong Encryption for the highest level of protection. Use this when top security is required.

  The higher the level of encryption used, the longer it will take to access the encrypted bases.

The **Do not encrypt locally** option turns off local database encryption.

An existing local database

- Open the local database that you wish to encrypt.
- **File**
  Database
  Properties
- Click the **Database Basics** tab  then click the **Encryption Settings** button.

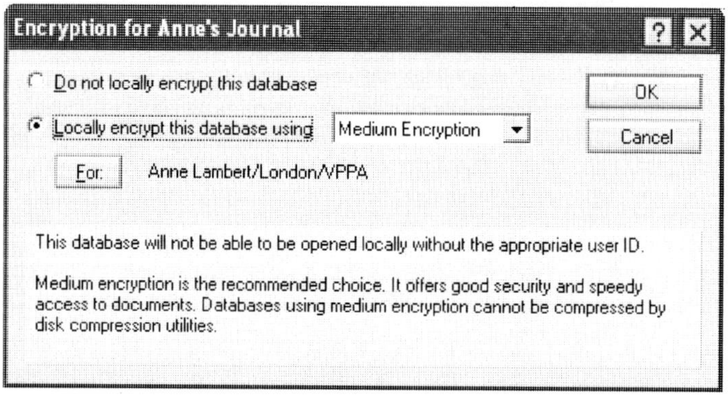

- Activate the **Locally encrypt this database using** option then select the required level of encryption in the associated list.

  You user ID appears next to the **For** *button to remind you that you are the only person who will be able to open the database once it is encrypted (this is Anne Lambert in this example).*

- If you want to give these access rights to another person, click the **For** button.

Notes reminds you that if it encrypts the base for another person's ID, you will no longer have access:

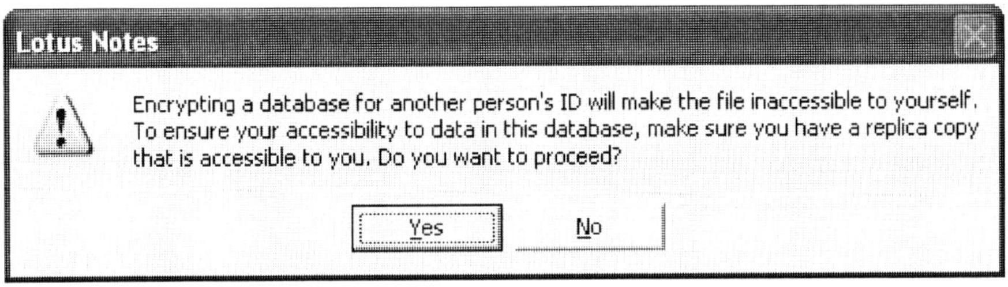

- If you still want to have access to the database, only click **Yes** if you are sure that you have an accessible replica of it. If you do not, or you are unsure, click **No**.
- If you clicked **Yes**, you can use the **Select Name** dialog box to select an address book then the name of the person to whom you are giving the access rights. Click **OK** to confirm.

  Remember that Notes uses the encryption keys within the user ID for which encryption is being carried out; this makes the data inaccessible to all other user IDs.
- Click **OK** in the **Encryption for** dialog box to confirm encrypting the database in question.

To turn off encryption for this database, tick the **Do not locally encrypt this database** option in the **Encryption for** dialog box.

Encrypting a document with secret keys

You may want to make a document available in a public database, but only to certain people. You can do this by encrypting the document with a secret key (from your user ID) and sending the secret key to your contacts so they can decrypt the document.

The document in question must contain encryptable fields (which appear in red field brackets). Only the contents of these fields can be encrypted: the other parts of the document will be available to all its readers.

Mail documents can be encrypted.

Creating a secret key

- **File**
  Security
  User Security
- If necessary, enter and confirm your password.
- Click **Notes Data** then **Documents.**
- Click the **New Secret Key** button.

- Enter the **Secret key name** in the corresponding box.
- In the **Comment** box, enter any comments you want to make about the key and the type of documents it can decrypt.
- If you are giving this secret key to a user of a non-American version of Notes prior to version 5.0.4, tick the **Use international encryption** option.
- Click **OK** to confirm.

*The characteristics of the new key are relayed to the **User Security** dialog box:*

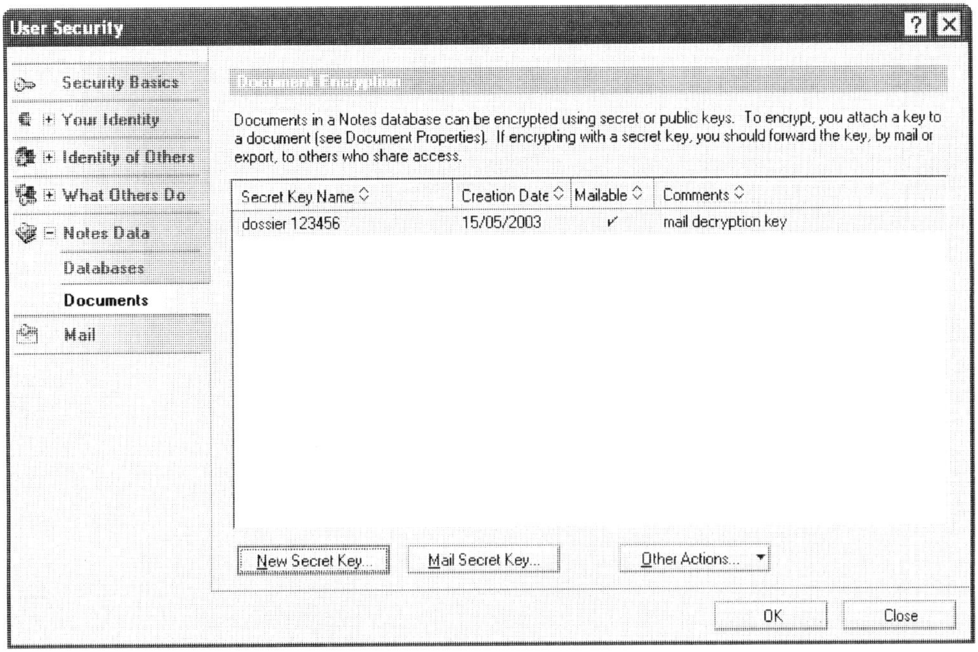

- Click **OK** to close the **User Security** dialog box.

Deleting a secret key

- **File**
  Security
  User Security
- If necessary, enter and confirm your password.
- Click **Notes Data** then **Documents.**
- Click the **Secret Key Name** that you want to delete.
- Click the **Other Actions** button then click the **Delete Secret Key** option.
- Confirm the deletion with the **Yes** button.
- Click **OK** to close the **User Security** dialog box.

Adding a secret key to a document

- Open the document that you want to encrypt.
- **File**
  Document Properties
- Click the **Security** tab.

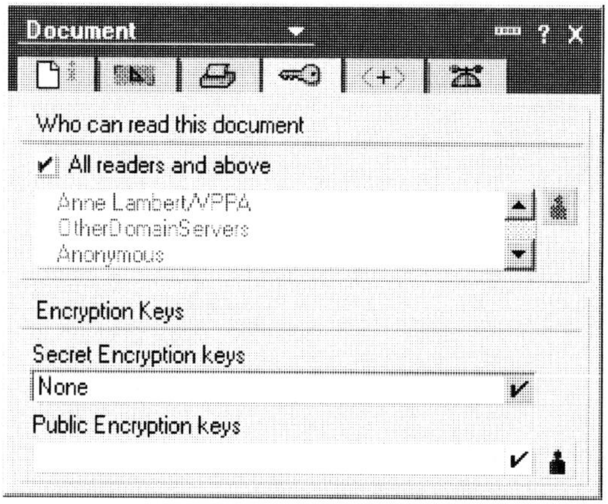

- If you wish, deactivate the **All readers and above** option.
- Click the symbol on the **Secret Encryption keys** field to see all your secret keys.

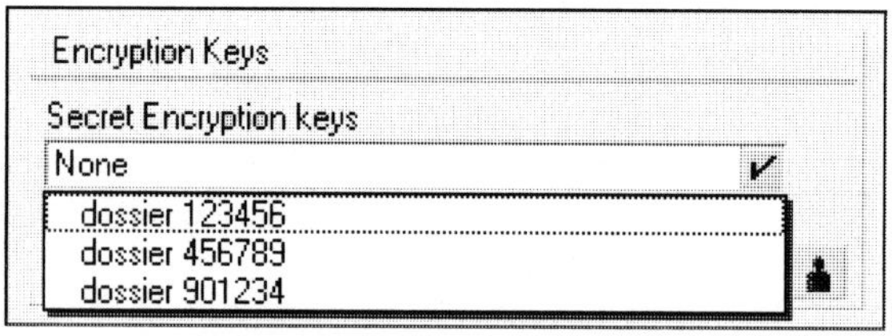

- Click the secret key(s) that you want to associate with this document.

  The selected keys appear with a tick.
- Click the symbol to close the list of secret keys.

  You can also authorise the user(s) of your choice to use their public key to access the document. To do this, click the button to select them.

- Click the [X] button to close the **Document** properties box.
- Save or close the document.

Sending a secret key by e-mail

If you want your chosen users to be able to decrypt a document protected by your secret key(s), they must have the key(s) in their possession. You can send them the key(s) by e-mail.

This method works only for users of Notes messaging.

- **File**
  Security
  User Security
- If necessary, enter and confirm your password.
- Click **Notes Data** then **Documents.**
- Click the **Secret Key Name** that you want to send by e-mail.
- Click the **Mail Secret Key** button.

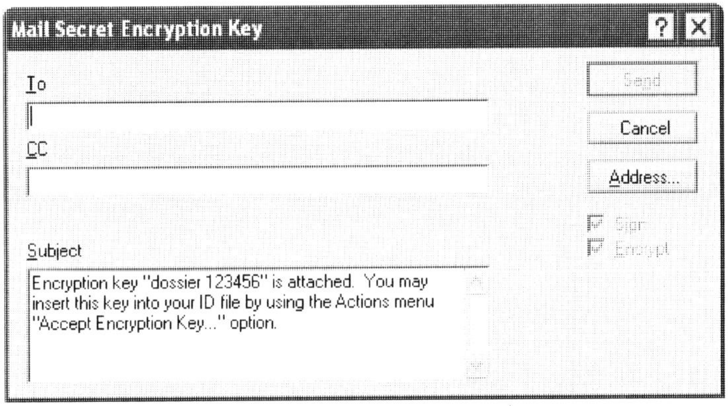

- To specify to whom the secret key should be sent, type the name(s) into the **To** box or click the **Address** button to select the name(s) from an address book.
- If required, use the **CC** field to enter or select addressees (see above) for a copy of the message; they will be notified that you have sent the secret key, but they will not receive the key themselves.
- If necessary, change the **Subject** of the message.
- Click the **Send** button.

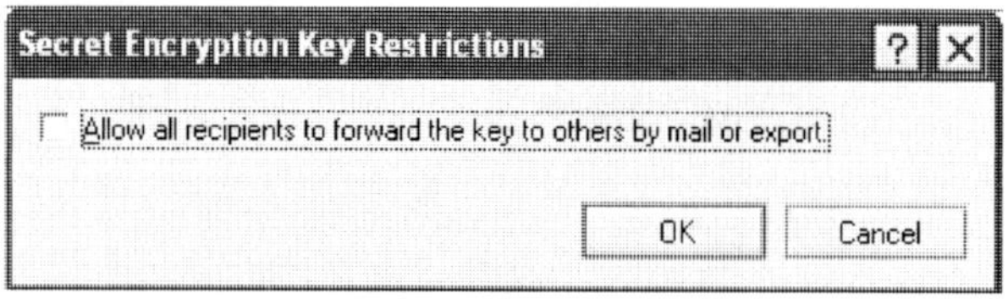

- Tick the **Allow all recipients to forward the key to others by mail or export** option if you want to allow the recipient to send the key to someone else.
- Click **OK** to send the message or click **Cancel** to stop sending the secret key.
- Click **OK** to close the **User Security** dialog box.

Accepting a secret key

Before you can use a secret key sent to you by a contact, you must first accept it. Once you have accepted it, the key will be stored in your user ID, so you can then read the corresponding encrypted document.

- Open the message containing the secret key.

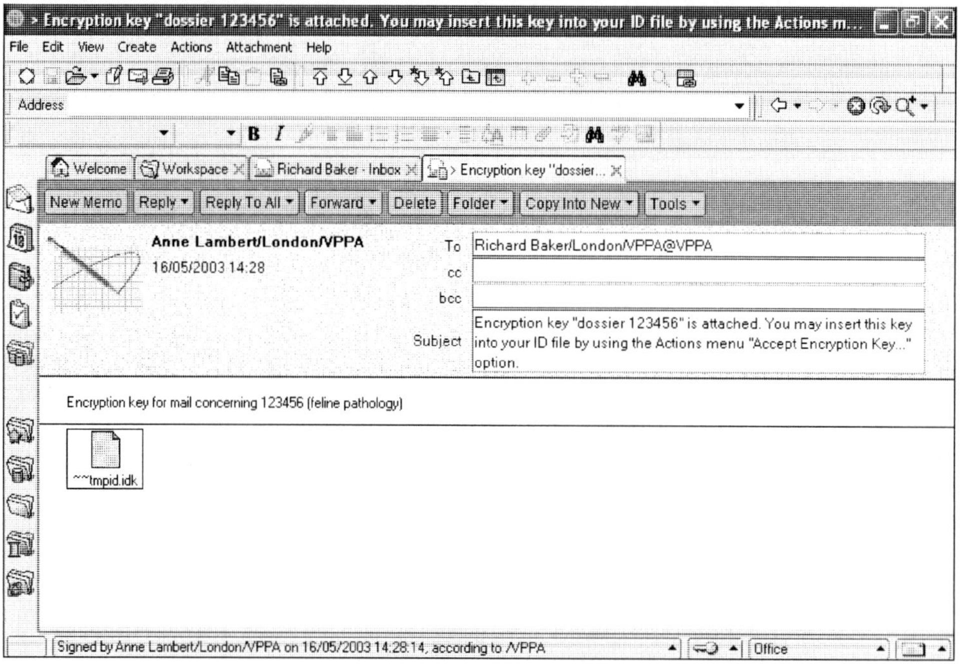

You can see that the secret key is presented as a file attachment.

- Open the **Actions** menu then click the **Accept Encryption Key** option.
- If prompted, enter your password and confirm with **OK**.

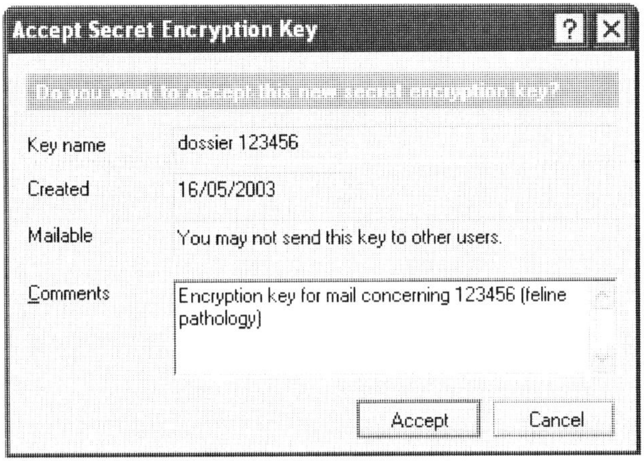

- Click **Accept** to confirm saving the secret key in your user ID.

  Once you have accepted a secret key, you would be wise to make a backup copy of your ID or to update any existing backups.

Windows

Alt F5	Restores the application window to its previous size.
Alt F10	Maximizes the application window.
Ctrl ⇄	Moves to the next window tab.
Ctrl F6	Move from one open window to the next.

Miscellaneous

F1	Opens the context help.
Alt F4	Leaves Notes.
F10 or Alt	Activates the menu bar.
F9	Refreshes the displayed data.
Ctrl M	Creates a memo.

Workspace

Ctrl →	Goes to the next workspace page.
Ctrl ←	Goes back to the last workspace page.
→	Selects the next workspace icon.
←	Selects the previous workspace icon.
Ctrl O	Opens a database.
Ctrl N	Creates a new database.
Esc or Ctrl W	Closes the current database.
F9	Updates the current document (in Edit Mode), view or workspace
Pg Dn	Goes to the bottom of the active page.
Pg Up	Goes to the top of the active page.
⇧ Shift Ctrl F9	Updates all the fields in the current database.

Views

F9	Refreshes the view.

Selecting documents

Ctrl A	Selects all documents.
Space	Selects and deselects a document.

Managing selected documents

F3	Goes to the next selected document.
⇧ Shift F3	Goes to the previous selected document.
F4 or ⇄	Goes to the next unread document.
⇧ Shift F4	Goes to the previous unread document.
Ins	Marks selected documents as read or unread.
Ctrl P	Prints the selected document.

Documents

Moving the insertion point and selections

Ctrl Home	Goes to the start of the document.
Ctrl End	Goes to the end of the document.
Ctrl →	Goes to the start of the next word.
Ctrl ←	Goes to the start of the previous word.
Home	Takes the insertion point to the beginning of the line.
End	Takes the insertion point to the end of the line.
Pg Dn	Moves one screen page down.
Pg Up	Moves one screen page up.

Copying/moving text

Ctrl C	Copies the selected text.
Ctrl X	Cuts the selected text.
Ctrl V	Pastes the cut or copied selection.

Character formatting

Ctrl B	Applies bold type.
Ctrl I	Applies italics.
Ctrl U	Underlines the text.
F2	Increases the font by one size.
⇧ Shift F2	Decreases the font by one size.
Ctrl T	Returns to normal text.
Ctrl K	Shows the **Text** properties box - **Font** tab.

<u>Paragraph formatting</u>

F7	Gives the paragraph a first line indent.
Shift F7	Applies a hanging indent to the paragraph.
F8	Gives a positive indent to the whole paragraph.
Shift F8	Gives a negative indent to the whole paragraph.
Ctrl **J**	Shows the **Text** properties box - **Paragraph Alignment** tab.
Ctrl **R**	Displays/hides the ruler.

<u>Replacing text</u>

Ctrl **F**	Opens the text search/replace feature.

<u>Managing documents</u>

Ctrl **E**	Toggles Edit and Read modes.
Ctrl **W**	Closes the active document.
Ctrl **S**	Saves the active document.
Ctrl **P**	Prints the document.

<u>Various</u>

Ctrl **Z**	Undoes the last action.
Ctrl **N**	Creates a database.

Index

Index

Index

Index

Index